How to Survive in International Marriage

by

Oksana Leslie

authorHOUSE™

1663 LIBERTY DRIVE, SUITE 200
BLOOMINGTON, INDIANA 47403
(800) 839-8640
WWW.AUTHORHOUSE.COM

First published by AuthorHouse 09/24/04

ISBN: 1-4208-0338-7 (sc)

Library of Congress Control Number: 2004097529

Printed in the United States of America
Bloomington, Indiana

This book is printed on acid-free paper.

In memory of Father, Vyacheslav Kornienko and Uncle Larry Nolder.
OKSANA KORNIENKO LESLIE with Keith Leslie

Table of Contents

CHAPTER 1
MY GOAL – AMERICAN HUSBAND. LEARN ABOUT YOUR PARTNER'S EXPECTATIONS.

"Each year, over 200,000 citizens of the United States marry foreign-born persons and petition for them to obtain permanent residence in the U.S." (http://www.shusterman.com/marriage.html)

This book written for those who seek or build intercultural marriage, for those, who just want to become more culture competent and well-rounded, for those, who look for a good spiritual story with some struggle, some humor, and some life advices. This book is for people who cherish true stories.

Have you ever seen a black hen sacrifice in order to help your finances? Have you heard about black ram sacrifice for the sake of the family? Have you lived among people who have two problems: "How to earn more money?" and "Where to immigrate?"

This book will answer all questions Americans asked me during last six years of my marriage to an American man!

Well, to answer your first question: "Who am I?" I am Russian. I look Russian. I speak Russian. I taught Russian. I love caviar and herring. However, I was born and raised in Uzbekistan. My grandfather's parents were Ukrainians and did not speak Russian, but they ended up in Uzbekistan, and from their heritage I got my last name Kornienko. Oksana is Ukrainian name, also.

Wait a minute! To clear the confusion, let me describe Uzbekistan in several words like bazaars, pilafs, baklava, lamb shish-kabobs, cotton and corn fields, pomegranates and watermelons, figs and quince-pineapples, minarets and mosques, mountains and deserts, Aral Sea and Silk Road. Uzbekistan has cities which much older Russian oldest cities. Russians look like Europeans, Uzbeks look like Asians (Afghans, Turks, and Iraqis). Most Uzbeks have black hair, black or brown eyes, and light brown to dark brown skin. The territory was conquered by Alexander the Great, Arabs, and Mongols. New Uzbek history textbooks claim that Russians conquered this region in the 19th century. During Soviet era Russians came to Uzbekistan for different reasons. Some came to the region to start a new life. Some Russians were evacuated with factories during World War 2 to Central Asia. In 1966, when earthquake destroyed the capital, doctors and builders from all over Russia came to rebuild the city and stayed there. My great grandfather was prosecuted during Stalin repression, and his wife was exiled from Leningrad to Asia. She was forced to leave her two bedroom apartment in Leningrad

(St. Petersburg) with her young daughters, take a train and arrive in Tashkent. My grandmother Nina was raised in poverty and fear to talk and question about her father.

Uzbekistan was the first country which gave their air bases to US air forces to bomb Afghanistan. I am very proud of this fact, by the way.

However, I am just starting. Russian from Uzbekistan sets herself a goal – to find an American man and leave her Motherland, relatives for better life.

Do you remember the CINDERELLA story? Where you satisfied with the ending? – "They lived happily ever after." Have you ever tried to imagine what could happen post nuptials? Well, this book is a modern Cinderella story, but it does not end like the old one. It will show what actually happened behind the curtains of the real life.

This manuscript is not just our love story. It is a story about my adjustment to American life, cultural differences, and my spiritual growth. If someone would ask you, what is this book about, your answer can be as short as nose hair: "This is a comparison book of three cultures: American, Russian and Uzbek."

You can learn a lot from it and even have fun. You probably do not know it yet, but it is a lot of fun to be married to a woman from another country! (My spouse certainly thinks so.)

Well, let start. How did we meet? We were introduced through mutual friends. There was a girl named Galina from my hometown Tashkent, who married an American citizen. Her goal was to find an American husband. She inspired me. After some time, they and Galina's mother decided to try to find a good Russian wife for their American bachelor, Keith Leslie.

Keith was going through a divorce at that time, so he was not interested in marrying anyone. However, he started to write letters to seven women from Tashkent. I had no idea that Galina would give Keith's address to a bunch of other girls.

I could not believe it happened to me! I actually got a letter from an American! Keith's letter came on my 23rd birthday. I got his first two letters in November and December of 1996. I wrote back to him right away, but I did not hear any news from him until August of 1997. I sent him a twelve-page letter in April of 1997 about my family and my country, but he never responded to it. Later, in the U.S., I found out that he had never read my super letter! He said that it looked too big and had too many mistakes.

When I started to write to him, I was looking for an American man. I was serious and honest with him. I believed that he belonged to me alone and that I had no opponents. I was so sure that I had no competition. I had low self esteem. If I would know that Keith was receiving letters from other girls, I could give up easily. Somehow I survived this correspondence.

Do you know what helped me? It was my passion to write. Most people generally stop writing to someone if they get no response. I continued writing to him even when he did not respond right away, because I had hope.

I call him Kiss or Kif, because the Russian alphabet does not have the diphthong Th. American alphabet has 26 letters, Russian has 33. Russian alphabet does not have Th, j, q, r, w, and y. That is why we have an accent, different pronunciation of English words.

Before my arrival in the U.S., I was searching for any magical or mystical signs that would make my way clear.

My good friend and Aunt, Lena Rashevskaya, who had two university degrees and was twice as old as me, spoke to me about life, values, and universal laws. I was told that with my negative feelings toward Uzbekistan and Uzbek people, I would never get out of the country. She explained to me that every country has its own energetic hierarchy, which serves as a local god. So if I despised my motherland, this local god would never let me get my visas and leave.

My friend also explained to me that my opinion that men were animals was wrong. She told me, "Oksana, if you hate all men just because some men are rude to you, it means that you will attract only bad men in your life. It is one untold law of the Universe. You think that in the U.S. you will find only good men. But you will get your prince only if you choose to give up your hate for the men who have offended you. You have to forgive. You have to stop looking back at your past. Then you will be able to see a terrific future with the best man of your life. Everything bad that happened to you before was your own fault. You kept attracting low-class individuals who had been humiliating you as a female and as a person, because you never had respect for any man or boy."

She was right, but it took me some time to pray and clear from my heart all the old injuries.

I was learning about the Holistic Dynamic Theory of managing your life by writing fairy tales. I started to write about myself as a bird that crosses a river, or escapes from a cage, or finds a new nest. I just knew that my life in the U.S. would be better than my life in Uzbekistan.

I was also forcing myself to go to church often. It was kind of like making a deal with God, because when I was giving bread and money donations to beggars, I was sure that He would help me win the battle for my happiness.

At one point I remember how I was showing my pictures to my adviser, and she told me, "Don't you know that pictures are what program your life? You want to find a good foreign spouse who will take good care of you, but you make pictures with your girlfriends! You should program you life with a new sort of pictures, Oksana."

I got the idea. So shortly afterwards I took my 15-year-old brother Stas to the mountains for a short vacation. We made some pictures in a pool, with him holding me outstretched in the air in his strong hands. I believed that this act had to work.

Now I am far away from my superstitious family and friends. However, these superstitions still affect me. For example, every time I make a picture, I make sure that I do not have an empty plate in front of me. I also make sure that men do not lean on me in pictures, because that would mean that I was programming them to take advantage of me or to be dependent on me.

I like to lean on my Keith. I even made one picture in which I kiss him while my hand is in his pocket. By doing this, I programmed the future so that his money will be my money.

I am also afraid to make pictures with empty chairs around, because I do not want to cause the death of any of my relatives by this unthinkable action. I destroy every picture in which my eyes are closed, because I do not want to turn my back to life.

Sometimes it seems to me very strange to believe in so many things and think about all these superstitious laws more than about God.

As time passed, my superstitions were somewhat damaged by some events in our life. For example, I was not able to prevent deaths in my family by making sure that I never had empty chairs in my pictures. And even though I did not let Keith lean on me in pictures, there came a point in life when he became dependent on me. So I changed some of my superstitious beliefs because of life events we went through.

Speaking of black rams and hens, I never sacrificed one or paid for the ritual like some people in Uzbekistan do. One my Uncle, who is Russian like me, did. He told me, how the rooster had to be mutilated in front of him by the Muslim female shaman. His construction business was going down the drain, so his last hope was is this superstitious ritual. Who ate the rooster? The lady-shaman and her family did. Did my Uncle's

Business improved? Unfortunately, it did not. Who sent him to this female shaman?

I did. Welcome to Oksana's world!

Now I'll share a secret with you. I visited a psychic in Tashkent and showed her Keith's picture. It was in July of 1997. At that time, I was looking for a job and for changes in my life. I did not have good luck in getting a high-paying job, but I wanted to believe that my life would change for the better at any time.

The shaman was a middle-aged Muslim woman who had six kids that were making repairs in their home during my visit. Their work was making a lot of noise, but it did not disturb her trance or her visions about my destiny. I was told that I needed to write to Keith, even if I did not hear from him for a long time. The visit with the psychic really made an impression on me and gave me hope. She told me, "I see that his soul is ready to open for you, and he will call you. You will meet him soon. Your future connects with his life."

I paid her what I could, but she did not seem to care about money. I brought her a big jar of homemade pickles and a little jar of honey. I had no money at that time, but I could have paid fifty cents or a dollar to this woman, and she would have been satisfied. People in my country believe that if a healer or a psychic takes a lot of money for a conversation or a healing, it is not good. People also believe that if they ask about charges for alternative body and soul healing, and the healer or psychic answers, "However much you can give," it means that this person has a gift from God. If a clairvoyant wants to earn a lot of money, it means that he or she has a devil's gift. This is just another example of the superstitions from Uzbekistan.

So after I visited this good person and she told me the encouraging news, I wrote another letter to Keith and he finally called me in August of 1997. Well. You can see that we had a long period of silence from January of 1997 until August of that same year.

He had gotten a divorce from his spouse, after they had been separated for over a year. He had also changed apartments. I had also been very busy at school that spring. I was working at the public school as a regular new teacher with a small salary. In March of that year, my father had to have surgery in a hospital, because he had developed stomach cancer. Then in May my brother was taken to the hospital for a fractured nose and a brain concussion. So I was very busy taking care of my relatives and visiting them in the hospital.

Time passed quickly, and Keith and I renewed our correspondence in August of that year. In other words, he didn't write to me for eight months! At that time, we started to use the Internet to communicate with each other without problems.

Since I had no computer, I had to visit the e-mail service at the Architecture University in Tashkent. The majority of people in the Soviet Union do not have computers because they are very expensive. Yes, a lot of people from the former Soviet Union have no idea how to use computers. Some people don't even know what the Internet is.

The Internet service in Tashkent is basically a free service for students and teachers to use. They simply must show their IDs to the service manager, and they can use the system for free at any time. Other people have to pay money to obtain an entrance to the service site and a password.

I can remember those three little rooms of the Internet service "PERDKA." One room was for the manager, who had to help people use the computer if they were just starting to learn how to use it. There were four computers in each of the other two rooms. Anyone could come in five days a week between 9:00 a.m. and 5:00 p.m. to use the Internet for twenty minutes. I remember very clearly how sometimes I would wait for an hour in a line to get a chance to read new e-mail from Keith and to write back to him. I used to type very slowly in English. Since I was using a dictionary,

I sometimes didn't have enough time to finish my message before the computer would switch off. Then I would have to stand in a line again and wait. Sometimes I would spend four hours of my day just to send an e-mail to Keith. This was because I had to wait for a bus for ten to thirty minutes, then spend forty to fifty minutes riding the bus, then walk ten minutes to the university, and finally wait in a line a couple of times before making the trip back home.

Now Tashkent has a lot of Internet café's, and my Mom sends me emails since 2001.

I want to tell a story. I will never forget it. One day I stood in line to get a chance to send an e-mail to my Keith. Some Uzbek students of the university were standing around their friend in a little crowd, which concealed him and the computer from people's eyes. When the first guy's twenty minutes were over, another guy sat down to use the Internet. Yes, they were acting like they were helping their friend on the computer so they could spend a lot of time and keep the computer busy for themselves without having to stand in line. It was a very good trick. When I saw what was happening, I told the manager. The manager told them all to leave the room. The guys got very angry with me and told me that they had stood in line and they hadn't seen me.

I felt very upset, because that day I had stood in line for an hour and fifteen minutes. Their words insulted me as a woman. I told them that I had stood in line for a long period of time and had seen their trick very clearly. One of the guys told me, "Woman, know your place." After he said these words, I had nothing to answer. I think that I have never been very good at coming up with quick answers. I just felt a lot of deep hate for all men in the world who are used to treat women like slaves for centuries.

"Know your place."

I was older than the boy. I was a teacher and a writer, and he was just a student with Uzbek appearance and Uzbek last name, and probably Uzbek parents with a lot of money. He did not learn from the Koran that youngsters have to respect older people. He was not a good Muslim, if he could say that to me. I have read the Koran twice in Russian translation. Koran as Bible teaches moral, respect to parents and to older people, unless they are enemies, those people. That boy made me feel that I was the enemy, white female one. However, it did not stop me from using this internet café again. I had a goal, - to meet Keith in Moscow and see if I like him in person.

Think and ask yourself: What do you know about Moscow?

Of course, you know that Moscow is the capital of Russia and the former capital of the Soviet Union. I believe that you also know that Moscow is the great cultural center in Russia.

I have not seen Moscow until I met Keith. I did not know that Moscow was also the most expensive city for tourists. Think twice before you make your trip to that place. After all, Keith and I think that the best place to meet each other and save money would be Bangkok. That is our advice for couples like us.

I was very excited about our date in Moscow. I was excited to see this generous individual who had sent me $800 for the trip. He didn't really know me. I could have been a con artist and just taken the money and disappeared, you know. Keith impressed me by his trust.

I was sure that if I did not meet him at the airport, he would have problems. There are a lot of cons of different nationalities that know of numerous ways to get money from tourists. If you are as clever and brave as to visit Moscow by yourself, and you do not know the Russian language, please do not trust anybody at the airport.

I came to Moscow on the 29th of October, 1997. I was shocked at the Domodedovo Airport by a lot of taxi drivers who wanted to help me get into Moscow's center. They were so overwhelming and demanding! They tried to take my luggage away from me and carry it to their cars! I felt like a little fly in a group of spiders. I could not find a bus stop. One man asked me very politely if I needed to get to a metro station. He told me that he wanted to find some more passengers. His price was $3.00, which was almost like the bus's price (friends in Tashkent had told me). So I said, "Okay!" I was sure that the other passengers in his car would pay him $3.00 each, and the driver would be satisfied.

He had a small, old car, and I was the only woman amongst four passengers. Two guys were Russian, and one was from the Georgia Republic. This old Georgian told us that he had never been in Moscow, and the two Russians believed him. I was born in the Asiatic Republic, so I know how to judge the characters of people of these nationalities. I know for sure that if a fifty-year-old person from Armenia, or from Georgia, or from Asia says that he has never been in Moscow, it is most likely a lie. Moscow was the greatest hub for cons from different republics, for both honest and sly sellers. It was the time before Perestroika, when all the population of the USSR aspired to visit the heart of the motherland to see Lenin's body in the Mausoleum, and to buy things that were absent in the provinces.

I kept silent, but I started to feel nervous. Soon, I found out that something was going to happen to us. Yes, soon the situation became clear. The old Georgian started to ask us questions:

"Where are you from? Have you been to Moscow before?"

One Russian passenger got excited and bragged about his trip to Italy. The old man asked him about the Italian casino, and what it looked like. The Russian man was happy to find an audience, so he started to explain about cards and teach us how to play.

The Georgian man showed a great interest, and he looked as if he didn't know this game. He got excited and said, "Friends, I have an idea! I want us to visit some nice place to eat! I will pay for our lunch, and then we can play this new interesting game for money, like real men would do!"

He was going to con us. I was only a shield for the driver, who wanted to make the passengers think that they had gotten a regular taxicab. The driver had an agreement with the sly Georgian! The men asked me if I wanted to play cards with them, and I said no.

Immediately, the driver stopped the car and asked me to get out. I could not control my emotions. I started to cry! Imagine! I was in Moscow for the first time, and I had to get out of a taxi in an unknown, out-of-town territory. The trees and the road were powdered with snow.

One guy asked me, "Why are you crying? We did not rape you. We are nice guys. You can wait on the road for a bus."

When the taxi driver helped me to get my luggage from his trunk, he whispered to me a short apology. "Sorry. He pays me by the hour. It is a man's game." It was at this moment that I told myself, *I hate Moscow and Muscovites! I hate men!*

I had no problem getting on the bus, because the bus driver saw me leaving the taxicab. I felt very frustrated. My first hour in Moscow was already a mess. After some minutes, I thanked God. *Thank you, God! You saved me from the cons! Thank you, God! They did not steal my money! Thank you, God. You gave me a chance to get on the bus quickly! Thanks, God!* I was alert about what was going to happen with a taxicab's passengers.

After my half-hour trip on the bus, and about twenty minutes on a metro train, I could finally take a rest. I came to a hotel about which I had gotten information at the airport. In the airport, I had paid thirty percent of the cost for the hotel, and I had to pay the rest at the hotel. When I got to the hotel, there was a sign that said: *No Rooms Available.*

There were several people around the hotel trying to sell me a hotel room cheaper than the price I had gotten at the airport. Later, I found out that these people were the representatives of the hotel. They had rights to find a customer and to have their percentages. When I paid at the airport, it was $50 a night, but prices outside of the hotel were $40 a night.

It seemed funny: I could reserve a room from the airport or use the service of the people outside the hotel. I could not buy room inside the hotel, because there was the note: *No Rooms Available*. I never stayed in a hotel before.

Maybe I just don't understand this system.

I liked the hotel. I got a nice room on the 9th floor without roaches and with toilet paper in the bathroom. However, my room was out of heat. I was cold for seven days. It was not funny. We loved Moscow's metro, the hotel's elevator, and the stores, because they were warm, much warmer than our hotel rooms. We enjoyed our time together, but Russian autumn made us quite uncomfortable.

Now I want to tell you about my first day with Keith.

I got up and looked in the mirror. I hated my appearance that morning. I had a rash around my nose, and bags under my eyes. I spent twenty minutes putting curlers in my hair and held them for about an hour. I put a lot of makeup on my face. I tried to cover the redness, but it was impossible. I did not feel very attractive. I had done a good job on my curls, so I tried to impress Keith with my blond hair. I was convinced that the first impression of a date was the most important.

I bought a $3.00 red rose and went to the bus stop Rechnoy Vokzal. I had one hour before my American would arrive. I got on the bus with the note *Sheremetievo-2*. A driver came in and said to the passengers, "I am not going to drive yet. There are not enough people. I have to make more money. You all have to wait about an hour."

I was angry and scared. I could be late to meet Keith! I had no money to pay for a taxicab, but I explained to an old taxi driver my situation. He agreed to drive me to the airport and pick up Keith and come back to the hotel. The price to the airport was $50, and from the airport to the hotel it was the same price. Moscow's taxicabs are very expensive, because it is a private service.

I came to the airport and got the news that Keith's airplane was late. The driver was waiting outside, while I was waiting for Keith's arrival inside the airport Sheremetievo- 2. I was standing in front of the exit, and my eyes were searching all the new people coming from the U.S. The driver could see me from outside through the airport's window.

Keith was in the last group of passengers. He held two bags in each of his arms. Later, I found out that Keith had taken with him for three days a lot of clothes and four pairs of shoes, including cowboy boots. He had even brought gifts for my family. He presented my mother a pair of nice slippers, my father got a bottle of whiskey, and my brother got a blue T-shirt that said, *Atlanta 1996*. I was impressed that Keith had remembered my relatives.

I had no time at the airport to kiss Keith. There was a big crowd of people trying to meet relatives and friends. I saw that Keith's hands were full. That was why I just said, "Hello," and grabbed his sleeve. I was very excited to see him. My English was not big enough to explain to him the situation with the crowd and the driver, who was waiting for us and looking at us through the airport's window. It was a funny situation when we saw each other the first time, and I showed him my bossy manners.

We got in the car, and the driver had some problems starting it. Keith was amazed to have to pay $100 for a taxi. It was not only for the ride to the hotel, but also for my ride to the airport to meet him. Well, now I understand that I could have saved him some money. I could have gotten up earlier to ride the bus. I could have come from a different bus station. I did not know Moscow and the places for buses that go to the airports! We could have just paid the driver $50 and came to the hotel on a bus. Actually, I had no idea that Americans cared so much about the word "economy" and that they save money and care about money. I was sure that for Keith, prices had no meaning, and he could buy anything he wanted!

I want to apologize to Keith and his relatives, and to all Americans for my wrong thoughts about them. I was wrong to think that all of them were "damn American rich capitalists." I had no idea that they were normal people who care about economy, face sacrifices, work hard, and try to save money.

I remember that before my arrival to the U.S., Galina's mother was always telling me, "Oh, Keith is rich. He will buy you everything, so you do not have to bring anything with you in the U.S."

I believed her. I thought that she knew Keith, because she met him during her visit to Atlanta! I was sure that I could trust her experience about the U.S.

When Keith wrote to me that he was saving money for my arrival and for our wedding, I was sure that he was just pretending to be poorer than he was. I had met that kind of people in the former Soviet Union. They like to complain that their knowledge is weak, but they always pass exams perfectly. They love to complain about money, but they have more money than they need. I decided that Keith was that kind of person! I did not know that $100 for a taxicab would bother him so much.

When Keith and I entered the hotel room, he presented me with a purse full of makeup. I was very glad. Later, I used this makeup kit for five months in Tashkent, before my trip to the U.S. Two-thirds of this makeup I gave to my mother and to some of my close friends. I could not use all of the makeup in the kit, because it was not my style or color. It was easy for me to share makeup with my mother, because we had always shared perfume and makeup under the same roof. My mom and I were close friends. Sometimes she would let me wear her clothes and she also used to borrow my sweaters. It was okay with me to give to her almost anything she wanted.

After Keith got out of the shower, I knocked on his door. I was going to present him with a very famous Russian watch. I asked him to sit down and to close his eyes. He was sitting on a chair, while I was sitting on my knees. I put the watch around his wrist, and I said to him, "Now you are the commander, because this watch has this note."

I believed that I had given him a magic gift. I thought that any watch would be the symbol of time. So my gift for Keith symbolized that his time with me was starting. You can roll on the floor laughing about this if you want to. It's okay. I believe that some gifts have meaning. Gifts can work for the giver. Well, this Russian winding watch with the word *commando* on it was supposed to bring Keith to me in time. To me, it sounded romantic and mystical. I did not know, that Keith does not like hand watches.

By the way, Keith and I had dinner in a small cafe on our floor in the hotel. I was so confused and my English was so weak that I could mostly just smile and use my electronic dictionary. It is so weird that after six years of learning English in school, and six years at the Tashkent State University, I still did not have the confidence to talk. It was easy for me to write and to read, but not to understand the American accent and manner of speech.

After dinner, we hoped to buy tickets at the Bolshoi Theater. I heard that Moscow's students used to buy all the tickets and sell them to tourists. It was a pretty good way for them to make money.

Keith and I met some students close to the theater who sold us two tickets at $60 each. I could see that the real price on the tickets was about $20 each. Keith was sure that we had gotten conned, because the Muscovites did not have the tickets with them. A guy had to run someplace and get them. We got tickets for Sunday, because on Friday the theater had no ballets, only Russian opera.

So we went for a walk at Red Square. Keith had a fancy suit and shoes on, and my dress was not warm enough for Moscow's October, either. The weather was very cold and snowy.

It was our first evening together. Keith and I met each other on the American holiday of Halloween. At that time, I did not know anything about that holiday, and did not care about it at all. Keith faced Moscow without any sign of celebration of that popular American event.

We soon found a place on the Red Square where you could take an evening excursion. We so much wanted to go someplace warm! We paid for the excursion and got on the warm bus! Keith could not understand anything about Moscow, because our guide in the bus was speaking Russian for the Russian tourists. Anyway, he could see through the window. The bus made some stops, and we had to get out and see Moscow's sights.

I remember when Keith embraced me for the first time. We were standing and looking from the High Hill of Moscow down at the city. Keith saw that I was shivering with cold. My black wool coat did not keep me warm. My legs were covered only by thin stockings. So as you can imagine, Moscow's penetrating wind had chilled my body. It was not fun, believe me.

Keith stood behind me, and his strong arms wrapped around me. I could feel his masculine energy. I understood during that evening in cold, snowy Moscow that I would have sexual harmony with this American man. You know, all hugs are different! You should know how important it is to feel somebody's energy. We know mother's hugs and sister's hugs, and we know friend's and spouse's hugs. They are very different and important feelings.

After the excursion, we came back to the hotel. Keith wanted to go to eat at the restaurant, so I dressed up. He showed me how much money he had. He had $60 cash. I had heard before that Moscow's restaurants were very expensive, and we could not go with so little money. So I explained it to him.

We were walking in a long corridor to get on an elevator. I will never forget this evening, this walking in the corridor. Keith took from his pocket some rings and started to try them on my fingers. The first, second, and third rings were too big for me. But when we got close to the elevator, Keith tried the last ring, with a diamond. It was a perfect fit for my finger.

I did not know what to say. I felt that it was a very important moment. I expected that such a special moment in my life had to happen in a special environment, with candles, champagne, flowers, and a man's sentiment. So I was ready for another situation. I had no idea that Keith, without any words, would give me an engagement ring before getting on the elevator.

Well, I only could say to him, "I never had such a beautiful ring. I never had any gold ring in my life. I could not even dream about a ring with a diamond. You are the first individual in my life who gave me such a special gift."

It was truth. I felt as if there were wings on my back. I was shocked that my American gave me a ring during our first day together. I was also very impressed. I thought that *God really gave me a future husband. It can't be just a coincidence.*

Keith did not think that he had given me an engagement ring. He called this ring a "friendship ring." He gave it to me because he liked me, not because he wanted to marry me right away. (Of course, I found out all of those details later.)

After we left the elevator, the ATM machine in the hotel's hall would not take Keith's Visa card, so he was very upset.

I tried to calm him by telling him, "No problem. I do not care about a restaurant so much. We can eat at a café, or we will find a good ATM machine in the morning at the closest casino. No problem."

You had to see how worried Keith was. Moscow seemed to him like a monster. Imagine that you invited your lady to a restaurant in Russia, but the restaurant doesn't take your Visa card because they take only cash!

How could you have a chance to buy your leather coat, your engagement ring, your car, your furniture, if the U.S. did not have a credit system? Capitalism is not so bad!

We had our first long conversation that night. Before the conversation, I decided to try to impress my American man some more. I took the TV and a phone off his table in the room. I gave him a camera and got onto the table. In a moment, he was taking pictures of me making weird yoga poses. When I finished, he took a picture of me showing how happy and proud of myself I was. Another day I walked on my hands and Keith got a picture of that, too. I was thinking, *I bet he never had a woman who could be so flexible and natural, and unpredictable.*

When people ask Keith how it feels to live with me, he answers, "Did you ever watch the TV show *I Love Lucy*? That show is like Oksana and me, but backwards."

Keith impressed me also by his delicate behavior. He did not try to have sex with me right away. It was very important. I had had boyfriends who could not control their physical urges. If somebody cannot control their desires, it means to me that they cannot control them with other women. I did not want to marry a playboy. I wished to find a guy with whom to create a family. I do not like swinging ideas, because I have an old-fashioned understanding of marriage. I feel that if I love my spouse, I am not supposed to play around.

I can like somebody's beauty and respect them. I can admire an actress or an actor, but I do not want to share my husband with somebody else. I do not want him to wish to share me with somebody else.

So Keith and I had a conversation about our hopes and principles. At our first real date, he asked me to be his wife.

Can you imagine it? He asked me to be his spouse before any intercourse! He did not know a lot about me. He felt that I was his style of woman, his size of woman, his dream. How could I ask him for some time to get to know each other more? I felt that this kind of man who already did for me so much could not be a sadist or a schizophrenic. I said to him that I had found my prince: him.

Later, in my e-mails to Keith, I told him often that he was my prince. It was not just because he could take me into the U.S. His behavior to me was unreal, as if I was Cinderella in a fairytale.

I could not imagine that Keith would ask me to be his wife on the first day of our date (especially on Halloween). I could not imagine that we would have so much in common.

So that is why I told him after our date in Moscow that I felt about us like people say about two halves of the same apple. It was a perfect match.

My mind knew it.

In the morning of the second day, I knocked at Keith's door and brought coffee to him. I usually drink tea. I had a plan to impress my American, so I brought him a mug of coffee. The mug was my gift to him, and had Moscow's symbol portrayed on it. It was Saint George on a horse, killing a dragon. I had my robe on and curlers on my head. I wanted him to see that behind all the makeup and yoga tricks was hiding a caring, average looking woman who curled her hair.

The morning of the second day, we started with a breakfast in the hotel's café. We had plans to find any information about ATM machines. We looked inside a couple of buildings of our hotel, and we finally found one! Keith could relax about his money. We went to see the famous Red Square.

We were lucky, as usual. An old lady, with a very intelligent appearance, came close to us and offered her services to be our English guide.

Oh, God saved me! I could relax and not think about the right translation to Keith about Moscow's history. I had headaches from my English conversations with Keith, and my attempts to understand him right, and to listen. Actually, I am the kind of person who cannot listen to another person without special efforts. I like to listen myself, okay? (Just kidding.)

By the way, our guide had a license to bring her clients to the Red Square's cultural objects without having to stand in any lines. So we did not wait in a line to see Lenin's body or to come on the territory of the Kremlin. She showed the security guides her license, and we stepped on the special land of Moscow.

Our guide was very nice, and she answered all Keith's questions. I remember her name: Lucia.

She took some pictures of us. We had to have a lot of pictures with different memorials and Moscow's special sculptures and churches as a proof of our date to the American Embassy.

We had a great day with our guide. We stopped to rest at the main store GUM, and we got coffee for Keith and Lucia, each cup for $4.00, and juice for me for $2.00. We also got a picture of our guide. I will never forget how pleasant a woman she was. It was $30 for her lecture and service. Keith was satisfied, because he got a lot of information in English. I was not listening to her English explanation, because my mind was just fried from the stress.

That morning Keith kissed me for the first time when we were under the Kremlin building. At the moment, I was shocked because I grew up in a Muslim republic. I had never been kissing or kissed in public before. I was 23 years old!

Keith kissed me, because he remembered my previous gift. I got him a column with a shape of the Kremlin. Keith was impressed. My plan had worked!

I was in a very good mood. I must tell you more about my plans. I wanted to give Keith a gift every morning and evening by which to remember me. I would be impressed by this kind of thing, so I thought that Keith would be impressed, too. So the next morning, on our third day I gave him another Moscow mug with coffee. In the evening, I gave him a little book and a little tiger made by the Gjel Russian factory. These gifts were small souvenirs for his parents. On the fourth day of our date, before he left, I gave him a little amulet with his Gemini sign. I really wanted to get married to an American guy with so many good qualities!

Our third day in Moscow was unforgettable. We spent 45 minutes in the metro to get to the paleontology museum. We also had our tickets for the ballet at 12:00 p.m., so we were in a hurry. The museum had opened at 11:00 a.m. Well, we had only a half-hour to look at all the museum's expositions and to take pictures. Actually, we had to pay a dollar for permission to take pictures in this museum. At 11:30, we left the museum and got in the taxicab. We were not too late to get to the Bolshoi Theater on time.

I enjoyed the ballet. It was a story about a girl named Anna who got married to an old rich man and forgot about her relatives. Her husband used his wife to get prizes from high ranks. A Russian writer of the end of nineteenth century wrote this tragic, true story. The last name of the writer is Chekhov. I read the story at high school.

After the ballet, we went to the GUM (supermarket) to eat pizza and to develop our new film. After one hour, we had to be in a hurry to get to the hotel and change our clothes. We had tickets to a small Moscow circus at 7:00 p.m. This time we were not late! We saw a great performance with animals and gymnasts, clowns, and dancers. I was impressed by the ice skaters on the real ice! Well, you can see it, too, if you go to Moscow. I remember that the tickets to the circus that we bought at the metro station were $4:00 each.

You have to know some more about metro stations in Moscow. It is a place where people can buy newspapers and journals, cards and books, perfumes and alcohol, and a lot of different stuff. You can buy at the famous central metro stations all kinds of tickets to the different places (theaters, circus, shows, and concerts). So Moscow's metro has a life of its own with beggars and sellers, singers and onlookers.

The fourth day of our date in Moscow started early for us. We wanted to visit the American Embassy before Keith left. Well, we got a taxicab, and came to the Embassy. We did not have to stand in line, because I told the security guard that I was an interpreter with an American tourist, and he needed to come to the Embassy to get help. The security guard was a

Russian man with a round, red face. He asked us to show our passports. After checking our passports, he allowed us to come inside the Embassy.

Keith and I did not know that we would not be able to get my K-1 visa to come to the U.S. that day. We had no idea that there would be so many levels of red tape to handle.

Then we went to the airport. Keith and I had some time left, so we went to get breakfast at the airport's restaurant. We enjoyed the food and our conversation. I did not understand a lot of his English, but I acted like I knew and understood everything. I think that if you have a chance to learn the Russian language in a group of American students with an American teacher, you will have a difficult time understanding the real Russian language in the republics of the former Soviet Union.

Keith gave me some money for my expenses. I spent it on Moscow's delicious candies, which I could not buy in my republic Uzbekistan. I bought some for my family, for my grandmothers, and for Galina's mother.

I felt as if I owed it to them. You maybe do not know that in Asia people expect gifts for the holidays, or after their relatives travel. People used to give gifts or expect them without any reason. It is one foundation of Asiatic culture. I remember that when I had my business travel to an Uzbekistan province, I was a guest from the capital in towns Khiva and Urgench, Turtkul and Nukus. Even though I was only there on business, the people showed me their towns and introduced me to their friends. I never knew where we were going to have lunch or dinner, because they took me to so many places.

We visited different houses, and often the owner did not even expect our arrival. How do you like that? We would arrive, and we would be treated as the best guests in the world. I will never forget that Uzbek hospitality. While the housewives tried to cook up very good national meals for us, I received gifts from the owners. Usually an old lady of the house would give me a bright Uzbek shawl or a handkerchief with warm words in Uzbek or Russian language.

Well, if you have a chance to visit Uzbekistan, you will be impressed by Asiatic hospitality. Please, do not forget to bring gifts. I do not want to say that Asiatic hospitality depends on your generosity! No! But I want to say that you would feel really bad if people were jumping around spoiling you if you had nothing to give in return. Okay? Really, I felt that it was my debt to bring gifts from Moscow with me to satisfy my relatives.

However, I think that without making any sacrifices in life, we cannot get anything special. In my opinion, sacrifices are any donations, any financial, physical, or emotional help to others, or any gifts to friends, family, or strangers.

I left Keith in the airport Sheremetievo-2 and felt that he was already in my pocket. I knew that I had impressed him, and he liked me very much. I also knew that I wanted to marry this kind of man, who had all the qualities I respected and needed. It was my goal to marry him not just to bridge my way to the U.S., but to create a family, and to not be alone. I wanted to escape from Uzbekistan and from my teacher's job, but I wanted to be happy with a wonderful guy. Keith was the man. I thought I liked him very much.

After I came back to Tashkent from Moscow, I had five long months to wait before my next date with Keith. We said goodbye to each other at the Moscow airport Sheremetievo on the 3rd of November in 1997. Then Keith met me at the airport in New York on the 3rd of April the following year. We did not see each other for five long months.

I want to talk about this time in my life.

I felt a lot of respect for Keith's actions. He saw me for only three days in Moscow, and he wanted to marry me! He wanted to help me financially in Tashkent. No one had ever treated me this way before. Never had I met a person who was as kind and adventurous as my Keith. I thank God that I got a chance to meet the man of my dreams.

I used to wear his gift, the friendship ring, all the time. I used to kiss the ring, and the nice little diamond, and think about my American fiancé. I didn't say anything about him to the majority of my friends. I was scared to jinx my luck. Most Russians and Asian people are afraid of other people's jealousy.

I believed that if my girlfriends who had correspondence with Americans during this time became jealous of my successful trip to Moscow, my future would go badly. The majority of my relatives did not know about my American fiancé either, because I still did not have my American visa. I thought that they would laugh at me, and my ideas about a foreign husband would get crushed. So I kept my secret about Keith. I kept all the excitement to myself. My parents, brother, grandmothers kept silence also.

Keith made a mistake when he wrote to me: I hope that you will always have everything that you want and need. I will always try to help you. If you need anything that I can help you with, please tell me!

19

Okay! I understood that Keith could fix all my problems and fulfill my desires. So I asked him to send me money, and I spent it all quickly without thinking about his sacrifices. My parents were upset when I was not very generous with them. So I filled our refrigerator with food. I also was buying food (eggs, chocolate, and veggies) every time I visited my grandmothers. I gave money to my father for gasoline, when he drove me to the Uzbek-Turkish bank to get more money from Keith. I paid for my English lessons and for my work-out classes. I had been visiting the Orthodox Church and the Internet service at the university, and every time I had expenses for public transportation. I also paid my publisher Igor Shelokov to satisfy my ambitiousness. I wanted to see my own books in hardcover very badly. It did not matter to me that they were as small as a matchbox! I did not care that nobody would be able to buy my books in bookstores. I could afford only one hundred miniature books of each series. I gave most of them away, and sold some to collectors of miniature books in Moscow. Now at least Moscow's miniature book museum Exlibris displays my five tiny books.

My grandma Nina and my cousin had birthdays in November, and in 1997 we celebrated them at my Uncle Valera's apartment. I bought gifts for the grandma and the cousin. Another thing that I spent Keith's money on was film to take pictures. It was important for me to have pictures of my family after I was gone.

You have no idea that in my republic people cannot afford to take pictures as often as Americans can. Pictures in Uzbekistan and Russia are fancy stuff, even for a middle-class person. People prefer to buy food rather than to pay for pictures. I remember that in Moscow we paid $4.00 to develop each roll of Adventix film, and for double prints we had to pay $20. Actually, it is much higher than in the U.S. In Uzbekistan I paid only fifty cents to develop the regular Kodak film, and each picture was twenty-five cents.

Such prices for pictures seem very good, but do not forget the salary most people receive in Uzbekistan. It is only $15 to $50 each month for food and bills. I spent $30 to take pictures not only for me, but also for my parents, for my brother, for my uncles, aunts, and for my grandparents. It was my New Year's gift for them. They were impressed that they got new pictures of the whole family together! They could not imagine that they could have something like that! They had not had pictures of the whole family together before! I was like a hero to them. We all should be thankful for my generous Keith. In fact, if Keith hadn't sent money to me, I wouldn't have been able to do any of these things.

On the 28th of November, I bought food to cook and celebrated my 24th birthday with my mother, father, and brother, my father's cousin, and my mother's mother (Grandma Mary). I also bought a roll of film to take pictures of my family. Later, I spent $60 to send Keith two pounds of important papers and pictures by Russian Express Mail.

By the end of December, I was out of money again. So I sent an e-mail to Keith. I asked Keith to send me money for my English lessons and for presents for my family.

He could not transfer money to me before the New Year. But God helped me, and I earned $20 by writing some course work for a student of the university. I bought some cheap gifts for my family.

You have to know that in the former Soviet Union, people celebrate the New Year as if it is the biggest day of the year. This is the most important holiday for them. Do not forget that they had seventy years of atheistic propaganda, and now they still prefer to celebrate New Year's Day rather than Christmas. Religious Russian people celebrate their Christmas on the 7th of January. Did you know that? People of the Soviet Union know when Americans celebrate their Christmas. Americans usually do not know anything about Russian traditions, people, or culture. Isn't that funny?

Finally Keith sent me $300 again in January, so I paid $100 for English lessons, and $70 for publishing my new little books.

I used to pay my father for gasoline. He had to pick me up five days a week after my English lessons, which were finished at 9:00 p.m. (Each lesson was three hours long.) You have no idea how much more expensive it is to pay for a taxicab in Uzbekistan, than for a civilian driver. Try to imagine yourself waiting for a bus or tram after 9:00 p.m. You would not know that any public transport in Tashkent slows down after 9:00 p.m. You wouldn't even know how much time you might have to wait: anywhere from ten minutes to an hour. Nobody knows exactly. It is like a gamble. You are lucky to get in a warm bus or tram without waiting long.

There is no republic in the former Soviet Union where the people have never seen snow. Even hot Asiatic republics have snow sometimes. So my dad was my personal driver during that very cold and snowy January of 1998.

People of hot Uzbekistan were amazed. We had snow for three days and three nights. The children were happy, especially the boys, because the snow helps them to make the girls cry. That is one reason that I never liked winter. It was the time that guys tried to hit me in the head with snowballs, just for fun. Even when I was a teacher, Uzbek students tried to hit me with snowballs before I got inside the school. Maybe, I was young and did not look like a teacher, just another high school white girl to hit on.

I think that our republics have so many problems because people don't care about each other very much, especially in the younger generation.

Strangely, I never wrote to Keith, *I appreciate your help very much.* I really did not know how to write beautiful thank-you notes. I just sent him e-mails like this: <u>Hi, dear Keith! I have received $770 today at the UT-bank</u>.

After such important information, I would write to him about how I was spending this money. I had no idea that it was not easy for Keith to save that kind of money for me. I was sure, like the majority of Russians, that Americans were "damn capitalists" with a lot of money in their bank accounts. So I thought that Keith had enough money to buy a house (I had no idea that people bought houses in credit in the U.S.), and to take me from Uzbekistan. I thought, *Oh, he can take money out of the bank any time and send it to me!*

In Moscow Keith told me, "Oksana, I am not a millionaire. Do you know that? $1000 is a lot of money for me." I heard, but I did not understand clearly. He was for me almost like a millionaire, because he had an expensive red car, and he had arrived in Moscow and paid for my expenses. He even sent me $800 before our date in Moscow! He never knew if I might be dishonest and keep the money. He impressed me by his generosity very much.

I thought, *Oh, I never met a person who could spend so much money for a woman he never met before!* However, I never wrote an e-mail or letter to Keith about my thoughts. I felt that he would not appreciate getting a cheap woman, who had never known a man's generosity. For me, he was like a prince from a beautiful story, who could save his Cinderella from her past life.

He just believed in our future and his good luck!

He wrote me an e-mail about his expenses. I was sure that to spend $400 a month for food in the U.S., and to have health and car insurance, was a luxury. I did not know that he bought his car on credit, and that he was paying every month for it. I could not imagine that in the U.S. there were so many places where you had to pay a lot of money for a service!

One day I got an e-mail from him saying, *I must save money for your Health Insurance ($500 or more). I also must save for our wedding (You* *will help me plan this???) We will marry after you have been here for two months. This will not give us much time to save for a nice wedding. You will need a dress, shoes, and other expenses ($1000), and I will need a suit, shoes, and other expenses ($1000). We will also have a party with food and dancing ($2000). I must fix some dents in my car before the wedding ($2000), and I have to buy an engagement ring ($3000). Do you want to wait until I can save more money before you come here?*

Oh, I was shocked. I did not want to wait! I felt that I did not need a fancy wedding or a car. I needed this man!

If I waited, I was sure that the super doctor, Mister Time, would make Keith forget about our Moscow romance! I could lose him! He was so attractive and kind that any woman would be happy to get him! Oh, no! He was also my bridge to a better life, so do not forget that important fact.

I wrote to Keith that I did not want to wait. I wrote that I loved him and missed him. I wrote him that I was sure everything in our life would be perfect. Also, I told him that Russians do not have a tradition of giving an expensive engagement ring to their brides, and Uzbeks do not either. I preferred to get a wedding ring without diamonds. *Get me out of here, Keith,* my soul was impatiently screaming.

However, I still did not understand very well about money. I really needed only $550 for my Moscow trip to get a visa. He sent me $900, because I asked him for this amount. Why? I was a selfish spender.

I bought gifts for my family again. I spent $50 for food for a "goodbye party" for my relatives and friends. I gave money to my mom to buy some nice fabrics to sew new dress clothes for me. I bought two luggage bags for $20 each to take to the U.S. My parents did not have dollars to give me, okay? My father was just getting better after cancer surgery. He owed a lot of money. How he could do anything for if he asked me to pay for his gas after English classes?

I knew that in the U.S. the majority of drugs and medications were available only with prescription, so I spent $15 for six months of oral birth control pills. I also bought antibiotics and pills to fight headaches, allergies, flu, and diarrhea. I had heard that in the U.S. medications were more expensive than in the former Soviet Union. So I tried to save Keith's money in the future for my drugs and for my fancy clothes, which were created by my mother's golden hands. My mother spent Keith's $100 to buy nice fabrics to sew new fancy clothes for me. Later I figured out that I could wear those only about once a year for special occasions.

23

After all I had spent, I brought with me to the U.S. only $20. So Keith thought that I did not appreciate his savings, and that I couldn't control money. I thought that I had done well. He would have spent more money for birth control pills (I did not have American insurance!) and for fancy clothes if I had come without anything. My friends told me that it was stupid to bring my clothes to the U.S., because they were out of style. I was told that maybe people in the U.S. would not wear that kind of clothes!

Also, my friends told me that I had gotten an American man who was not poor like the majority of Russians. "Come on, Oksana, he can buy you a lot of new American clothes without any problems," they told me.

Keith was able to make my last five months in Tashkent such a gorgeous time. Yes, I squandered his money. Yes, theoretically I could have saved it. To be honest, I wanted to feel that I had an American fiancé, and I did not care about the money. Keith expected me to save and be practical. I expected him to pay for everything, because, from my point of view, he was earning dollars.

Okay, I want to finish this chapter. I want to end with a short conversation between my grandmother and her neighbor, who saw Keith's picture for the first time in her life.

The neighbor said, "Keith is not beautiful."

My grandmother responded, "Oksana is not beautiful either."

CHAPTER 2
COMING TO AMERICA. HELP YOUR PARTNER TO COPE IN NEW ENVIRONMENT.

I was anxious during five months of waiting for my interview at the American embassy in Moscow. I had a neighbor-psychic with beautiful name Irina Borisovna.

She was a widow, her spouse died from cancer. Her son was killed in his twenties.

She lived in one bedroom apartment with her granddaughter and a dog. I explained to Irina Borisovna about my concerns and hopes regarding my American dream. She gave me several good advices. One of them was to go to a cemetery and wash tombstones of Tashkent Orthodox bishops. I took the advice seriously, talked my grandmother Maria to accompany me. We bought flowers by the cemetery, several cheap carnations. We brought with us our own bucket and rags. Inside the cemetery gates we filled our bucket with water. I felt very religious at that time, like I was really pleasing bishop's souls.

I washed about four tombstones. My grandmother was watching. Then I went into small church there and prayed to clear my way to America.

Moscow on the 14th of March in 1998 was very snowy. I got on a bus, and in a half-hour I was at the subway station in Oktyabrskaya.

I had only one hour to find the hospital of the U.S. Every metro train in Moscow has a map of the city inside. I had no problems finding the station I needed. I found the street (I don't remember its name), but before I got to the hospital, I had an adventure. Muscovites tried to con me using a very popular method. I read about this method in an article from a newspaper and in a chapter of the book *Police Academy* (about all methods of cons).

A young, skinny guy with eyeglasses, maybe eighteen or nineteen years old, asked me, "Woman, is this your wallet?" He showed me a man's wallet.

I said, "No."

He whispered to me, "Woman, there is money inside. We can share it!"

I answered, "Keep it." I left him and went into the hospital.

Now I want to tell you what was supposed to happen to me if I had agreed to share the money.

There would suddenly appear some strong guys, the boy's partners. They would say that they had lost the wallet, and that they had the witness who saw how I shared the money with the boy. The boy would leave me very quickly. Then I would be surrounded with the strong, angry guys. Then they would say that I should give them their money back, and they would be very upset, because I only had half of the sum. They would make me show them my wallet, and they would take all my money. Then they would beat me and say that I was a thief! Witnesses would not come help me, because they would not know that I was a victim of a con! They would believe that I was a thief! Do you think that you would try to fight with four or five strong, angry guys who could trample a woman? Do you think that you would not be scared to get some hits on your attractive face, sweetheart?

Okay. God blessed me. I entered the American Medical Center in time, and said to a girl at the front desk, "I am Oksana Kornienko. I have an appointment at 3:00 p.m."

She said, "Yes, how are you today? Please write down your information and pay $100 for your medical examination."

I filled out a questionnaire and paid $100.

A nurse, I believe, took my blood. There is enough AIDS in the U.S. already, is that clear?

A medical technician took an X-ray of my lungs.

The doctor was very nice. He asked me about the situation in Uzbekistan. I answered with pleasure that we had no civil war, and that our wise president Islam Karimov kept peace in the republic.

I was confused when the doctor asked me to take off my sweater and bra. I did not know that the exam included a test for breast cancer! I took off my clothes. Do you know how I felt? I felt shamefully. I was not going to flirt with anybody. I never was a stripper. I never was a nudist. Doctors had never checked my breasts. I feel disgusted thinking about male gynecologist. I was raised in a Muslim country, ok?

I felt that he took advantage of me. I was sure that he did not check old women's breasts. I thought that his exam was only for young breasts. It was so embarrassing to me! I was thinking, *When will he finish it?* I paid $100 to be insulted like this and could not do anything about it.

Okay. He finished his job. After that, I had no desire to be nice or to talk about my republic. I did not want to see him any more. When I left his room, I found an old woman who had been examined before me.

I asked her, "Excuse me, I am very confused. Did he examine your breasts?"

The old woman smiled and answered with pleasure, "Yes!"

Okay, I will have to forgive this doctor.

So I spent 30 minutes at that center. I was told to come back on the 16th of March to get an envelope with the results of the analysis. I waited for two days. I was very worried. How could I trust these strange doctors? They could make mistakes and write that I had some terrible sickness! I could not relax, because I was so scared. Those two days were full of praying and hope.

Then, on the 16th of March, I got my analysis in the envelope, which I was not supposed to open. I was fascinated as if I was carrying a bomb.

I knew that if there were something bad about me in this envelope, I would not get an American K-1 visa. I do not know why I was so upset about the secret results of the examination!

I bought different cans of soda, smoked sausages, pineapple, and bananas, and brought the food to the hotel UZBEKISTAN and ate like a pig. It was my first time to try Dr. Pepper.

You might be thinking, Why was Oksana so hungry for all that food? Hadn't she ever seen it before?

Yes, of course, I had seen bananas and pineapples in Tashkent, but I had not ever had enough money to buy this fancy food in my motherland. Uzbekistan imports pineapples and kiwis. When Keith sent me money, I did not feel that I needed to try to save it. I felt like a queen who could buy anything I wanted to eat.

I found out that prices for pineapples and bananas in Moscow were much lower than in Tashkent. I even met a person from my city. She bought pineapples for $3.00 each to sell in Tashkent for $5.00 to $7.00 each to the rich customers.

Oh, do not think that in Uzbekistan the salaries are higher just because the prices are higher! No! Salaries in Moscow are higher than in Tashkent, but still some sellers buy food and books at the capital of Russia and sell them at the capital of Uzbekistan.

We call that kind of people *chelnok*. In Russian, that means, *canoe*. Chinooks take lemons, garlic, pomegranates, and herbs for cooking from Tashkent to sell in Russia. It is like having a business without paying taxes to the government. Imagine yourself not having to pay taxes! Did you imagine it already? Okay, relax. You are not in the Soviet Union, where there are people who know many ways to hide their incomes.

I didn't sleep peacefully that night. I had dreams in which I went to the American Embassy and forgot some of my important papers.

The second day in Moscow, I went to see the Olympic Center – the big building for sport games. I knew that people sold a lot of books inside very cheap. Can you imagine? The place for sport games wants to earn money, so it allows people to rent a place for trade! Yes, I found out that it was a good place to find good bargains, journals, and cards. I understood why smart shoppers prefer to buy some stuff at the Olympic Center! They sell the goodies at the Moscow metro stations, or they take them home to Tashkent, to the provinces, or to other republics to resell. That is a chelnok's job.

The capitalism is growing in the formerly communist Russia. You can be glad that the Soviet Union has elected capitalistic ways of economics. Twenty or thirty years ago, people like chelnoks were considered to be criminals, not modern businessmen.

The Soviet Union gambled away this war against capitalism. Do you roll on your floor laughing with happiness to know that? I feel very sorry for my motherland! I have no idea when circumstances in Russia, Ukraine, Uzbekistan, and the other republics will change, and the sick economy will breathe free. I left my motherland like a rat fleeing from a sinking ship! I did not want to share her problems. I never liked communist ideas. I was a teenager when the period of new reforms started. I felt like the young generation feels now in the former Soviet Union, as if they were fooled by ideas of equality. Socialism destroyed the greatest strong country and her economy. I felt like I didn't want to rebuild something that I was not responsible for having destroyed.

I bought some books for my family at the Olympic Center, because I cared about their intellectual needs. I found some good math books for my brother, some famous Russian modern detective stories for my grandparents, for my father, and for Uncle Andrey.

For me and for my mother, I bought books about karma yoga and about the diagnostics of karma. Each book cost $1.00, and that was a really good deal. I found a lot of books by the American writer Louisa Hey, and I bought some. I was impressed by her ideas and her style. She is a great woman, and I respect her very much.

Yes, my family expected to get gifts, so I couldn't shatter their hopes! I couldn't save Keith's money. For me it was very important to make my family happy. The thought of coming back from Moscow to Tashkent with empty hands seemed impossible. I felt like I was Santa Claus, giving gifts and making people happy. Even he can only make people happy temporarily, though, because human beings are never satisfied.

After my best buy at the Olympic Center, I saw a church and decided to enter. I had never been inside of this church before. I had no money to buy candles and to order some special graces. While I was listening to the liturgy and getting warm (outside there was a lot of snow and the temperature was 20 degrees (F), one old woman asked me to give her some money. She did not believe that I had nothing. She looked at my bag full of books, and her old eyes were full of admonishment.

On the 16th, I got my envelope at the hospital with the medical exam. The warning on the front said, *Do not open the envelope! A representative at the Embassy of the U.S. in Moscow will open it!*

On the 17 of March, I awakened early and went to stand in line at the American Embassy at 7:00 a.m. Later I realized that that was stupid. I had an appointment at 8:00 a.m. I thought that the paper said that the Embassy opened at 8:00 a.m. In Tashkent, the American Embassy used to have long lines from 5:00 a.m., so I was sure that I needed to get in line beforehand.

There were two lines at the Embassy. One line consisted of people who wanted to get a guest or tourist visa. The majority of those people would never see the U.S., because they wouldn't be able to prove their "attachment" to the motherland. They wouldn't be able to prove that they would come back to Russia or that they would not try to stay in the U.S. illegally. How do you prove that you have enough "attachments"? Well, applicants for visa have to prove that they own not only a car or an apartment, but that they have a business, a very high income, some property (stores or restaurants, for example) and that these things would hold them to Russia. Do you understand?

The other line had people who came to get a visa without a lot of problems because they had relatives in the U.S.

I came in when the security guard told me to enter. I gave my passport to the woman at window #11, and she told me, "We haven't got the Affidavit of Support in your file. You can't get the visa without it."

I was shocked. I felt like my knees were shaking and my mouth was dry. All I could feel was hate for everybody in this place! I said to the woman, "Please, check again, because I called the Embassy last week and a man told me that they had received a fax with the Affidavit of Support!"

She asked me to wait. I was waiting for ten minutes and felt very upset. I prayed that God would fix the new problem. God helped me again. The woman from window #11 returned and told me that my papers were found and I just had to wait for the interview.

The interview was at window #8. The American asked me what language I preferred. I said, "Russian." He asked me the following questions:

- *Why do you want to speak Russian?*
- *How long have you known your fiancé?*
- *How did you meet him?*
- *When did you meet him?*
- *What language did you use with him?*
- *Can you show to me something that proves your correspondence with him, pictures of you together in Moscow?*

Yes, I answered all of his questions. I showed him Keith's phone bills ($400 each month), Keith's letters to me, our e-mail correspondence, and our pictures. They already had everything, because Keith had sent it to them! They wanted to make sure that I was really Oksana, Keith Leslie's fiancée, and that our relationship was true. After seeing all my papers, the American asked me if I had any boyfriends in Uzbekistan.

"No, I have not," I answered.

"Aren't there men in your republic?"

"Yes."

"Are Americans better?"

"I think that I have found the man whom I can respect and appreciate. I cannot brag that I know a lot of men in Tashkent that I could trust or that I would want as a husband or as a father for my children."

"Okay, you will get the visa. Come to get it after 5:00 p.m. today."

Thank you, God! I felt really happy! I had gotten the visa! I called Keith and my parents so they could be happy for me. I had gotten the visa! I felt as if I had grown wings to fly, to love, and to create new worlds!

I came to the hotel Uzbekistan and took my bags from the room. I paid $2.00 for the hotel's storage to keep my bags until I returned.

Well, I had five hours before I could get the visa! So first, I visited the famous Moscow art gallery, the Tretyakovskaya. I paid $3.00 for the ticket and enjoyed everything I saw. If you have a chance to visit Moscow, you should see the Tretyakovskaya Art Gallery. You have to know that for foreign speaking tourist prices for tickets are a little bit higher. Sorry, guys!

After going to the gallery, I felt sleepy and went down to the subway. I fell asleep in a metro train. I love Moscow's metro! You don't have to use a taxicab in Moscow, because the metro is like a big spider web. You can get anywhere in this huge city by the metro.

I woke up at 4:30 p.m. and went to the Embassy. I got my passport with the fiancée-visa and did a little more food shopping. I bought some sausages, blueberries, cheese, and some delicious Moscow candies for my family! I had never seen blueberries in my life before, and I was excited to share this new discovery with my parents and my brother!

I came back to the hotel and got my other bags. I had come to Moscow with only one bag, but I left with three. I had books and food to impress my relatives. I didn't think that I could have impressed Keith if I saved his money. I felt, like all Russian women, that if he gave me money, it was my money, and I didn't have to save anything. I didn't connect our lives yet, and Keith was so far from me that I really hadn't any idea that I needed to help him with money.

I flew to Tashkent like a winner. I had gotten the American visa, the bridge to a life I had never had before!

Three days in Moscow ended with the best results for me. I could think only about my new future, when I would be able to eat cheese and mushrooms, chickens, and oranges any time I wanted! I thought about my classmates, who would die from jealousy to hear about my success. I felt as if I had won the lottery. Keith was my jackpot. I did not care about my family, or how hard it would be for them to lose me. I wanted to get out and to love. Thank you, God!

Did you ever feel as if your body had lost its soul? Did you ever have an experience that made you realize that your past is already over, but your future, your next days are yet unknown? Can you understand how difficult it is when you do not feel enough love? I felt that something was missing in my life.

I had a hole in my soul for my first couple months in the U.S. I wanted to check my mailbox every day and receive a lot of letters from my family and friends. However, mail from Uzbekistan usually takes weeks to send or receive. I had a lot of friends in my motherland that could write to me and support me. I waited for two months to receive my first letter from one of my friends. It was not until I returned from my honeymoon with Keith. I got a wedding congratulation card from my friends.

Keith bought me stamps and envelopes, nice stationary, so I can stay in touch with everybody. He supported my hobby to write and my need to stay connected. He started to teach me how to use internet, to search, to answer emails. He drove me to Russian restaurants and stores in Atlanta, bought me Russian newspapers, so I am not falling apart from being alone. He drove me to his friend's houses, so I can get more comfortable around Americans. He could get me Russian TV channels, but I never asked, never cared for those. I wished to fit in my new English American environment. Keith taught me some manners, too. For example, he taught me to hold the door for a person behind you. When someone is paying in a restaurant for my meal, I should not order more than one drink, and not to order the most expensive meal on a menu. Keith was the one who took me for the first time to see a three dimensional movie, to try Japanese food. I was stunned to see huge supermarkets like HOME DEPOT and SUPERWALMART. As a former bartender, Keith could mix some drinks at home. I was getting better-rounded by trying cocktails I never had before in my life. Keith let me chose to rent videos I saw in Russian before. It helped me to understand English more, since I knew what was going on already. Keith tried his best to help me to cope in a new environment.

To confess, I did not truly love Keith when I came to the U.S. I thought that I was in love with him right after Moscow. I felt that he was a very special and original individual. I was impressed by his generosity. His unpredictable sense of humor overwhelmed me. I understood in Moscow that my life with Keith would be full of laughs and kidding. Keith was 39 years old when we met, but his thoughts and behavior were not old and obsolete. Keith is an open-minded person. We played like children in Moscow. We even beat each other with pillows. He did not act his real age. It was terrific to know that my man had a young soul and that my future life would not be boring.

First of all, I wanted to be a happy person, because I escaped from Uzbekistan. I was very proud of myself, as if I had gone shopping for an American husband and gotten the perfect purchase.

It was a great fortune to marry an American. I did not know that my feelings for him would grow like healthy tomatoes. It took time for me to find out that Keith reminded me of my family.

He is like my mom, because he has great taste and the opposite opinion about my "Uzbek taste." He can criticize me exactly like my mom. Like her, he organizes things neatly and keeps everything as clean as possible. I am a slob compared to him. However, he does not tell me, like my mom used to, that I am a fat pig.

He reminds me of my dad by his desire to create things, to work with tools, to carry me on his shoulders. He is very practical, like my dad. He also knows how to save money. He can control my spending attitude and help me to understand American money and budgeting. He teaches me about bills like my dad tried to teach me.

A lot of times I called him "Stas," because he is like my brother, and he can make me scream and run away from him. He is as fun as my Stas. I feel very happy about it. Yes, I want to highlight that before falling in love with my own spouse Keith, I was in love with the idea of my new life in the U.S. I was in love with my rosy vision of America.

I never thought that Keith was my bridge, which I would use however I wanted. I believed that breaking up with a person who loves and appreciates you would never be a green light for a happy future. I felt that I would never leave a person who took me from my Uzbekistan, where I did not have a future as a writer or as a happy woman. I believe that it is almost impossible to create a happy, lucky palace of a new love and marriage on the bricks of broken hearts and injured feelings. I always pray to God to keep my marriage strong and healthy. Do you do the same thing?

CHAPTER 3
COMPARISON STARTS HERE. LEARN ABOUT THE ENVIRONMENT YOUR PARTNER CAME FROM.

Dear American reader!

I want to talk about restrooms.

Imagine, my friend, that you are the tourist of Tashkent, Samarkand, Bukhara, or Khiva. You are looking for the sign, *RESTROOM,* but at the stores you cannot find it because it does not look familiar at all. Probably, you will spend a lot of time looking before you find the sign close to a subway station.

Please, be careful inside. There are no sinks, no toilet paper, and no toilets. Some people already did their business on the floor. I hope you will not step in it.

Sit down, please, or squat. Do not complain that strangers are sitting close to you, and everybody can see you, because there are no walls, and no doors.

However, libraries and theaters have restroom cabins with toilets, sinks, and water. You have to be practical and carry your toilet paper and soap with you. Hotel rooms, as a matter of fact, have everything. Do not worry, if you are going to be staying in a hotel.

When I stayed in Moscow at the Hotel ($50 a night) and at the Uzbekistan Hotel ($30 a night), I was very happy, because I had good service in those hotels, including restrooms!

Moscow has a lot of public restrooms. They are not free. I remember that at the restroom at the Domodedovo Airport, I had to pay fifty cents to use it, but I was disappointed because there was no toilet paper, no soap, and no hand dryer machine. Maybe other Moscow airports have this fancy stuff.

Well, you also do not need to worry about restrooms if you are in a restaurant. Restaurants usually have everything in their restrooms for your pleasure. If you are not a customer at the restaurant, you should not try to go inside to use the restroom. You will be thrown out!

Here in the U.S., I was absolutely amazed by the supermarkets and little convenient stores, which have nice restrooms. But in the beginning I always had bad luck with them. I got stalls with broken locks or stalls that were out of toilet paper.

Funny, I got what I used to have in the Soviet Union!

My pet peeve is seeing urine in a toilet. People often do not care to flush the toilets when they are finished. To me, it is like an insult. It has been my bad luck in American restrooms to get the worst stall!

However even in the worst stall, with urine, poop, or worse, I sit down and thank God that I am in America.

Then, I want to thank God for my dishwasher, which I had never had before! I remember that in my old country it was unpleasant to wash dishes after having company. I would be very tired from cleaning and cooking for my guests, and I definitely hated to wash stuff afterwards. Also, I did not have your fancy "anti-germ" and "anti-grease" liquids! I had to use hard soap. Thank you, God, for the people who created the dishwasher machine!

I also have been impressed by the microwave oven. Yes, Keith spent enough time to explain to me how to use it. I remember that in my country we used to defrost meat outside on a balcony or under the table in our kitchen. It used to take a lot of time. Here in the U.S., the microwave makes your life more comfortable and you do not even think about what kind of gift God gave to all people by letting somebody invent the microwave oven!

In my country, we used to boil water on the stove to make tea. Here, my microwave takes only two minutes to give us this pleasure!

In my country, my parents and all my friends and fellows used to heat up food on their ranges, because they did not have microwaves. That meant that I used to make a cooking pan dirty every time I had to heat up my lunch or dinner.

Do not think that all Russians or Uzbeks have no idea about microwaves. My friends from Tashkent Larissa and Gennady sent me a book in Russian called *1000 Recipes of Microwave Cooking*. Well, some rich people could use this book, but not my friends. None of my friends or family has a microwave.

Wait one second! Now, in the former Soviet Union, supermarkets of the big cities have different kinds of goods, but only rich people can afford to buy them. The middle class is very poor in the republics of the former Soviet Union since Perestroika! A good education does not necessarily mean a good job, satisfaction, or confidence in the next day. It is painful to know that my family and friends spend a lot of time in the kitchen and their university education does not make their life better. It is not their fault. It is the country's deep crisis. It is good to feel that I escaped from my motherland, and I appreciate everything I have now in the United States!

In the Soviet Union, in Uzbekistan, people used to drink hot tea. They did not have refrigerators with icemakers. They had no knowledge of your American habit of putting some ice cubes in your glass any time you want a cold drink! I had to learn to tell a waitress: "No ice, please." My teeth were very sensitive to ice cubes in my drinks. I am very happy to go shopping in the U.S. and fill my refrigerator. My family never had enough money to buy everything we needed. We never used to buy expensive overseas products. We had no idea about avocados, papayas, or a lot of other stuff. I wrote a letter to my family about these products, which they had never known or had before. We also never had credit cards, so we could not charge now and pay later.

Now let's get back to my former home.

Well, I did not like to clean toilets with rags in Tashkent. It was my mom's dirty job. She always complained about this part of her duty.

Let's take a moment to imagine a situation. First you take a bucket and pour water and some detergent inside. Then you take a rag and wash your toilet by hand. You also have to wash out your dirty rag by hand and think about all the germs and urine on your skin because you cannot afford to have gloves or paper towels.

Thank you, God! You created the genius that invented paper towels! Now I love to clean our toilets twice a week, and I am not embarrassed to talk about it! I can spray bleach in the toilet and on the floor around it.

I like to clean it with the amazing paper towels! I do not have to wet my hands or get germs on my skin! I do not need a basket, water, and soap, so I save a lot of time! Thank God that I live in the U.S. and have a lot of American goods! Do you guys feel disgusted with cleaning? It is just because you were never in a worse situation. So now you can appreciate what you have!

Why did I write about paper towels in the chapter about my kitchen? I keep them in my kitchen! Also, I keep under my sink a lot of different treasures, which to you are simply bottles of liquid to clean the floor, the furniture, the carpet, the windows, and the mirrors! You are lucky, because you can have everything you need at the same time! I feel even luckier than you because I grew up without having all these goods and helpers, and I can really appreciate them now.

Keith is not always happy about my housekeeping.

In fact, I was never a good housekeeper in Tashkent. I did cleaning only when under the lash.

My mother was always unhappy about my laundry and cleaning. I hated to do laundry in my country.

Here I love it. I want to explain to you about my past and the reality of most Soviet Union people. Most of them do not have a laundry room. They have to do their laundry in bathrooms. That is where people usually keep their washing machines.

First, I had to open our old-fashioned washing machine to take out its wires and to plug it in. After that, I had to take two hoses out of the washing machine. One tip of one hose I used to connect to the bottom outside of the machine. Then I had to screw another tip of the same hose into the washing machine.

I used the other hose to put water into the washing machine from our bathtub's tap. I had to be very careful because it was easy to make a flood if I left the hose in the washing machine too long! I had to stay in the bathroom. I would watch the water pour down into the washing machine. I had to turn it off in time to avoid flooding.

Then I had to put the detergent and clothes in the clean water. After about six minutes, they were ready to go through the squeezing machine. Our squeezing machine was connected to the washing machine. I had to transfer clothes from washing machine to it by hand or with help of wooden long tongues.

After three to five small loads, I needed to change the water. I had to take out dirty water first, so I would take one tip of the hose out of the machine and put it into the sink. I cannot brag that I enjoyed holding the hose for five to ten minutes until all the brown-blue water would come out into the sink. Then I had to clean the washing machine and sink after draining out the water. While the washing machine was working, I had to pour cold water into the bathtub.

After the spinning cycle, I had to put the clothes into the warm or cold water in our bathtub. I had to do that because our old-fashioned washing machine did not have an automatic rinsing cycle! So I had to rinse the clothes out in the bathtub. Later, I had to take them out and put them into the spinning machine again!

Yes, it was a lot of hard work. I knew that if it was my turn to wash clothes, which my mother, brother, father, and me had saved for two weeks, it could take me four to six hours. The washing machine could not fit very many clothes at one time. I had to change the dirty water several times.

After washing, I had to starch some of the white shirts, pillowcases, and sheets. It was my mom's rule that all the sheets and pillowcases had to be starched. We could not buy a bottle of starch, because it was fancy, expensive stuff. We used to boil starch powder in a pan and later put the clean clothes inside the pan. After starching, I had to wring the clothes out by hand. One thing I hated about doing laundry in Russia was the fact that my hands were wet all the time.

We did not have a dryer machine either, so all the families used to dry their clothes outside on their balconies or on a clothesline. I remember that we always argued about who would have to hang out linen?

Here in the U.S., I was so happy to find that there was an easy way to do laundry! I already wrote a letter to my family about how happy I was to not wet my hands when I do laundry! I save a lot of time, because I do not have to use hoses, plugs, or rinse stuff by hand! I even have a fabric softener, which I never had before in my country! And I also have a bottle of starch, so I do not need to boil starch powder or dip clothes in a pan with starch!

I also do not have to dry my clothes outside now, and I do not have to follow my mom's rule about starching all the sheets and pillowcases! I am so happy that I do not have to spend time ironing the linens! Americans have fitted sheets, which they stretch over their mattresses! This helps the

Americans a lot, and they save a lot of time on making beds, and they do not spend a lot of time ironing their sheets!

Oh, thank God that I live in the U.S.! In my country, two well-educated people usually could not make enough money to buy enough clothes and food to eat. A lot of people have to work very hard just to get paid once in three months. Their domestic work is very hard, too. Many people dream of having a better life.

A lot of people in Uzbekistan and Russia cannot even imagine how spoiled Americans are!

Are you an American? Do you have to get your hands wet when you do your laundry? No? Say, "Thank you, God!"

Are you an American? Is it possible for you to pay money to someone to clean and iron your shirts for you? Is it normal for you to do it? Say, "Thank you, God!"

During my first couple months in the U.S., I had a difficult time understanding how to use the washer and dryer. I could not figure out how to make them start!

I also had difficulty understanding how to use bleach. In my country, we only have powdered bleach, and my mother used it only for white clothes. Here I did not know that the liquid bleach was only for white stuff! We had two bottles of the bleach in Atlanta. One had a lot of flowers on it, so I thought that it was for clothes with colors! Oh, you just do not know how boring it was for me to try to translate every new word on a bottle! You just don't know. I was using bleach for the first time without reading any instructions at all. I did not even want to take the time to translate the meaning of the word "bleach." So some of the clothes were ruined, and Keith still reminds me about it.

In Tashkent, I never knew about the existence of fabric softener. But I am sure that if Uzbekistan markets now have this kind of fancy stuff, lots of families still would not be able to afford to buy it. If they had a choice between buying a piece of meat for dinner or some fabric softener, which they had never used before in their whole life, they would never buy the fabric softener! Now I have started to understand what this fabric softener does, and I like it!

For several years of our marriage, I was doing Keith's and my laundry. If I would forget to take the clothes out of the dryer in time, I would have to spend some time by the ironing board. Actually, after Keith got his job in Arizona and started to work at home, he did not have to dress up and wear white shirts at all, so I did not have to use starch on his work clothes like I used to have to in Atlanta when he worked at Lanier.

Oh, I was a happy homemaker! I had detergent, bleach, fabric softener, and a bottle of starch! I never dreamed that I would have these things! I had no idea that my life would be so easy and filled with so many American goods! That is not all!

When I arrived in the U.S., I had a big cultural shock. A lot of new things impressed me. I wrote a bunch of letters to my family about those things. I will tell you about those new things, so that you can see the difference between the former Soviet Union and American cultures.

First of all, the food stores seemed to me like museums of food. I saw a lot of fruits all year long and wrote about them to my family. They were surprised to know that you could buy and eat strawberries, grapes, and peaches all year long in the U.S.

I wrote to my family about how happy I was buying meat in the U.S. First of all, meat in the U.S. supermarkets has been packed and cleaned of dirt and skinflints. I remember that in Uzbekistan I could spend one hour cleaning meat from skinflints, or tiny bones, before I could start cooking it. My family used to shop at local bazaars in Tashkent; we could not afford expensive new markets with packed meats.

Another thing that was amazing for my family and friends to find out from me was that Americans eat different salads and use different dressings. Sour cream, mayonnaise, and vegetable oil are regular dressings for most of the people in the republics of the former Soviet Union.

I had difficulty understanding that in the U.S. dressings were more delicious than what I had been used to before. It wasn't easy to figure out how to use Ranch, bleu cheese, and other dressings, which I found in Keith's refrigerator. I used bleu cheese on pasta because I thought that it was just a rotten cheese which had to be used somehow. I used to smear bread with ranch dressing for Keith's sandwiches. I did not want to ask him how he liked his sandwiches, because I was sure that hungry men could eat anything.

It took me months to figure out that he likes his sandwiches with mayonnaise, lettuce, a piece of tomato, and a piece of turkey. I was sure that he was a picky eater, since he did not like my experiments with American food. Later I started to cook the way he wanted and liked. I was definitely changing.

My family and most of the Russian and Uzbek people I know do not eat sandwiches. In the Soviet Union for many years, butter breads were popular. Russian people smear a piece of bread with butter or horseradish and put a piece of cheese or smoked tallow (pig's fat) or a piece of sausage on top of it. Russians do not put another piece of bread on the top of their "sandwiches."

When I tried to eat sandwiches in the U.S. without bread on the top, Keith was very angry. He called me "toady." It was just part of my culture, that we did not eat two pieces of bread at the same time. It took some time for me to change my eating habits. That is why I am overweight now!

I discovered new products like cereals and oatmeal. I was overwhelmed with doughnuts! I did not like cinnamon rolls. Celery and peanut butter were new to me.

Uzbeks and Russians are not used to peanut butter and jelly sandwiches; cereal milk bowls for breakfast or bacon. American sausage links and sausage patties do not exist in Russian menu. My Regular Russian breakfast was buckwheat or barley porridge, omelet, or bread and butter. Here, in America, I discovered foods like hash puppies, corn bread,

hash browns...

Russians love four kinds of salads very much. The first one is sliced tomatoes, onions, cucumber, red or green peppers with sour cream or mayonnaise. The second one is boiled, chopped eggs, potatoes, carrots, meat, yellow onion, sliced sour apple, pickles, and sweet peas with sour cream or mayonnaise. It is like an American potato salad, but with more healthy ingredients. The next is boiled, chopped eggs, chopped green onions, and fish with mayonnaise or the fish sauce from the can. The last salad is boiled, chopped eggs, fresh chopped radishes, and onions with mayonnaise.

The most famous Russian salad is called Herring under Fur Coat. I love it very much. We had this salad at our wedding, because we had a chance to order it in the Russian restaurant Moscow, in Atlanta. This salad includes boiled, sliced potatoes, beets, eggs, and herring. This salad has to be covered by a sour cream. It is a very rich food.

I had to explain to my mom that in the U.S., doctors would never be medical technicians. In the U.S., you do not have to be a doctor if you want to be an ultrasound specialist. In Uzbekistan, she worked as a pediatrician first, and after several years she got training to be an ultrasound specialist. She writes prescriptions, she checks on her patients, and she has a full-time job in the hospital. Every two years she attends more training.

I gave my family and friends a chance to learn about the things they never knew. For example, in Uzbekistan they do not have or use in their system any kind of insurance.

I learned from my Mom, that my brother in Russia bought health insurance. He was obligated to do it as a foreign student. My mom kept telling me in her letters that I needed to go to a doctor, without having any American ID or health insurance. She could not understand that it is very expensive. She could not stand to hear from us the word "expensive." She wrote to me in one letter, *Stop writing to me about what is expensive.* She had a difficult time understanding that we could not afford to buy and do a lot of things.

She used to give me advice about what kind of hair-removal kit that I should buy. My Grandma Nina saw advertisements of American products, and wrote to me about products that I should buy to lose my extra twenty-five pounds. I had to explain to them that I could not just buy whatever I wanted. I also cannot simply believe in every advertisement that I see on TV. They were sure that Americans could afford to buy any products they wanted. My family had a difficult time understanding that my husband and I did not want to pay $50 or more for weight loss products. Later, we actually spent close to this amount for another quick-weight-loss product, but it gave me diarrhea, and I did not lose a pound.

My family could not understand why Keith did not send me to a college right away. It is pretty easy in the former Soviet Union to get an education. It was free for years. It was easy to change your university or school. You did not have to be a resident for a year to get a cheaper tuition. My family could not understand that when I just got to the U.S., I did not have a regular American ID card. I was not considered a resident of Atlanta. Keith was busy organizing our wedding. My family could not give a penny for the wedding, and they still expected Keith to send me to college and send them money.

Actually, my English was not good enough yet for any college. I was too shy to ride a bus. It was three months of staying at home, overeating and oversleeping. Actually, it was also a time for watching cartoons, whose language I could understand.

My family believed that if I got to stay in the paradise of the U.S. that I would never know about any sacrifice. So they thought it was my turn to be charitable. Father very smoothly wrote me a letter, and told me how much he needed to fix his car. It was going to cost $400. I wrote him back that we needed more than that to paint and fix our car, but nobody could send money to us.

My mom believed that with my Uzbekistan University's education, I deserved to be at least a secretary in a nice office in the U.S. She was angry that I did not pass a test at the Motorola factory. She wrote back to me, *You did not even pass a simple test at the factory! That means your English is very bad. Stop playing with your stinky rats. Go to college to learn English instead.*

She still did not understand that we moved from Georgia to Arizona, and I had to become a resident of Arizona before I could take college classes. She did not realize that we were in the process of buying a brand new house. We were in the process of saving money for a lot of things. My family could understand this simple fact from my letters: if we have money to save, it means that we do have extra cash to share, too.

We did not have another car for me to drive to work or to school. We could not even buy another car, because then we would not be able to get our loan for the house. For my mom, the most important thing was my American education, so that I would be independent from Keith.

It was not easy to correspond with my totally ignorant, lovely relatives. Thank God, I love to write letters. Thank God, I have patience. Thank God, I have Keith. He helps me to buy as many stamps as I want so that I can stay in touch with all my relatives and friends. Keith also helps me to ignore my mom's orders and useless suggestions on how to live in the U.S. Keith was always my Kleenex supplier, when I used to cry after conversations with my mom or after reading her letters.

Another thing that I wrote to my friends and family about was American holidays like Christmas, Halloween, and Easter.

I also shared with them incredible information about sales in stores. People do not have sales in Uzbekistan or in Russia. They have only inflation, and prices go up every week.

I explained to them about the American credit system. I wrote letters about health, life, and car insurance. Russians do not have to deal with things like that. True, they do not pay house insurance, but they can lose everything during a fire accident. Can you imagine life without car insurance? Russians can, but most of them do not even have cars, as they take a subway or bus to go to work.

I wrote to them about the credit system and how you can go on a trip or buy furniture and pay for it for months and years. This credit system saved Keith and me from bankruptcy when he was sick or unemployed.

I wrote to my family and friends about how you can get stamps in the mail and do not have to go to the post office. I wrote them about how we bought plane tickets from priceline.com with a credit card, and how we got our tickets to a ballet through the mail. It is so amazing how the American system is so safe and doing business is so easy.

Another amazing American service that I wrote to them about was the Post Office's change of address. You could never transfer your mail to a new address in Uzbekistan or Russia. First of all, most people do not even have any mail to get or to send, because they do not have checkbooks to send checks to pay the bills. They simply walk to special offices to pay their bills. Actually, in Uzbekistan people can pay their phone bills at local postal offices. Here you get mail every day, a lot of junk mail. In me country I did not know what "junk mail" was. Our mailbox could be empty for days.

Keith always showed me attention and listened when I was telling him about the environment I grew up in. Listening and learning helps to understand each other's backgrounds. All foreign spouses have to learn how to operate new equipment. The spouse, who is teaching those skills to his /her partner, have to be patient and be ready for foreign partner's mistakes.

CHAPTER 4
START OF INTERNATIONAL MARRIAGE. DO NOT EXPECT A LOT OF HELP FROM YOUR FOREIGN PARTNER.

Keith's notes– April 1998

Anticipating Oksana's arrival to the United States, my friends' and family's true characters came out. One family member was very upset that I could possibly be marrying a non-Christian. Other friends were very cautious and reserved. Others were sincerely excited for me. And yet others were sincerely concerned.

Prior to this, a year of correspondence through letters, e-mail, and phone calls had led up to a meeting in Moscow.

Moscow was every person's romantic fantasy. It was beautiful. We met in November, and I began to fall in love.

The day has finally come. My friends came over and helped me clean. I have cleared out a closet and dresser for her. I have tried to make my simple one-bedroom apartment into a home that is inviting, pleasant, and cheerful.

I met Oksana at JFK airport in New York. She surprised me from behind at the airport with a big hug. She looked as if she had a serious thought on her mind. She told me that she must meet her friend's daughter here to deliver a letter. We did it.

Then we took a taxicab to our hotel and met my brother and sister-in-law for dinner in the northern part of the city. Oksana did not know what to order, and I had very little success in explaining the menu to her.

She seemed to be very tired. It was cold from the draft coming in the door behind our backs. We had a very good dinner, and went to the hotel. In the hotel, she was again cold and tired. We took a shower and went to sleep, because we had to get up at 4:00 a.m. for our flight to Atlanta.

Upon arriving in Atlanta, we were met by our friend Rick. He and our friends Galina and Dewitt met us at the airport. I wanted to show Oksana how many people were so eagerly awaiting her arrival, so I had planned a small party for those people who had helped me in the preparations.

This turned into a disaster rather quickly. Oksana overdressed for the occasion, despite my advice. She became cold and tired and uncomfortable very fast. This was a big disappointment to those guests. I found her in the bedroom by herself soon after she had eaten, sulking. She asked me gruffly, "When will they go?"

I asked everyone to leave, explaining that we were very tired, especially Oksana. She needed more rest after her eighteen-hour flight, her first New York experience and all the excitement of coming to America.

OKSANA'S NOTES ABOUT THE WEDDING

For the first time in my life I saw blooming magnolias and friendly squirrels all over place! I enjoyed seeing tall pines and flowers, but I could not breathe. It was too humid for me. I could only breathe in conditioned one bedroom apartment in a buck head area, Keith was renting.

If my Russian friends and family knew what kind of wedding I would get, they would have pitied poor Oksana and Keith.

I learned about American life from movies. I watched a TV show called *Santa Barbara* for some years. I was sure that my wedding would be something gorgeous like the weddings on this show.

I had no idea that stupid flowers would cost so much money! The majority of people in Russia and Uzbekistan do not get paid $400 in a year! Here in America, we spent that crazy sum for some small bouquets.

My rosy vision about the U.S. started to disappear day by day after my arrival. I was disappointed by the U.S. even before my wedding. I found out that we never had enough money for the kind of wedding and fun I wanted. I thought that my first months in the U.S. would be full of restaurants, museums, and theaters. No. Keith had to work as a computer programmer at Lanier, and I could really only spend time with him in the evenings and on weekends. He was trying to entertain me, but I heard a lot about saving money for the wedding. I was sure that the words "sacrifice" and "savings" existed only in the socialistic society back in Russia.

I could not imagine that Keith and I would have to spend some days cleaning the restaurant where the ceremony would take place.

Before my arrival to the U.S., Keith told me that he was going to buy a restaurant with his friends. He wanted to be one of the investors.

This information impressed my father very much! He loved the idea that his son-in-law would be an owner of a private business. We had no idea that "the restaurant" was a big, old building in poor repair without any kind of equipment. When I saw this place for the first time, I got very frustrated. I have never seen such dirty windows, walls, toilets, and so many flies. There were not enough lights, and there was no water. It was just a piece of dirty land covered with bricks and beer advertisements.

No, I did not like the idea of having to clean the place where my own wedding would take place. However, we did not have money for a nicer place, because Keith had invested money in this restaurant. He could not get more money before our wedding. Keith trusted his partners, but they ripped him off. We did not have a really nice wedding because of Keith's sneaky, black "friends."

I thought that I came to the U.S. to enjoy my life and to not care about money. It was hard to see that things were different than I had thought. Preparation for the wedding was hard work. Some of our Atlanta friends were helping us. At that time, I did not think about how much they did for us and for me in particular. I was so surprised by everything that I could not think clearly.

I had just come to the U.S. and already had to hear from Keith words that I never expected to hear from an American: "We have no money. We have to save money."

All my life in Tashkent, I had heard the same thing from my parents! I thought that I had changed my life radically! I changed the country, the language, and the culture, but I could not change the rules of life! I still had to be practical and think about money.

You cannot imagine how bad I felt. I was thinking that all Russian women try to escape from the different republics of the Soviet Union, and they do not have to think about money at all in the U.S., the country of paradise! Poor American guys do not know that their Russian brides have too many hopes about them and their life in the U.S.

Well, let's get back to my wedding. There were not enough lights in the restaurant. You should see our wedding video. It is pretty dark! We had no money to pay for a professional one. Keith's friend said that his gift to us would be our wedding video. I thought that he would pay to have a professional take the video. No. He used our videocassette and our video camera! He chose a position right in front of the windows, in front of the sunlight, and stood there without moving through the whole ceremony! Our wedding video came out really bad. He made a video of us taking pictures and eating.

He was so irresponsible that he was in a hurry to go out on a date. He had the responsibility to make a video of the most important day in our life, and he ran out on a date. Do you think I could forgive this? We do not even have the video of our cake, of all our guests, of people dancing, and of all the fun! All Keith's family members flew in from Ohio and Pennsylvania to be at our wedding! Do you think our wonderful video man took the time to videotape this important moment when all the family was together? No, he did not, just because he had a date. How can I respect people who cannot keep their promises or control their physical needs? Well, I was upset that Keith had depended on this kind of weak and good-for-nothing person. He was to me like another "face of America."

Keith's brother Kevin Leslie from New Jersey was our photographer at our wedding. He worked hard, and he used seven rolls of film to take pictures of our guests and events. We appreciated his help a lot. At the time, I had no idea how much money he had saved us. Thank you, Kevin!

Thank you, God. Keith has a very good and helpful family.

Do you know that Keith's sister Kim and his parents Richard and Joann helped to make the restaurant nicer, too? Oh, Kim bought toilet paper, napkins, trashcans, and hand soap for the restaurant.

Do you think this sounds funny? "Sister bought trash cans and toilet paper for brother's wedding." To me, it sounds somewhat embarrassing, but on the other hand it sounds respectful. I got to know Keith's family in an extreme situation!

Keith's Uncle Larry from MacClenny, Florida, made it to our wedding with his beautiful wife Joann Nolder. Uncle Larry was a very sick person, so he could not make it to his sons' wedding. However, he was my honorary "father," because I did not have any relatives at the wedding to give me away. Keith's brother Kyle and his family flew in to be at our wedding, too! It was really impressive, because they had just had a baby in April of

1998! They came to see us at the end of May with a two-month-old baby! I do not think that I would be as brave as that.

Now I want to say several words about my friend. I grew up with Alina Groysman. We used to go to the same childcare center as well as to the same public school. We were neighbors and friends since we were five years old. She came to the U.S. with her family and started her new life in San Francisco. I will never be able to forget her financial help to me while I lived in Uzbekistan. She used to send me $50 for my birthdays. It was a real help to me when I was a student and later when I was a teacher.

I had a dream to be in the U.S. and to see my friend Alina as the maid of honor at my wedding. My dream came true! Alina and her husband Alex were able to fly out from San Francisco to be guests at our wedding. Just think about it! I had a plan to be married to an American and to have my best friend Alina at my wedding as the maid of honor. I was so sure and so lucky! She could have just sent me $25 and a nice card with excuses like, *Sorry; we do not have the money to fly to Atlanta from San Francisco.*

Other special guests we had were Galina and Dewitt, who introduced us, and who helped us to meet each other through correspondence. If Dewitt had not married Galina from Uzbekistan, Keith would never have had the possibility to think of having a Russian woman as his possible soul mate, as his pen pal, or as his wife. Sometimes I feel that God let Galina meet Dewitt just because He had a plan for me to be married to Keith.

God blessed us with help. A lot of people helped us.

I want to say special words about Dawn Barkett. She was Keith's girlfriend for four years before they broke up. They stayed friends after their separation. She knew that Keith did not have time and money to rent tables, chairs, tablecloths, plates, and glasses, so she rented everything for us. She has a big heart. She wanted to see Keith happy. Her gift for us was a night in the hotel Marriott Marquis. It was my first time ever in a really nice hotel. Dawn tried to do everything she could to be the greatest friend in the world.

We did not have enough money to make our wedding super unforgettable for our guests. However, we got them some small souvenirs – famous Russian dolls called Matrioshkies. It was Keith's idea. Russians do not have the nice custom of presenting appreciation gifts to wedding guests.

I saw that a lot of the guests left our party before we cut the cake. In Uzbekistan early leaving would be considered an insult. I am sure that I was a bad hostess. I did not have enough confidence to speak with strangers.

Keith's brothers and sister had difficulty understanding my accent. I was afraid to go from one guest to another to talk, to ask questions, and to thank them. I was stressed out from being in America! I was surprised by Keith's dad, who led the wedding ceremony. I did not know how to behave. I only cared how I would look in the pictures and on the video, and I wanted to talk to my Russian friends from Uzbekistan, Galina and Alina.

We had a Russian disk jockey that we invited from the Russian club. His name was Igor Kopnar. He was the owner of a travel agency. He was the guy who helped Keith to get his Russian visa and tickets to Moscow. Igor did a great job at our wedding by picking up some really good Russian, American, and Italian music.

I did not know that newlyweds were supposed to dance at their own wedding. Keith and I did not have any training to dance. However, our dance amazed everybody. People were sure that we had gone to some dance classes.

We were a perfect match for each other. Our bodies knew how to move, and what to do. It was an incredible discovery for me and for Keith. I had no idea that somebody could dance with me with so much understanding and passion. It was like a miracle.

The biggest miracle was my wedding. I knew that I had worked it out. I knew that God had helped me. I knew that God wanted me to be with Keith. I knew that I deserved a better life. I was sure that my wedding was not bad, but I had no idea that I would have to clean the place after the guests left! Did you ever meet a bride who had to clean the place of her wedding party after guests left? I was that bride.

I took off my white dress and put on my T-shirt and shorts right in the restaurant to clean everything up with Keith and the group of our friends: Chet and Thad Barkett, Carey Cox, Sherry, and several others.

When I think about my wedding, I think about a lot of cleaning and sweating. For Keith and me, our wedding was a lot of hard work.

My favorite aunt, Lena Rashevskaya, who practices holistic healing and psychology, wrote to me in one of her letters about my wedding.

Oksana, you have to be happy and proud that your marriage started with hard work. It is a very deep symbol of your life. You and Keith have cleaned your past. So your future will be clean and hopeful. The problems in your life drew people whom you can trust in the future. You did not know the personalities of Keith's relatives and friends. So you had a splendid chance to see who is who!

However, if my wedding took place in Uzbekistan or Russia, I would not have to think about things like does maid of honor's dress matches my wedding colors. In Uzbekistan or Russia a bride has only one maid of honor, who picks what she wants to wear. There are no matching bouquets. Brides get all kinds of flowers from guests as gift attachments. So, brides do not choose any flowers for their weddings! We do not have flower girls, also.

Bride does not have to wear "something old, something borrowed and something new" in Uzbekistan or Russia. I would not have to throw flowers to a crowd of single ladies.

I was a maid of honor at my friend's wedding in Tashkent. My friend was half Tartar and half Uzbek. She was 17. He was 17 also, Uzbek, and a very handsome and intelligent young man. It was their first love. The couple was driven with some close family members to a civil court, where they signed papers. Their marriage was registered. Then our little crowd visited some famous places in Tashkent, where newly weds left flowers and took pictures. Then we went to the apartment of bride's parents and had feast, which was prepared by her relatives. It means, that this family could not afford restaurant. Anyway, my present was a flower bouquet and an envelope with money. I could not give her a lot, because I was a student, who was getting little stipend. When later I asked my friend to give me her wedding picture with me in it, she told me how much it will cost me. I did not have the cash, but offered her a book about sex of the same value. Her husband agreed, and I got the picture.

My other, 20 years old, friend got married a different way, more traditional Uzbek-Muslim one. However, it was not arranged. I remember, that bride's parents weren't very happy with the fact, that her chosen man did not have a university education like she possessed. However, they later grew more satisfied then he started to take some evening classes at one college. Bride's parents told her that they can not afford a big wedding, involving a feast in the restaurant, car rides to Tashkent sights and a honeymoon. She had to make a choice. She chose to have a honeymoon. So, mullah, a Muslim priest, was invited to their home. He said a prayer and announced young couple as husband and wife. The bride with covered face was sitting on the carpet besides her groom. The mullah got on the floor also. Mullah did not tell them to kiss each other. The same day, newly weds traveled to another republic to stay at some lake's resort. I was not invited to this wedding, since guests were not invited. I gave her my gift when she came to visit me after her honeymoon.

51

One Russian girl I knew fell in love with one Uzbek guy. They started dating. His family was against their relationship, and condemned him. Her mother was not very happy either, but daughter's happiness was everything. So, Russian family made all the wedding arrangements with financial input of Uzbek groom at one of the biggest restaurants of Tashkent. Their wedding was rich and big. The happy couple went to civil court to register first, then visited famous city sights, then had a party. Groom's relatives did not come. Newly weds were young, the man was trying to avoid mandatory service in Uzbek army, and rushed with his Russian wife to Moscow to start a new life.

My American wedding was different from Russian or Uzbek tradition. Keith expected me to help him to plan the wedding, to have ideas. Since I did not know much about American wedding traditions, my ideas and imagination were worthless. My family could not help financially or arrive to the wedding. It was impossible to get a visa for my parents or pay for the airplane tickets to the US.

Later, Keith's cousin married a Japanese lady. She was born in Japan, but lived in the USA for sometime. She knew the language, American wedding traditions already. In this case, they combined American and Japanese wedding traditions. The bride was wearing a white gown; the groom was dressed in Japanese kimono. Groom's family organized the wedding. Bride's family arrived, but never asked how they can help out financially as American family expected. This is what I am talking about, do not expect,

DO NOT EXPECT, DO NOT EXPECT, before you find out for sure, what is your future foreign spouse is capable of bringing to the table of your relationship.

KEITH'S NOTES FROM OUR WEDDING

To me, our wedding was one of the happiest and most beautiful days of my life.

Even it was raining. The water was not turned on until the day of the wedding. Even though I spent all of my savings and had to borrow money. Even though my mother and I argued the day before the wedding, and Oksana and I argued the morning of the wedding. Despite these negative things, there were so many positive, good things.

Oksana did not know anything about planning an American wedding. I had to arrange everything. I chose to have the wedding at our new restaurant site. I thought it would be a great way to combine fixing it up to open with my event. Time was critical, as we were planning to open the restaurant in weeks. We had originally planned to already have it open. However, no one was really doing anything, except me.

I later lost over $2000 on this deal, along with some very valuable time. I was promised by T.C. to receive this money before my wedding, but he never paid me. This left me short of funds. I could not afford to do the things I had wanted, and I had no money for a honeymoon. Thank God, some friends and family sent money. Without it, we would have had no honeymoon. The $600 I received in gifts helped us to travel to my uncle's house in Jacksonville, Florida, and to visit an amusement park in Atlanta. I had to use the other money to pay back my debt.

I was not really able to enjoy myself as much as I wanted. I was so stressed. Oksana had told me she was bringing a wedding dress from her country. Then I found out that she had not. Not only had she not brought a dress, she also had not brought any good clothes or shoes, or anything. She had expected me to buy her all new American things.

I waited to plan the wedding so that Oksana could give her opinions and input. This was a mistake. I found that Oksana was uncaring about any of this. She expected me to magically arrange everything to her dreams. She expected me to use ESP to know what her dreams were. She would answer, "I do not know," to every question I asked her. I asked her about location, food, decorations, etc. She really had no opinions.

I read of her criticism and broken dreams. I was shocked. I do not think she had a clue of what I had to do. But for me, my wedding was a beautiful day. My friends and family are great.

OKSANA'S BOOK CONTINUES

I feel that it is important to give our readers some Keith's and mine backgrounds.

Keith was born in 1958, in Florida, and I was born in 1973, in Uzbekistan.

When I was three years old, Keith joined the U.S. Army.

When we were growing up – each of us in our own time and place – neither of us had computers, VCRs, Segas, Nintendos, cell phones, microwaves, remote controls, or Palm Pilots. However, Keith's childhood was filled with his mom's piano playing. My dad was a professional musician and was teaching me how to play, too.

Keith remembers times when his mom was sick and tired with nothing to cook. He told me, ". . . and fifteen minutes later someone would ring our doorbell and bring us food. It was like a miracle. Sometimes a family from our church would invite us over for dinner. That was a big deal for the six of us. I would say that we were members of the lower middle class."

This support from church members is not common in Uzbekistan or Russia. Relatives usually live close enough to provide such support to needy family.

When I was growing up, I remember how my father used to spend extra cash for stocking food (rice, carrots, potatoes, pumpkins, melons, apples, flour, beans, sugar, canned meat, onions, and pasta), in case of inflation or unemployment, and because his parents had done the same thing. I remember days when we had no meat to eat, but I also remember days when we ate caviar with bread every day for breakfast. My favorite breakfast was fried eggs or buckwheat porridge. Some families served to themselves a piece of bread with butter and sugar on top.

If my brother and I ever got tired of our parents' cooking, we would take a tram and spend a weekend with our grandparents. I remember that grandmother Nina could fix unforgettable soup with mushrooms, soup with barley and pickles. I remember one day I ate ram's cooked brains and mash potatoes for lunch. Grandma Nina could fix pirogies with cow's heart. I liked fried chicken gizzards or beef liver with onions on my bread.

Keith was taught from the time he was a little boy that the most important thing in life is God. When Keith was young, his social activities included church, basketball, and baseball.

I was taught by my parents and grandparents that education is the most important part of life. My social life revolved around more cultural activities such as going to theaters, museums, and the zoo, as well as attending music school.

When I was sixteen or seventeen, I was sure that I would never get married. Sometimes I had fantasies that one day an alien would take me into his spaceship and we would travel to the stars.

When Keith was sixteen or seventeen, he was sure that he would never get married before he was in his thirties.

When I was sixteen, I planned to become a writer. From the time that I was eleven, I occasionally had some of my articles and poems published in local papers.

When Keith was sixteen, he had no idea what he would like to do with his life. So he started as a soldier in the infantry. He was in training for four years, learning how to fight U.S. enemies (Russians). He never suspected that he would be married to a Russian in the future!

Keith told me one story, how a piece of a broken mirror was a prize possession for an army guy. They would use them for shaving. I grow up with a superstition that looking into a broken mirror will bring bad luck!

Our common hobby was reading. Keith and I as teenagers loved to spend time with historical novels and fiction. I enjoyed Mid Evil novels about torture and fights for the throne! Keith liked war strategies.

I never liked romance novels, and Keith did not either. Why? We both did not believe in love. We did not know that one day we would meet each other and love would happen to us! Even after we met and fell in love, we still did not enjoy reading romance novels. However, international marriage is not a romance.

It is a hard work.

CHAPTER 5
DEALING WITH THE FAMILY
AND FRIENDS OF YOUR
FOREIGN SPOUSE.

Imagine how naive I used to be to think that my honeymoon would be something extraordinary!

It could be a trip to Hawaii or Miami, to Egypt or to Italy. I did not know that something extraordinary costs a lot of money. I did not care about money. I forgot that Keith's father was a preacher and that he was not a millionaire, and his son was not rich, either.

I could not imagine that we would not be able to travel to another country. It was not just because of Keith's money situation. For traveling, I had to have a travel document, which could be an "advance parole" for a non-immigrant like me. Advance parole gives permission to a non-immigrant to come back into the U.S.

To tell you the truth, it takes time to get this document. You have to wait three to four months after applying and paying $95 to the INS. I believe that there is no way for a person who came into the U.S. as a fiancée to travel until she has applied for her travel document.

My honeymoon was great anyway. Keith tried to do everything to make me happy. I wanted to see his Uncle Larry and Aunt Joann in Florida. I wished to see the ocean for the first time in my life. I wanted to pick up a lot of shells and swim. I desired to try seafood, to taste all kinds of cocktails.

We were driving to visit his Uncle Larry and Aunt Joann Nolder in Florida. Keith was driving. I remember that day very well, because I was impressed by Florida's bogs and palms and by all the guts of dead insects on our car's windshield. We hit a small crocodile that was crossing the highway. It was scary and unusual. I said that it was a good sign for Keith and me.

Keith was telling me some stories. I had a headache from trying to understand all this American talking and slang. In my head, I had to put it all together and to imagine how to write the spoken sentence. I had to translate each word separately in order to grasp the whole sentence. Later, I did not have to write sentences in my brain. I started to catch the meaning of the whole phrase or sentence right away if I listened.

So while we were driving our little blue Plymouth, Keith told me very seriously, "Your feet are on fire."

I was listening at that time, and got surprised and said, "Why? How can that be?"

Keith was happy and exclaimed, "You listen to me! I kept telling you that your feet were on fire for a long time, and you would just agree with me. I see that you do not pay attention to what people say."

Keith realized that I could answer his questions without listening or understanding. I was always telling him, "Yes."

This is a quality I still have. Keith can catch me not listening to him or to other people.

My honeymoon was full of discoveries for me. Keith was like a magician. It was so romantic. He knew exactly what kind of food to order to impress me, to open new horizons for me in American food and alcohol. If you are waiting on your fiancée to come to America, remember that she will be like a child in a candy store.

I could not stop myself from trying and tasting, eating and drinking. I learned about marshmallows and French fries! I ate shark's meat and snails! I ordered shrimp and crab! In my life in Uzbekistan, I could not even imagine such luxurious eating. My honeymoon started with it.

When I close my eyes and think about my honeymoon, I see a bright picture. I can still picture Keith and me riding a roller coaster. I can see us screaming and later, kissing right on the beach by the Atlantic Ocean.

Before our honeymoon, we did not really have a lot of time to spend together. Of course, Keith took me to a mall, to Atlanta's botanical garden, and to his friends' houses.

I feel that we got married before we really knew each other's personalities well enough.

We sensed each other's strengths, values. We knew that we can get alone. We talked before our marriage, that we want to start a family in a couple of years. We planned to be parents one day! However, it was our business, when we will do it.

You know that it is a tradition to wish something for a married couple. People wished us to have a lot of children soon. At first I thought that it was a normal tradition to say the same thing over and over again.

My family and friends kept asking me in their letters about my health and any possibility of a pregnancy. It seemed that everybody was very interested in my becoming a mother. It made me very angry. I had to write to my family and friends and explain why we were not going to have babies right away! I had to explain to them why we were not going to follow Russian and Uzbek traditions about getting pregnant right away after our wedding. They thought that it would be very easy to start a family in the U.S. I thought so, too.

I came to the U.S. as a non-immigrant with a temporary fiancée visa. The visa was going to expire on the 3rd of July in 1998. We had to get my status and visa changed. It takes a long time, though, and we could not start my paperwork right away, because we were waiting for our marriage certificate. By the time we got the certificate, it was too late. We already knew that Arizona would be our new place to work and live. So we moved to Arizona and sent our papers to California. We had the address of the Immigration Service, which was also responsible for the state of Arizona.

Our papers included copies of my passport, visa, our marriage certificate, Affidavit of Support, applications signed by Keith and me, pictures, and checks. So this was a very good way for the American government to make money. We had to pay $70 for my work authorization temporary card in 1998, and $130 for my new Permanent Resident Status (green card).

California's INS office returned all of our papers to us with directions to send them to INS in Phoenix. However, they did not say anything to us about what we should add to our package with the applications and documents. So we believed that everything was all right, and soon we would get my status and visa. That meant a lot to a non-immigrant who had no American picture ID at all.

Did you ever think that you could live in the U.S. without a Social Security number, without health or car insurance, or without a driver's license? Can you imagine getting pregnant in a situation like this? You would not be able to get insurance, you would not be able to drive or to work, and you would be completely dependent on your missing papers. It would make you feel very frustrated. Your baby would be able to feel your fears and unhappiness, okay? How would you like this? I hated this idea.

Russians have bureaucracy, too. We even have a saying: "You are a bug if you do not have papers."

My parents did not understand that my situation was putting too much pressure on my mind, and I did not want to get pregnant as quickly as women in the former Soviet Union normally did.

We had rented a two-bedroom apartment in Mesa, Arizona. I did not like the idea of becoming a mother before we could buy a house and furniture for it.

After my first six months in the U.S., I still did not understand English well enough and was scared to meet new people. I was uncomfortable to have a business conversation with callers from Cox Communications, to order pizza, to talk to children. I feared that they would think that I was stupid when I would answer, "Oh, I am sorry. I do not understand your speech. Please call back when my husband is at home."

You should have seen me during my first two months in the U.S.! I used to switch off our phone because I did not want to answer it! I felt as if I had forgotten all my English vocabulary and people could not understand my accent. Even Keith sometimes could not understand my speech, because I had difficulty saying clearly what I felt and thought! I often used wrong words. Some of them were old, and Americans were not using them anymore in their speech, but my Russian/English dictionary still had them.

My friends and family had no idea that I had the most difficult time during my first year in the U.S. I could not take care of myself, but they thought that I should be starting to take care of a child!

When I had been in the U.S. for a year, I got a letter from my friend asking, *When are you going to have a baby? You might spend all your time taking care of your pets.*

I was sure that my friend, who is already a mother, got sarcastic with me. I had to write and explain to her, as I had to everybody else, why Keith and I did not want to have babies right away. We wanted to get to know each other better, and we wanted to save money for a house. I wanted to get my American ID and health insurance, and I could not wait to start driving and become a social human being. I did not get any jobs at that time. It was too early for me to think about jobs without a Social Security number, work authorization, or driving privileges.

God helped us to realize our plans before Keith and I became parents. I was adjusting to my new American life.

Every day during my first year in the U.S. was separated in two parts for me: before and after the mail arrived. It is hard to imagine that I was so dependent on letters from my family and friends. I used to look out the window to try and see the arrival of the mail truck. I was always thinking about mail. I thought about nine relatives who wrote to me. I kept in mind my fifteen friends, who wrote to me every two to four months. My other five friends wrote me once a year. Some of my best friends never wrote to me. One of them sent me a birthday card once. Another friend called me twice a year to talk for a couple of minutes.

I write to my friends every three or four months, and I never forget their birthdays. I cannot leave a letter unanswered. When I lived in Tashkent, I expected to get a letter or news on the day I saw a spider. The spider had to be small and drop on my face or head from the ceiling. This superstition sign did not work in the USA.

My spouse Keith got a computer program for me with the Cyrillic alphabet, so now I can type in Cyrillic. My keyboard has two kinds of letters. I can type in English or in Russian. I am very happy about it. Keith cares about my writing hobby!

I like to write letters with information about the U.S. (laws, TV shows, schools, post offices, credit cards, police, jobs, Social Security numbers, journals and newspapers, coupons, holidays, and culture). I type these informative letters and send them to my friends and family.

Sometimes before their letters arrive, I already have three pages front and back printed with news about the U.S. and my life, so I do not have to write a lot. I take a page from a writing pad and make a short note answering their questions and mail it.

I want to share with you some secrets about international mail. It coast me 80 cents to mail a letter to Russia, Uzbekistan with 6 pages in it. If you are planning to mail a lot of pictures overseas, I would recommend going to the post office. There you can get the exact price for mailing your letter.

Now I want to talk to you about sending packages to the former Soviet Union. Do not think that it is as cheap, as it is to mail a package in the U.S. I want to give you an example. When we sent a five- or six-pound package, it was $20-$25 for surface mail (2-3 months), and $35-$40 for airmail (2-4 weeks). Sometimes our gifts would cost less than the price of mailing them. It was very frustrating to us.

I love to get letters from my family with their opinions about our new videos or their appreciation for our pictures and gifts. Keith and I love to give, to be generous. We just hate the idea that international mail fees are so high!

When I write, I have this feeling that my family is with me and that I am talking to them.

I try to write to my family often instead of talking to them a lot on the phone. I think that I was in a mail trap, which I created myself.

Honestly, I do not miss my motherland a lot. I do not miss my parents' home. What I do miss is my family, my friends, and my trips to the mountains to search for herbs and berries. That is why I so much enjoy the letters from my family and friends. They bring me sweet memories from my childhood and my student life. Sometimes, they are full of complains and sadness. This is the worst part of being a spouse from the third world country.

Here are some letters I translated for you, my readers.

From my mother on April 2nd, 1999:

Good afternoon, Oksana.

Hello to Keith. Today I got a letter from you. The letter arrived in sixteen days. The whole letter is about your rats. I do not understand it. You do not know how to express your love. Your rats and your dog turned out to be more important for you than your brother with whom you grew up. When I talked to you on the phone about him, you answered that you cannot afford to send him some food by mail. You surprised Dad and me very much. If trains would still go from Tashkent to Novosibirsk, we would send Stas some preserves, honey, and pickles with an attendant. It would be faster and cheaper than to send the package by regular mail. Stas would not complain to you or ask for anything. You forgot about your family during the first year of your American life. I feel that you want to forget everything and think only about yourself and what you have now.

There is never enough money. I know it by my own experience. The more money you have, the more desires and plans that will come into your life. It is sad to realize that parents and brother for you are "nagging flies." All our friends think that you send us money and gifts. Yes, you are changing fast. Maybe it is good to forget your Tashkent life.

From my Grandma Mary, my mom's mother on July 19th, 1999:

Hello, dear Oksana.

I very much appreciate your attention. I cherish your every letter and phone call. Thank you very much. Oksanochka, you wrote to me that Keith got upset about our family friend's letter. Oh, my darling. You should not translate to him everything if you know it could upset him. Of course, Oksana, to live life is not to cross the field. You have to know when you should be quiet, especially if it would keep your spouse from getting upset. There are no perfect people in the world. Nerve cells do not get rebuilt. You have to control your big mouth, because that is very important in a marriage.

You wrote to me that your parents sent Stas to a prestigious university in Novosibirsk. You know perfectly well that they did not plan it. They did not even talk about it in April 1998, when you left us for Keith and the U.S. Stas passed very difficult exams at the Russian cultural center in Tashkent and got an invitation to spend one year and graduate from high school at that university.

Oksanochka, just think, if they would not let him fly to Russia, how would he react? Stas was so happy about his little victory. He would not forgive his parents for their lack of support. They would feel guilty for all their life that they had closed a road in the future of their son. Parents have to help financially and psychologically in situations like that.

Oksanochka, please be careful. We do not want you to have arguments with Keith because of us. Please, do not get upset with Mom. She is a very good person. She loves you all. I do not know how I would survive here with my ridiculous pension after 40 years of work at the factory. She helps me with food and money. She is my only child. I am very proud of my daughter. I wish you would try to understand her depression without her babies (you and Stas). I wish you would not have any confrontations with your mom.

I love you. I miss you.

Letter from my university professor of Russian language and literature on July 7th, 1999.

Dear Oksana,

We enjoy reading your colorful letter about the U.S. and your life. Thinking about your American lifestyle, I see that your life is better than ours. In the U.S., a man is always a part of the business, events, news, and shows. I believe that the life of American residents is kind of a chain of interesting, attractive events.

Our lives do not have this chain. Our lives are just detached links. There is emptiness between those links. People fill this emptiness differently. Some people drink. Some people try to be philosophers. Some people simply kill time by spending days in idleness. I write short and long stories, or tales. Most of them are fiction. I write without any hope of being published. You know, here writers have to have money to see their books published, if those books are not government ordered.

I think about the future with the mind of an expert. I have a feeling that I have been in the future already, and nothing can surprise me anymore. We look for your letters and check our mailbox every day.

Letter from my high school mate, who lives in Ukraine now. June 1999.

Hello, Oksana and Keith!

Thanks for your letters and pictures. After a pretty long silence, I got the chance to send a letter to the U.S. I did not have any money to pay for international fees or even for the envelope. The time of starving came. We eat potatoes every day. Thank God, we grow them in our back yard.

To tell the truth, I do not know what I can write to you about. The life is so bad here, in Ukraine. I hate to complain about it. I have some passport problems. I still have my old red Soviet Union passport. Here, without a Ukrainian passport and citizenship, I cannot get a job. It costs $100 to get this passport.

My spouse Stephan does not get paid at his job. You know he works at an alcohol factory. My in-laws get their retirement money only once every three months. It might sound cool to get plenty of money for this time. But think, Oksana. During these three months inflation will turn this money into almost nothing. We have to use it all to pay bills for the three months ahead. My parents have been living in Russia, in Petersburg for the past six months. They are trying to earn money for my brother's wedding.

It is so difficult to make money now. Life has never been so bad. I feel like I live in hell. I wish you would help me to get a job in the U.S. I could be a housekeeper and a baby sitter. I do not need you to spend your money for me. I will borrow from some rich people here for my plane tickets and for my passport. I wish I could stay for one or two years with you or with a family for whom I would work. I would work for just $500 a month. I would send this money to my spouse for my two sons, and to pay off my debts.

Please, maybe you can find something for me. I am so embarrassed to even write about it. I understand that you have your own problems and plans.

Letter from my colleague from public school in November 1999.

Hello, Oksana!

I heard about your new house and all the pets you take care of. Are you looking for a job? Do you want to work? Do you have to work? I believe that a woman should stay home and take care of her marriage and kids. Ten years ago, I used to be a homemaker, too. I cherish my memories of that time.

I am very happy for you, that you live in such a nice environment and have such a comfortable life. We try to live with only basic needs and wants. Maybe we are closer to God because of this.

Oh, I want to talk about God. My daughter started to take religion classes in church. She studies the Bible with some American missionaries. I got to see some amazing events. Some students turned out to be the wives of Americans. I think these lessons caused some strong emotions to develop in my daughter.

This is my question: will my girl be able to impress an American heart? I am afraid she is too shy. I wish she would leave this country. I wish she would have a normal life, because she deserves it. I believe that all good men are extinct like mammoths of prehistoric times. It is impossible to find an intelligent man who is also a good businessman. That is why we are seeking good men from overseas.

Oksana, my daughter does not like that idea. She does not think she should try to flirt with an American. Maybe you can explain it to her. She should not be afraid of taking brave steps! Our modesty keeps us from having a better life.

Letter from my university mate from Kazakhstan on July 30th, 1999.

Dear Oksana!

Excuse my silence. I spent my salary on our house repair, and did not have enough money to send a letter to you. This summer did not bring a lot of fruits and berries, because we had unexpected late frosts this spring. That means that the fruits and berries that survived cost way too much at the markets. This summer we had another problem here in Kazakhstan. Farmers had to deal with hordes of locusts. As a result, prices for bread went up, too.

I have no idea what to expect this winter in this new millennium. We can only pray to God. There is no stability this summer in anything. I am afraid to hope. I am afraid to dream. I am afraid to be happy out loud, because I might scare away small and rare nice moments from my life.

I know you will say with a smile, "Oh, she is nagging again." You know my personality too well. I cannot change myself. I am not as optimistic as you are, Oksana. Events in Yugoslavia have overwhelmed us. The media has been talking about the American government as a monster that interferes in other people's business. I do not like politics, but I hate to hear about innocent people starving and civilians suffering.

I tried to send my pictures and brief in one of the bride's catalogs. I also tried to find pen pals from Germany. You should remember that I have been in Germany two times, and I speak German. I should not try to get an American spouse, because I do not know English at all. Nobody has written to me so far. I have lost all my hope of changing my life. I am aging. I am twenty-eight! My work at school takes all my time. Life is just passing me by.

I am sorry for nagging again. Good-bye.

Letter from my dad in March 1999.

Dear Keith!

Hello from Tashkent! I wanted to write you some of our news. Here in Uzbekistan, all land is the property of the government of our republic. If the government plans to build something on your land, you have to move without any negotiations. That is what happened to my garage. I had my garage for fifteen years. Now somebody else will build something on my space.

The government gave me a new space, where government workers had to cut trees. My brothers helped me to take out the stumps from the dirt, to dig a basement, and to cement it. We use the garage's basement as a storage place for vegetables and fruits. It is impossible for us to afford to buy onions, potatoes, melons, and apples all winter long. That is why we buy several sacks of those goodies in autumn and keep them in our nice, cool basements throughout the cold season.

My garage was moved to the new place. Nobody paid for my expenses. Nobody apologized. I never got any money for what I had to go through. It was a lot of stress and a lot of work. Oksana might have told you that I had surgery and lost most of my stomach. Since then, I have not been able to work as hard as I used to, or to carry heavy stuff. It is very frustrating for a forty-nine-year-old man like me to depend on my neighbors, friends, and family. Thank God that I had a lot of people to help me rebuild my garage.

Letter from my university friend, who lives in a province town in Karakalpakistan by the Aral Sea.

Dear Oksana!

I miss you so much! I want to tell you so many things! I write to you mentally, and I talk to you mentally. When I try to put my thoughts on paper, they seem to disappear. I have a lot of news to tell you, because I did not write to you for a whole year.

I gave birth to a baby boy on Sunday, the 9th of May. We gave him the name Shodirbek. It means "joy" in Uzbek. My in-laws are happy that I had a boy. He was born on the day of the Russian victory in the Second World War. That is why my in-laws are twice as happy.

My mother-in-law has not had too much happiness in her life. She has been losing her relatives each year. She buried her brother, her daughter-in law, her sister, and her daughter. She has been wearing all white for seven years, since that is the Muslim tradition for mourning. She ceased her mourning after I married her son.

Since I gave birth, none of my relatives have been with me. There have been only my in-laws. My spouse went to Tashkent to graduate from the University of Tashkent. After the delivery, I felt great freedom and a desire to sleep. But the doctors and my in-laws would not let me sleep. I was told that I would sleep forever, if I did fall asleep.

Now I have a goal in my life: my son. I do not have friends with whom I can be sincere and pour out my heart. I even started a diary. At this time, I live with my husband as a cat with a dog. My mom says, "It is good that he does not beat you yet." I answer her, "Like I would let him!"

Here in Karakalpakistan, people have not been paid for September and October yet. I am writing this letter on the 28th of November. People get paid here not by cash, but by food (flour, sugar, rice, and butter). That is another reason why I do not send letters to you. I do not have any money! I have just food! I can get money from my elders, as they get their pension in cash.

My news is that I am rereading all our classic Russian literature (Tolstoy, Pushkin, and Lermontov). It helps me to not get down and to not go crazy from my life. Sometimes I cannot believe that I got married to put up with "all that." If you only knew what kind of compromises I have to make to keep my marriage for my son! I wish I could leave and start my life over again.

My spouse is unhappy that I visit my parents every week. He thinks that it is because I am not used to my new home and family. He tells me that I am lazy and that I read too much. My husband very often criticizes and reproaches me. I explain to him very calmly that with that behavior, our marriage will fall apart. I told him one day, "If you do not like it, then let's divorce. I do not care anymore. Now I know what it means to be married. It is enough, I am tired!"

Oksana, maybe it is my fault that I got married. I never loved this man. I just wanted to be a wife and a mother, and to make my parents happy. Also, I feel bad that you are the only person on the planet that I trust and love. My spouse is already jealous. He thinks that we had a sexual relationship with each other before you left for the U.S. These ignorant people do not know what a real friendship means. He thinks that I love you the most in the whole world. He believes all kinds of stories and gossip about me. You know we live in a small town, and everybody knows everybody, or thinks that they know them.

My method in dealing with my husband is to ignore him and not talk to him. I perform my marital duties in silence and then go to my room to be with my son and my mother-in-law. I act like they are more important to me than he is. I see that he suffers from that, and I feel somewhat vindicated *(you see what kind of person I am now). When he tries to talk to me, I start to sing songs.*

He even tries to explain our problems as Zodiac incompatibility. My spouse is a Libra, so he can be very moody. I have to understand that and be patient. I am a Taurus. That means that I am stubborn as a bull. So we have to forgive each other and place the blame on the Zodiac.

By the way, it seems like the majority of people love my son and me. My parents love my husband because he is my spouse, and they want to see me happy.

Well, Oksana, this is just a little bit of what I wanted to tell you about my married life.

Last year the winter was very warm, almost without snow. On your birthday, today, we got snow. This autumn passed by very fast. We had problems with gas. Some people on our street did not pay for their gas. Well, the whole street lost the gas service until the debtors paid their bills off. My family had paid for the whole year up front, and we could not even use it!

We had been cooking food outside in our back yard over a wood fire. It is so nasty to cook lunch or dinner outside while it is raining or muddy. One week we did not have gas, water, or electricity. Our life is a struggle of survival. I was so scared that my son would die while we did not have heat, electricity, and water. I burned herbs, since they are disinfectants.

Here in Karakalpakistan, almost every other woman lost a child this summer. I heard that Karakalpakistan has the highest child death rate. It is because of diseases of the stomach, brain, and blood. Here a lot of newborns are aborted. My son's birth was one week premature.

In Karakalpakistan with dirty, salty air, we also have very bad water. We get unrefined water, so it looks like green tea, with a yellowish color, and has a salty taste. One time our neighbor got water with a snack! A small fish dropped down from the faucet into his pan. People were laughing about how he got tea and dinner together.

This summer was very hot and very dry. Irrigation season took all the water for our cotton and cornfields. Sometimes we have had water at our homes this summer only early in the mornings, between 3:00 and 5:00 a.m. People were searching for water in our town, asking neighbors from other streets, standing in lines to pour this "life-giving liquid" into their buckets or pans. We were safe, because we have a well with outdoor plumbing. So our back yard always had lines full of suffering neighbors. People started to get tap water only at the end of August.

I do not go out too often unless I want to visit my parents and grandma, or if I have to go to a clinic to get shots. This is the story of my life. Good-bye. I always wait for your letters. I miss you.

Every time I tell Keith, "I am going to check the mail," he answers, "I will check the female then."

KEITH'S NOTES – SEPTEMBER OF 1998

Okay, we just celebrated our fourth month of marriage. I have had the chance to really get to know this woman I married. I know that we truly don't know each other yet. But I still feel that I know her much better than before. She is definitely a beautiful person inside and outside.

I do have some funny memories of her housekeeping that I would like to share with you. Imagine trying to learn all these new gadgets and foods and cleaning supplies.

Oksana had fun learning American ways. I remember when she put too much dishwashing liquid in the dishwasher and flooded our kitchen with bubbles.

Another time she put bleach in all the loads of laundry and managed to get little white spots on a lot of clothes and turn my white underwear pink. Even my jeans turned pink.

She washed my wool suit and shrank its jacket and pants.

She made me such wild combinations of sandwiches that I could not even imagine what she would make next. I ate a fried chicken gizzard sandwich with horseradish. It seemed completely normal to her. Some Russians just put horseradish on a piece of bread and eat it like that.

One day Oksana made me bleu cheese pasta. It took me a while to figure out what I was eating. She saw a big bottle of ranch dressing in the refrigerator, so she put it on everything I ate until it was gone, and then she hurried me to buy a new bottle. The first time in her life that she cooked a frozen pizza in the oven, she left it on the cardboard. Then she asked me to get it off.

She jumped every time the phone rang. She called me one day at work in panic because the smoke alarm was going off. She had never seen round lettuce heads before, and she thought it was cabbage. She tried to make stuffed cabbage in the microwave! In nine minutes, the lettuce began to smoke. She did not know what was going on, because Russians do not have smoke alarms!

Oksana kept all our napkins and straws in the living room like a McDonalds.

She washed our mop head in the washing machine with lots of bleach, and then it unraveled in the dryer.

When she saw that the vacuum bag was full, she tried to empty it, because she did not know about vacuum bag replacements!

We had some Crisco and she asked what it was, so I explained to her that it was like oil. She cooked a very nice dish with it, but she did not know how Crisco smelled. She did not know that it was rotten.

Oksana had never heard of permanent press, so she dried everything too much, of course. It took her some months to get used to this idea.

We had a security gate in our apartment in Atlanta. It was very funny trying to get back in one time when I forgot my remote control for the gate. I was with a friend. He called from the gate's phone and said that it was he and Keith. Oksana said, "Keith is not." She did not understand that I was sitting in the car with him, so then the next time I called. I said, "Oksana, do not hang up. It's me, Keith. I am at the gate. Push five." She said, "Where?" Oh, my! On the phone! She thought that she needed to push five on our security pad by the front door.

She could not close Tupperware containers or storage bags right! She could not open the "easy-open" stuff. Everything was opened in a torn fashion.

She used dishwashing soap to clean windows. We never could get the soap off those windows.

Oksana burned a few pans trying to get used to the stove.

When we moved to Arizona, I neglected to tell Oksana that the new dryer had a lint filter just like the old machine. Well, a couple months later I saw a bunch of stuff stacked up in front of the lint filter. I opened it to find an eight-inch layer of lint. When I asked Oksana about this she said, "Oh, I thought this new machine was a fancy one."

She wants to help so much, and she tries so hard. She is a lover. My Oksana is special, and I love her.

OKSANA"S BOOK CONTINUES

Oh, I hated Americans until they started to understand my speech. The problem was hiding inside of me. I got a lot of help from the TV and from Keith.

I can even tell you which channels were my teachers. They were HBO, SCF, and the Discovery Channel. After being in the U.S. for one and a half years, I started to prefer the News World International Channel, and Court TV. I would watch a TV with a note pad, to write some sentences down and get an explanation from Keith later. For example, one day I asked him: "What means…Do not pee on my hush puppies?"

In September 1998, I started to think about getting a job as a baby sitter. I could not get any job until my paperwork was finished. I felt bored doing the same housekeeping and watching TV every day. Keith supported me in me desire to do something. He never pushed me to look for a job. He was very sensitive man.

God helped me, and I found an advertisement: *Need a Baby Sitter.*

I called and visited the American family. Margaret and Bill had two children. Their little boy, Kyle, was in the hospital at that time for five weeks. During this time, I babysat his sister, a six-year-old named Debbie. It was pretty easy. Every evening from Monday through Friday, I made the short walk over to Bill and Margaret's apartment. They lived in the same apartments as us.

I used to take Debbie to work out or to swim. We enjoyed going to the Jacuzzi and sauna together until the middle of November. I taught her how to dance and how to say some Russian words. I watched Debbie until 9:00 p.m. After this time, she had to go to sleep and stop bothering me. So I was pretty busy with this little girl for two to three hours each night.

I had to sleep in their apartment, which I did not like. I could not take Debbie to stay at our place too often, because our second bedroom was Keith's office. Keith used to have the habit of working all night long or watching TV until late. Keith loved this time when I was not at home. He could get a lot of work done, and relax without me interrupting him with questions. He did not care about my salary. He understood that I was working for fun and not really for the money. I felt great that Debbie could understand my English very well.

Debbie's mother and stepfather both worked the graveyard shift. They used to not get home until after 7:00 a.m. That was when I would get back to my apartment and find my spouse sleeping on the sofa with his clothes still on and with the TV on.

I know you do not care about all these details. But I write about them not only because I love the warm memories, but also to make you smile. Are you ready to smile? Are you ready to think about something very important?

I am not going to say how much Margaret and Bill paid me. I am embarrassed by how cheap I was. I wanted to get this job to have something to do. I was sure that I would make more money with baby sitting after their infant son Kyle got out of the hospital.

However, God is the only one who knows the future. I never had a chance to baby-sit this boy. He died on October 13th, 1998, just a week after entering the hospital. He just stopped breathing during the night.

I wrote a story about this sad event. I hope that you will understand the right meaning of my words.

Thank you, thank you, thank you, God!

Dear reader! I hope you will never lose your child. It was so painful to see a little body in a casket. Kyle had a blue casket and blue clothes on, and his head was covered by a little Taz cap. A blue teddy bear was sitting in the casket, ready to sleep forever.

I know that people do not care too much about other people's lives. I am not going to write all the details about the funeral. I just want to remind you of something. Do not forget to thank God for every day that you have with your child!

I wrote a story about this little boy. When you finish reading, your mind will be full of different emotions and thoughts, just as mine was.

Last Show of Kyle or Monologue of the Baby Sitter, by Oksana Leslie, February 22nd, 1999

You are pretty in your blue casket.

In a black dress, I am bending over you.

Your features are traced neatly by brown lines. Your last makeup is fondly trying to hide the colors of decomposition.

I did not use my makeup today. I knew that I would sob.

Your mother is unexpectedly beautiful today. I was very amazed. She fixed her hair and put on a lot of makeup. I did not know that she could be such a pretty woman.

Your casket is surrounded with flowers and people. I guess that you would be offended to die without the knowledge of the world's flowers' fragrances and colors.

Your skull is disfigured by the kisses of Death and covered with a cap that is too big. The hero from the cartoon *The Tasmanian Devil* has the nerve to grin from the cap. He is a fast, sneaky, unpredictable creature. Why is it that he is your companion in death? What were your parents thinking about?

I can see a blue plush teddy bear sitting on your legs. He could have been your favorite toy. Maybe he will be. Egyptians believed that all the things in a pharaoh's grave would be used by their owner after death. God bless every belief.

You lived only three painful months. For three months, you could breathe. July. August. September.

October cut off your days. You suffocated in your sleep. You suffocated in your mother's bedroom, close to your mother. I bet she will never forgive herself.

Your six-year-old sister is the only dry-eyed person here. She has prepared very well for your last show. Her cheeks are red from blush. Violet eye shadow makes her eyes have a stupid expression. I notice that she used her mother's red lipstick. The feeling of hate punches me in the face.

I do not have any words to describe her. Please forgive me for my crudeness. She looks very happy now. She knows that she will be able to sleep at night now without hearing you bawl. She knows that her parents' salary will not be on your necessities any more. She will never again hear, "Think about your brother!" She does not have her brother any more!

I am sorry because I did not want to upset you today.

People around you cry and blow their noses. It irritates me very much. What a joke of a nature that tears are married to noses! It is a defect of the human body. People blow their noses. These sounds are like sacrilege in this moment of bemoaning your cold body, your untold story, your first steps that will never be taken.

If you think deeply, you, who did not ever come to know the world or appreciate the difference between wrong and right, are not alone. You could have become a serial killer. Maybe God took you before you had the chance to choose the evil side.

People around you are your relatives. They are not bad. They are just simple American citizens. They were good to me most of the time. Sometimes they treated me like a piece of furniture. Yes, out of tradition baby sitters do not get much respect. People usually are not discreet or embarrassed in front of baby sitters.

I can just imagine what an enraged swarm these nice, sobbing and nose-blowing creatures would have been if your death had occurred during my night of duty. These nice people would have messed up my future. Who knows how many pieces they would have torn from my soul?

Kyle, you died and did not steal my happiness and calmness. Thank you, Kyle.

Thank you, God. Amen.

Four months of my baby sitting for an American girl was a very good learning experience for me.

This girl used words that my spouse never used. I would have to ask her, "What does that mean?" Then she had to explain them to me. It was one of many different ways to learn English. Her explanations were very simple, and I liked that.

On the other hand, she showed me as much disrespect as she could. She did not like to listen to my side of an argument, so she would always win easily. She always said to me, "You do not know."

One day when I got to Margaret's apartment, we could not find the key that I had always taken with us to go work out or swim.

It was like a sign to me. The sign was that I no longer had the key to this situation or this job.

At 9:00 that evening, Debbie did not want to sleep alone in her room. She was disturbing my sleep and pestering me like a mosquito. Do you love mosquitoes, my friend? I told her, like before, to shut up and to go to sleep. This time her reaction was different.

She fired me! Imagine that! She told me, "You are mean. You are crazy. I don't want this baby sitter any more!"

That was like a knife in my heart. Debbie fired *me*, the best baby sitter in the whole world! It was hard, I can tell you. I was so angry that I wanted to take the video of her dances and destroy it. I wanted to break my Christmas gift to her: a child's makeup kit! I remembered all the times that I had read to her or taught her how to cut paper, or how to make pretty art! After all I did for her, she said that I was crazy because I was strict and my voice was loud and bossy.

So I responded that I would quit the next morning. She told me to get out right away! Imagine that! Ten minutes before, she could not stay in her room without me!

I had a difficult night. I decided to quit and never come back to see this girl again. Later, her mom tried to bring me back, but she really did not kiss my butt. Neither Margaret nor Debbie ever apologized. They had no idea how much Debbie had hurt my feelings.

My best friend and neighbor, Pat Durbin, said to me about my situation, "It is always like this with kids. The more you spoil them, the less they appreciate you. Kids do not respect their baby sitters at all."

Sometimes, on the sidewalks of our apartment complex, I saw Debbie. It was irritating.

In April, an interesting situation occurred. I met Margaret at our pool. She told me that she would like to get my address and Social Security number for her taxes. I would not give her this information, because I wanted to talk to Keith first. He told me that my work had been "under the table." I did not have my Social Security number at that time, and I did not have permission to work from the INS. Margaret had known that, and she had hired me anyway.

I had to go see her and tell this information. She was very calm and nice. Her answer was simple: "It is not my problem. I knew that you did not have your Social Security number, but I did not know that you didn't have permission to work."

It was the first evidence of her stupidity. She was a thirty-year-old woman, the mother of three kids, and she did not know that without a Social Security number people are not allowed to work in the U.S. Excuse me, but how would they be able to pay their taxes without a Social Security number?

Margaret told me that I should not worry about my taxes. Why? This was proof of her ignorance. She told me that with the small amount of money I made as a baby sitter, I would not have to file any taxes. Well, I am married. In the U.S., a married person is not an individual any more, guys! I would have had to add my baby sitting pay to my spouse's tax records!

Keith and I had already paid a tax accountant to do our taxes, okay? If Margaret was late with her decisions, it was not our problem, right?

She was going to call a 1-800 number and find out about this situation. We did the same. Margaret had always paid me in cash. She could not prove how much she had paid me.

She had saved so much money by using me as a baby sitter, and she still was trying to get her money back. She did not even pay me minimum wage, because I was a naïve immigrant. I agreed to get paid only $10 for twelve hours. No, I did not charge a penny for nights! I entertained and taught Debbie from 6:30 p.m. until 9:00 or 10:00 p.m.

But nights with Debbie were like working a graveyard shift. Do you think that Margaret ever cared about my sleep? She only cared about paying me as little as possible. I did not make more than $400 in four months.

I even felt sorry for her. Every time I used to come to their place, I felt sorry for those people. It was amazing to me that they never had a spray deodorizer in their bathroom. Their furniture looked old and crappy. I wanted to work for them for so little because I felt like it was my little deed to help them. So what did I get? A bad experience, disillusionment, and disrespect from my first employers in the U.S.

If you hire a baby sitter, you become an employer. If you want to report this on your taxes, remember that you must pay the baby sitter in checks for at least the minimum wage per hour. Make sure that your foreign baby sitter has not only a Social Security number, but permission to work, too. Permission to work for a foreigner is essential. It is like a stepping stone to independence and confidence in this country.

Independence is a very sweet, strong word. A lot of my friends were writing and telling me about the necessity of being independent. They were always reminding me about my spouse's age and his future retirement.

They did not understand that it takes time to start over. It was difficult for me to answer all their questions: "Do you work already," "When are you going to work," etc. I could not work for the first ten months that I was in the U.S., as I did not yet have the government's permission to work.

I got my Work Authorization card in January 1999. It was my first American picture ID. One day in one supermarket, I wrote a check to pay for our DVD movies. A young cashier could not take my check because she had never seen a Work Authorization card before. Luckily, Keith saved me with his driver's license when he finished looking around in the store.

Keith decided that I should get my driver's license. He made me study the book for two days. I was sure that I wasn't ready to drive, but Keith helped me to fight my fears and uncertainty. He has always believed in my ability.

It all happened during the last week of February. I got my driver's license, my health insurance, and my first credit card. I had to take the test for my driver's permit twice. The first time I missed nine out of thirty questions because I did not understand some of them, but the next day I only missed three.

Keith used to explain driving rules to me by using my limited vocabulary. So the result was that I did not learn the new driving vocabulary from the book. Keith was my teacher and interpreter. He was able to translate the book for me in such a way that it was easy for me to understand. It took him three weeks to teach me how to drive a car and obey traffic signs.

I got my driver's license on March 18th. The old man who gave me the driving test said, "I am going to pass her, but don't let her drive!"

I was very proud. Although people in the U.S. are used to getting their driver's licenses and driving cars from the age of 16, most of my friends and family in Uzbekistan cannot drive and do not even have the opportunity to buy a car. Former Soviets think that Americans are very lucky.

After I got my Social Security number and driver's license, I felt very good about myself. It is not that there is anything special about having a number. It is about being a part of society. It was a small step toward independence.

I had thought that I was independent from my Russian family. Every time I did anything, I thought about my parents and grandparents, and how they would react if I wrote to them about those actions.

For example, we sent them a box of gifts. I was very excited before my family got it. I was wondering if they would like and appreciate it.

Yes, they loved it very much. Very soon, my mom was annoying me, asking me to send anti-wrinkle cream for her, and a box with food for my brother Stas in Russia's Novosibirsk University. Yes, I knew that my family had a difficult financial situation. Yes, I love my brother very much. Yes, I wished to help them.

However, we could not. It was frustrating for me. I used to write and explain in my letters to my family all the details about our life, and about the American system. They had read that we planned to buy a house. Do you know what my mom said to me when I told her, "No, we cannot send anything to you or Stas right now"? She told me with sadness and irritation in her voice, "Yes, now you are buying the house, and later you will buy furniture and start a family. It will just continue. You will never have money to help your family here."

I cried after this phone conversation with my mom. I love her so much and I think about her a lot, but she does not understand anything about our marriage or our attempts to realize our dreams. My mom has a great heart. She always helps her mom with money without waiting for special events. She would spend most of her extra money for her son Stas, a student of Russia's Novosibirsk University. Occasionally, she sends us gifts. Always when I am walking through Wal-Mart, I think about things my dear mother would love to have. I think about things that I would love to send to her. I love to give, but it is hard to be generous when people always ask you and pester you to give them something.

I have always known what my mom loves and needs. I do not need for her to tell me. Keith and I love to surprise people, but we felt that my family did not appreciate anything we did for them. Why? Because they were sure that we could give them even more. If we could order pizza every Sunday or afford to go to a restaurant, we were supposed to have extra money to help them, too. They felt this way even when we explained to them that we did not have our house yet and needed our car fixed, and a lot of other things.

One year we sent money to my family for Christmas. They loved it. My Grandma Nina thanked me in her funny way for this monetary gift: "Thank you for not forgetting us."

I was upset. Do you know why? She never calls me. I call her every two or three months and on holidays. She does not write to me as often as I write to her. I send my Grandma Nina two to three letters a month. It is important for me to share with my family news about the U.S. and our life. Still, she did not feel that it was enough. She told me exactly what she was thinking.

I got the message very clearly. If we do not send them a lot of stuff, they assume that we are selfish and do not care about them. I can understand it, because my Grandma Nina is a helper. She helps her sons and grandsons with money all the time. She has helped my father a lot with money, and also my brother Stas in Russia. She has a good heart. She raised her passed sister son Andrei. But she does not understand that we care about her even if we can't help the family a lot financially.

I hate to complain about my family, but it is an important part of this chapter. They do not understand our life. It is as if we are talking to each other in different languages.

Do you know that Russian VCRs cannot read American videos? It is because of their system. The U.S. uses the NTSC video system, and the Soviet Union VCRs use PAL and SECAM systems. It means that we have to convert videocassettes from NTSC to PAL or SECAM when we want to send my family a video about us. When I came to the U.S., I brought with me several cassettes with Russian movies and music concerts. We could not watch them for a long time. Then one great day came! My Keith gave me an expensive new VCR which can read a lot of different systems of videocassettes, and convert from one system to another.

My problems with my family are like this difference between our VCR systems. I can tell that they speak in PAL and SECAM systems, but we speak in NTSC. They cannot understand that it is not easy to survive here, because you have to work hard and think about your future. People in the U.S. can plan their futures and try to save money in their bank accounts, for example.

Most of the people in Uzbekistan and Russia don't trust the banks. They always pay cash and get paid in cash. They do not have ATM cards or credit cards. They think only about what they will eat tomorrow or the next week. The majority of the population in Russia and Uzbekistan can only dream about buying a new refrigerator, buying new furniture, or traveling overseas. Most of the people have the strong belief that in the U.S. money almost grows on trees. They do not want to hear that you cannot support yourself. They do not want to listen when you say that you do not have enough money to send them. They do not understand how their daughter cannot find a good job.

My mom knows that there is no guarantee in the former Soviet Union that mail and packages will arrive from the U.S. We sent my dad a cheap audio player for his birthday. The player cost us $10, and the airmail charge was $8. Well, the gift was lost in the mail. I say that it was stolen. Anyway, Dad never got it. My mom knows that once we sent her a journal and a calendar, but she only received the journal. So I was very angry to hear that she ordered a jar of preserves for Stas, since she knows for sure that there is no guarantee for mailing gifts into poor, hungry Russian dormitory!

Yes, it is all my independence. My mom could make me cry with her misunderstandings, complaints, and needs. Sometimes I felt like I did not even want to open her letters. Later, it was easy for me not to call her every week, but once every two weeks. It was difficult financially for her to call us, so she was always begging me to call her more often. She did not care that we had bills to pay. She did not understand that we were sacrificing by calling her every week in the first year. I should tell you that during the first year our bills from AT&T or MCI were between $200 and $300 every month.

After I figured out that talking to my mom only made me feel more depressed because of their problems, it was easy to call her less often. She could not control me on the phone so much.

Well, in her letters I always read the same sad song: *Soon you will forget about us. Do you even miss your past with us? I feel that we and your childhood are hidden very deep in your memory.*

She would write it to her only daughter, who had no real job, just learned how to drive, and was totally dependent on her spouse. My family expected my spouse, who never met them, to be caring and generous to

79

their needs. We have friends, who are in debt, rent an apartment, and still send $100 every month to Russia. Keith did not plan to support financially my relatives, I never discussed with him before the marriage this issue, and I was stuck with disappointed family. We both agreed that we will send them money for holidays and for emergencies, but not on a monthly basis.

Every week, during my first year in the US, I sent my mom a letter on three pages on both sides. Occasionally, Keith wrote to her in English, and she translated with a dictionary. We send her pictures and videocassettes of our life.

Now you know what makes me feel that my family expects a lot of financial help from us. I know that they need help. I am very upset that they are so far from me, and they still are able to control me emotionally. Their criticism can make me feel bad for days. Is there such a thing as independence from my family?

How can I have independence in my marriage? I do not believe that there is such a thing. In a marriage, people depend on each other, and it does not matter how much money they make.

I have always cared about people's opinions of me, especially Keith's opinion. I see that there is really no true independence in our life. We all depend on each other, on our government, on our family, and on God. Keith was a big support to me. When I would complain to him about my Mom, he would comfort me. He would say: "She does not understand." He did not get angry with my family or went further to fulfill their dreams and requests. Keith was doing hid best to helping me to adjust to his country.

Keith taught me how to pay bills, how to manage our checking and savings accounts, and how to work with our home banking program. He told me to keep all our receipts, so I kept them for some time. Once I had checked their existence in our bank statements, I threw them all away. Those receipts were always in my way. I did not know how to organize them better or why we needed to keep them.

Later, when the time for taxes came, Keith asked me for those receipts. Oh, I found out that I had thrown our money in the trash! Keith was working from home. We could have deducted from our taxes all of our business expenses. I did not know that those expenses could be deducted from the taxes to the government, because in Uzbekistan we did not have that law. I could not conceive in my mind, that you could get money from your own government.

What a wonderful country! Your taxes can be recalculated! You can get some money back if you have home business, if you help your relatives overseas financially, if you make donations, if you pay for child care, if you move to another state for a job, if you lose money on your rental property. Did you ever think about this great system? I am impressed, honestly.

I feel that my first year in the US was very interesting. I have had learned so many things. I had two friends – Galina from Atlanta and Alina from California to talk to in Russian. My other friend flu to this country to get married an American man, too.

I have to tell you this story.

We met in Tashkent State University in 1996. We used to study Russian language and literature there. I will call her Olga, because I do not want to use her real name here.

She was a very intelligent, alert, serious, and pretty woman with some Asian features. Every time I needed money, she would help me out. I could borrow money from her and not pay her back for months. She would never remind me about my debts, but I would always return her money with a little gift to show my appreciation and respect.

Olga got a very good job, because she could speak English pretty well (better than me), and she knew how to use a computer. Interpreters can get great paying jobs in Uzbekistan, especially if then can speak Russian, Uzbek, and English or another foreign language. Interpreters make more money than teachers, doctors, engineers, musicians, or drivers. Olga was a very successful woman. She was making $500 a month, compared to a teacher's salary of $10 to $15 a month. Her salary was high because she worked for a private Uzbek-English business, not in a government office. She could afford to buy any jewelry or clothes she wanted, pay all her bills, and pay for repairs in her home. She lived with her mother and brother in the apartment they owned.

Of course I was jealous. I did not even have $100 to pay for computer classes (Windows 95, Word). I still did not feel comfortable with English. Yes, I could read and write in English with a bunch of mistakes, because I had taken courses at the university for five years. However, I could not pick up English speech, and I would not understand or recognize the sounds of words. Unlike Olga, I was lazy, so I didn't study enough to improve my English. She led a very busy life, and when she was working she felt very important.

I told Olga about my dream of getting married to an American. I gave her addresses of bride catalogs, and she sent her pictures and briefs to those places. One day she got a phone call from an American guy. She was lucky to have an e-mail service at her job, so that the American could write to her. I'll call him Matt (not his real name).

She told me that she was dating different guys in Tashkent, but she had never met anyone she could really love. Well, she was falling in love with Matt through their phone conversations. Soon she wanted to meet him just as I had met Keith. Of course I told her all the details about getting my visa in Moscow.

She and her American decided to meet each other in Bangkok instead of Moscow. They had a wonderful time together and decided to get married. Matt had to start paperwork for Olga to get into the U.S. just as Keith had.

The most important document in this paperwork is the Affidavit of Support. An American has to prove to the government that he is financially stable and able to take care of his foreign fiancée. He also has to prove that he is not a criminal and that he has met his fiancée (proven by pictures and copies of letters attached). Well, Olga went to Moscow as I had, got her K-1 visa, and flew to the U.S.

Olga had enough money to pay for her own trip to Bangkok, for her trip to Moscow, for her visa and medical exam, and for her trip to the U.S. She told me that she had brought $3000 with her. Actually, it was against the law to take more than $1500 from Uzbekistan, but she was sneaky and smart.

Keith paid for both of my trips to Moscow, sending me $800 through the Uzbek-Turkish bank each time. He sent me money for my birthday and for Christmas, and paid for my flight to the U.S. Altogether, he spent $2500 on me in six months, and that is not counting how much he spent in Moscow just for fun. To be honest, he reminds me from time to time about all his expenses and my ignorance about money. Yes, it is true that I was very selfish. Olga was an independent fiancée who was not a financial burden on her American.

She even brought her wedding dress and shoes to the U.S.! Did I? I misled Keith about my wedding dress. I told him that my mom wanted to sew my wedding dress for me, so he sent us a package with two American fashion magazines full of pictures of wedding dresses. My mom had a lot of fun looking at those fashion models. We thought that it would give her some good ideas about styles and designs.

Suddenly, she changed her mind. She came down with a very bad case of the flu, and during that time she came up with the idea that in the U.S. there were much better dresses than she could create, and they came with shoes and all kinds of accessories.

Nellya Ilinichna, a family friend whose daughter married an American in Atlanta, was telling us that Keith would buy me all new clothes because he was rich. That is why Keith had so many more expenses with his Russian fiancée.

My flight was from Tashkent to New York. I was scared to get lost at the New York airport, so I begged Keith to meet me in New York. I knew that Dewitt from Atlanta had met Galina in New York, too. I thought it was no big deal, so I made Keith spend more money on his ticket to New York, our hotel in New York, and our tickets to Atlanta.

Olga and Matt spent three days in New York City. Olga told me that they both helped pay for their expenses. She actually did some shopping while they were there.

It sounded funny to me. I believed that a man should take care of his lady and pay for everything himself. My friend Olga had strong ideas about partnership and money.

She came to the U.S. on December 21st, I believe. She and Matt got married before Christmas. After that, she called me and invited us to her second wedding, which was to be held in a church the following month.

Honestly, I did not want to go. We were saving money for a down payment on the house, and we had not planned on any traveling. However, we had one free airplane ticket. Keith convinced me to fly to Panama City for my friend's wedding. He was supportive of my relationships with my Russian friends.

Actually, a couple days before my flight, I had an appointment with the INS for my work authorization card. It was my first American picture ID. I had not had a valid American ID in the U.S. for ten months. That meant that everybody who asked me for my driver's license would make me feel like I was nobody, like I was not a number yet. So I did not feel confident or comfortable during those months. I was so scared that something would go wrong during my flight.

Keith and I sent our gifts by mail. We bought a nice set of expensive crystal vases and candleholders and sent them by FedEx. I had never sent anything by this service before, and I could not believe that it was $37 to send one package. Why did we send crystal? Olga's family in Tashkent had plenty of this nice stuff. Like a lot of Soviets, we love crystal. I knew she would love our gift.

When I arrived in Panama City, Matt and Olga met me at their local airport. We got in the car, and I started to speak English with Matt. Olga interrupted my speech and tried to correct my mistakes. That is how we started our friendship in the U.S. She felt that she knew everything about the U.S. and that her English was perfect. I could hear plenty of Olga's mistakes, but Matt was very nice and did not try to correct her. I believe that even Americans make a lot of mistakes in their speech, especially when they are upset, angry, or worried. So what can you expect from immigrants?

I did not try to speak perfectly or impress anyone. I wanted to be comfortable with my friends. However, Olga made me feel uncomfortable right from the beginning. I came to visit her and support her, but she started this contest to see whose English was better?

Of course, I took some revenge. For example, when she was getting her nails done, she said, "I am so exciting!" I told her that she should instead say, "I am so excited!" She became very angry, and told me not to irritate her. She could not accept any of my knowledge about the language.

She even tried to be my interpreter at her own wedding. When her new American relatives were trying to speak to me, she would try to translate their speech to me. Even at her wedding, she would not relax and stop interpreting. When I told her that she made plenty of mistakes herself, she answered me with irritation, "Remember, I was an interpreter in Tashkent, and I know how to speak English."

This was one of her new ways to put me down.

When I saw the environment in which she was living in the U.S., I could understand her mood and behavior with me. When she got to the U.S., Matt was already unemployed for a couple of months. He brought her to live with his mom in a very old, small house trailer. The only thing that impressed me about it was the giant bathtub.

Something happened to the trailer's pipes, and this family had to deal with a hole in the wooden floor right in the middle of the kitchen and laundry room. I thought that Olga was like a princess before, and now she had turned out to be a Cinderella. In Tashkent, she had lived in a bigger and better apartment, believe me. Even I had lived in a bigger and better place in Tashkent than this trailer without ceiling fans or lights. To me, this place was a big shock.

I bet that my friend felt the same shock during her first months in the U.S. Just like me, she was excited about affordable oranges and bananas, and about seedless watermelons and oranges.

Olga told me that she started to take classes for immigrants. She even wrote to my mom about it. So my mom started to mess with my brain and ask me why Olga went to a college, but I didn't? My friend told me that those classes were for people who didn't know how to speak English. Olga needed to visit this place to dress up and show off so she would not feel lonely and worthless.

She loved to meet new people, and be the best student in the class. She told me that people in the class would ask her what she was doing in that class with her great English. She would tell everybody that she needed to pick up an American accent, because she used to work not with Americans, but with English businessmen. Since Matt was unemployed, he had time to drive her every morning to this place.

I had to write a long letter to my mom to explain that I did not want to go to free classes for beginners, that I did not yet have my residence to go to a college, and that we did not have enough money for a good American education. Olga made my mom think that her spouse took better care of her than mine, because he drove her to her "classes."

Olga loved to talk about the necessity of getting an American education in order to be independent. She could not understand why Keith didn't care about my education and place in society as much as her Matt. She constantly reminded me that since Keith was not young, anything could happen to him. I hated to hear this. I also did not like how Matt was always talking about Olga's future jobs. To me, it sounded as if he could not afford to support both of them and he brought her in the US to help him out.

Yes, I know, I was wrong. I kept forgetting that she had not married a successful computer programmer, so she did not have the choice to work or not to work. I just hated the idea of having to make sacrifices or of "having to work." I did not like or appreciate her telling me what to do with my life.

Well, in appreciation of my coming to the wedding, Olga gave me a cheap silver bracelet and ring. She told me, "I know you like this stuff." I acted as if I liked her gift, but deep in my soul I was insulted. I liked to wear silver when I was single, because I could not afford to buy gold for myself. Keith was the first man who ever gave me a gold ring with a diamond. After I got married, though, I started wearing pearls and gold, and I stopped wearing any silver, especially if it was as cheap looking as her gift. I was nice and wore it at her wedding, even though it did not match my pearls. It was the first and last time to ever wear her present.

Olga had no idea that I had changed. That is why we could not get along. She treated me like the same Russian girl I was who could not speak English, could not communicate with English-speaking people, and liked cheap jewelry.

She told her mother-in-law that I would not want to stay in a hotel because I was a "very simple woman." She repeated these words three times to make her mother-in law feel comfortable with me. Maybe she was trying to make herself feel good, but I was very upset. My spouse had spoiled me for ten months with nice hotels and good food. I was not simple; I was already a spoiled-rotten, unemployed Russian wife.

My first night in Panama City I shared a bed with Olga. They had no other place to sleep for me. I did not mind. I was acting "simple". Olga showed me her clothes and told me how much she had paid for them. This information was extremely irritating to me. To me, it all sounded as if she was bragging: "Look, I am better than you are. I had my own money to buy all this stuff." I loved to talk about her new clothes in Tashkent, but here I was relaxed about clothes. They were not as important to me as they were in my past. Olga was reminding me of my past, and it was hurting my feelings.

I do not know what was wrong with me. I knew that I lived in a better apartment and that my spouse made more money than hers did. I could not stop myself from hating my friend. If I had owned her nice, dressy clothes, I wouldn't have been able to wear them anywhere!

Before her wedding, she told me that my wedding video looked very crappy. I explained to her why it was not great. We just did not have the money to pay for a professional video. Do you think she had the money for a professional video? No! She asked me to bring my video recorder and camera. So I felt very silly to be her maid, her photographer, and her video person. Of course, I could not spend the whole time making the video and taking pictures, so I asked one of Matt's friends to hold the camera for a while. He did. Olga's wedding video came out even worse than mine!

Every time she had a chance to say something to the camera, she would talk to her mom. This part irritated me, too. It was a video of her wedding, not a special video for her mom! It was my video about my travel to Panama City, which I was going to send to my mom, too. My mom did not need to hear all of Olga's hellos to her mom. Okay?

In a normal American wedding, the bridesmaid does not take a video and pictures for the bride. I did, and sent all this stuff to Olga. When Olga sent me some pictures from her wedding, which her relative had gotten developed, they all were of pretty poor quality. She even sent me one big picture of her, Matt, and me, so I could frame it. How could she even think about framing this cloudy picture in which I looked horrible? I would never put a terrible picture of myself on the wall. I do not know if she was trying to be the best again, or if she had not even looked at me in this picture.

Now I want to talk about my second night in Panama City. Olga and Matt decided to put me in a motel. My friend told me that it would be their gift to me. I did not want such a gift, because I was satisfied to stay at her mother-in-law's trailer. However, I was told that her mother-in-law needed a rest. Olga and Matt put me in a motel by the beach. It was a dirty, single-floor motel with no hot water, shampoo, or towels. My room had dust everywhere. The art was leaning against the walls instead of hanging on them. The bathroom looked like it needed repairs, and the floor was slippery and dirty. I felt disgusted to be in this room. I did not feel any security. I looked through the window and saw that only two cars were parked in front of the motel.

Olga told me, "We are in the Holiday Inn. You can find us there if you need anything."

The next morning, she and Matt came to pick me up to make a video of them on the beach and in their hotel.

I had on Olga's jacket, which I had borrowed from her because I came to Florida without any jacket. I knew that I would need one for an early morning on the beach. What did Olga do? The first thing she told me was how cold she was, and then she took her jacket from me. I knew I would get very cold. On the beach, she continued saying stupid hellos to her family again, and she told them that in January people swim in the ocean every evening when the water gets warmer. I still have this video.

You see, even such little things were driving me mad.

When we came into their room, I saw that it had two beds. Olga started to tell me how she and her spouse were making love. I stopped her. I was different before, okay? I loved to hear about sex when I lived in Tashkent. Now I do not talk about it. This is a very private thing. Olga was so happy about her spouse as her lover that she wanted to share her happiness with me. I did not have enough tact to listen and be simply for her.

However, I was rude and told her to stop. I felt that it was wrong to talk about her wedding night right in front of Matt, who did not understand

Russian. I also think that it was stupid of her to show me their room. I was cold and angry. She saw how I felt and was upset, too.

When I told them that the motel they had put me in was the worst motel I had stayed in during my entire life, and about all my better experiences with American hotels, Matt asked me not to tell Keith about it. He also told me that he had paid $120 for my room and that their room at the Holiday Inn on the beach was $300 a night. Of course, he lied. Keith used to stay in hotels in Panama City during the wintertime, so he knew the prices. Keith still cannot forgive Matt for risking my life by putting me in such a cheap motel with no security.

Matt offered to take us to breakfast. I said that I liked Waffle House. I did not want to make him spend more money on me. At the restaurant, they let me know how much the bill was, as if I cared. That was another thing that irritated me all the time. I usually like to know how much things cost, but Olga and Matt were constantly talking about the prices for everything. Matt was the kind of American who, like many Russians, liked to tell everyone about his financial business. I hated it. I can still hear their voices about their purchases: "Oh, how nice! Look! It was only $12!"

When we were at the airport, Olga hugged me and apologized for her behavior. I saw her real tears, and she told me that she felt like I was her sister. However, my heart was closed to these sincere words and actions. It was too late. I knew that we could not be friends any more. She did not know it yet, but maybe she felt it.

After my trip to Panama City, I still called my friend occasionally, and she called me. I figured out very quickly that Olga did not know how to listen. She could only talk about shopping, restaurants, and her classes. I did not like to talk about how many times we had been to McDonald's or other fast food restaurants or about shopping.

She thought that Keith did not take me anywhere. She would ask me questions like, "Have you ever been to see Home Depot?" or "Have you been in a mall?" I hated her opinion of Keith and me.

I actually did not even call fast food places "restaurants." I called them "cafés." I was sure that if there were no waitresses, then it wasn't a restaurant.

Olga was excited about all the new stuff. Her questions would make me mad. I just could not understand her behavior.

When we were trying to talk about the credit system in the U.S., I told her that Keith might have bad credit. Actually, he did not. I had never seen his credit report, but I thought that if we had only one credit card, that it meant he could not get more. I remember telling her that if he had bad credit, we might have trouble buying a house. She was trying to act smart. Olga told me that we could buy the house in my name only. Of course, she did not know that a non-immigrant without a stable job or a good credit report could not get a loan for a car or a house on their own. When I wanted to explain this or other secrets of the U.S. credit system to Olga, she got angry and said, "Stop patronizing me! I knew all about the credit system in Tashkent, and I worked with foreigners!"

After this conversation, I saw clearly that she did not need me as her friend anymore if she could not appreciate my knowledge and experience. I told Keith that I would not call her again. He went to our second bedroom, his office, and wrote her an e-mail. It was like my e-mail to her, but more clever and sarcastic than I could have created at that time. This e-mail was supposed to make her understand why I was upset with her. I had never told her about my feelings before. Even this e-mail did not contain all my feelings about our relationship. I was just keeping dissatisfaction to myself. Had I been wrong? I probably should not have kept all my disappointments to myself, and I should have talked to my friend in order to sustain our friendship.

That e-mail finished our relationship. Olga did not feel like changing herself or apologizing to me.

When she sent us an Easter card, we did not respond. I simply put the card in the trash. After some time, she told one of my other friends that her mom was going to visit her in Florida and my mom could send with her a gift for me if she wanted to. I answered, "I do not want anything from Olga, not even a piece of garbage. She is not trying to recreate our friendship and be nice; she just wants to show off again."

Yes, I really thought this way about her. Maybe I was wrong. However, this was how I lost my good Tashkent friend in the U.S. I am not proud of myself. If I could change my past, I would just stay home from her wedding to keep us from ever getting into a stupid competition about spouses, clothes, language, and knowledge about the U.S!!! Why didn't I ask God for guidance, strength?

I bet at that time I did not think about God much. I was proud that I have an American husband, who finally taught me how to drive! He also taught me how to be a pet - lover. When I lived with my parents for a quarter of the century, the only pet I was allowed were turtles. Keith was buying me pets during our first year of marriage. He started with a rat, then we had more rats, then we bought a dog and a cat, and a fish tank.

My life was busy with taking care of pets. I learned new words like leash, collar, fleas,

Shots, paws, kitty litter… It was a great think, that Keith got me pets. I definitely was not boring. I was very satisfied how things turned out.

We were married already for a year! Two days before our anniversary, we went camping with friends and with our Labrador, Shok. This was another test for us. We had never gone camping before, and we had no idea how we would handle each other in the wild. We were lucky to find out that we both are good campers and did not get on each other's nerves too much.

However, I want to talk about our anniversary day. We went to celebrate it at a restaurant in Mesa. The hostess had a strong Russian accent, which got us interested. We started to talk to her, and she told us her story. Her name was Nina and she was from Russia. She used to make lots of money as a "chelnok." She would travel to Turkey and buy goods there, which she would sell in Russia.

She did not need to escape Russian poverty, because she was financially stable, but one day she met an American guy and fell in love. They spent five days together, and they wrote some letters. Soon he fixed some paperwork for her to come to the U.S. She got her K-1 fiancée visa in Moscow's American Embassy and arrived in the U.S. with $30,000 of her savings. She hid the money on her body to avoid paying taxes on it.

She was excited about her new life in the U.S., because she was sure that her true love was here. Very soon she found out that the guy was lazy and expected her to work and make money for them.

I still remember her saying to us, "I did not have permission to work for months, since my English was too poor for any job. We were spending my savings on my vehicle, our wedding, stereo, videos, and food. Very soon we did not have any money, and my son and I were hungry for days. My new American husband would disappear for some days, and we would not know if he was alive or dead. I hate him. As soon as I get my green card, I will divorce him. Without my green card, I am his slave. I work to feed three of us and send some money to my parents in Russia. I work seven days a week, ten to sixteen hours a day.

"In my life, I never cried so much, as I have cried in the U.S. I hate Americans, and my spouse. I have been humiliated so many times here by Americans, just because I speak with an accent. My coming here was a terrible mistake, but I am not going to fly back. Are you happy, Oksana?"

I was glad to answer, "Yes, I am."

Nina was ready to leave, and said, "Remember, it is very rare. I know a lot of Russian wives who are unhappy and just waiting to get green cards to be able to get rid of their American spouses. These women are just being patient and hypocritical until the right time comes. Happy anniversary! Good luck. At least I met someone who is happy in their marriage!"

Keith and I felt that to meet Nina and to get to know her story was very important. It was like a sign. It was a sign from God that we should cherish each other and our relationship. All the problems we were facing with our friends or families, we solved by ignoring, forgiving, adjusting.

CHAPTER 6
COMPARISON CONTINUES.
LEARN YOUR PARTNER'S
VALUES AND TRADITIONS.

Do you know that Russians and other people in the former Soviet Union do not celebrate a terrific holiday like Halloween?

I am very impressed by the American Halloween. I love how people prepare to celebrate this holiday.

I had a lot of fun looking through all the costumes in the supermarkets! I thought, *Poor Russian children! They do no have such a fantastic holiday!* Even if they started celebrating this holiday in Russia now, it would not work because the majority of the population in the republics of the former Soviet Union has financial problems. Adults would not be able to buy costumes for their kids! A lot of people could not afford to give away candy! People there have to always think about how to earn and save money to buy bread, milk, and meat. Most of them can't afford to buy candies except on holidays and birthdays.

Now ask yourself, are you thankful enough to God that you have enough money to celebrate Halloween? You probably never thought about it. It is very difficult for you to understand the idea that candy could be a fancy, expensive thing and your college education would not help you to buy it as often as you wanted!

Do you feel happy, very happy? I do not even want to talk about how impossible it would be for Russians, Uzbeks, Ukrainians, and others to buy Halloween decorations and other stuff. There are so many thieves there who would steal door decorations to resell in order to have money to buy food, and there are also vandals who just like to destroy things.

Okay, let's continue. The Russian Orthodox Christianity celebrates Easter and Christmas. However, Easter in Russia is not a special holiday with selling Easter cards and rabbit toys everywhere. Children love this holiday, because they get the chance to eat a lot of special baked treats and painted eggs. I do not understand how the Americans can mix Jesus' death with rabbits at Easter. Personally, I like this holiday because of the white chocolate bunnies and eggs. I never cook at Easter, so I miss my grandmother's cooking.

Birthdays in the republics of the former Soviet Union are great days. People do not have surprise parties. People love to plan and to prepare for the celebration of their birthdays.

When I was a young girl and a teenager, my birthdays always began the same way. My parents gave me gifts in the mornings, my grandparents called me very early, and my friends called me in the middle the day to wish me a happy birthday! I always expected phone calls! I would have been very upset if somebody had forgotten my birthday!

Well, when my parents and my brother Stas had their birthdays, I loved to present my gifts at the beginning of their great day in order to put them in a very good mood! A person has to know right away in the morning that people did not forget his birthday! When I was a schoolteacher, children gave me gifts twice for my 23rd birthday! Some students congratulated me on the 27th of November after lessons were finished, and other students congratulated me on the 28th of November before lessons started. Do not be surprised! It is a tradition to congratulate favorite teachers on their birthdays in the former Soviet Union. I have good memories of these days when the children gave me lipstick, a box of candies, flowers, nail polish, body sprays, lotions, and hair sprays. Yes, their parents bought these gifts for them to give me, because the kids wanted to make their teacher happy.

If my birthday or a birthday of any member of my family was in the middle of the week, we had a celebration with guests on Sunday. Most people in the republics of the former Soviet Union work on Saturdays, so gathering relatives and friends together is only possible at the end of the week. In Russia, Sunday is the end of the week for everybody. The majority of women used to do their laundry on this day. As I have already explained, laundry is long, hard work.

The birthday parties are always the same. The hosts clean up their apartment or house. Then they cook and bake a lot of food. It is a very important tradition to feed the guests, so they can eat as much as they want. Sometimes it is not advantageous to spend a lot of money and time preparing a special dinner. Guests can bring very cheap gifts and eat a lot. Sometimes it is better to save money by not celebrating.

There are no tradition of offering snacks like pretzels, chips and salsa. Russian dining table offers to the guests snacks like sliced cheeses, kielbasa, canned delicatessens like sardines and herring, caviar, cooked cow's tong, salads before the main meal arrives.

Sometimes it is wonderful to come together and introduce all your friends and relatives. It depends on what you want. In fact, birthday celebrations are usually cooperation between the closest relatives.

For example, when my Grandma Nina or Grandpa Alexander wanted to celebrate their birthdays, my mother always baked a cake and my father and Uncle Valera would bring the alcoholic drinks. I would help clean the house, cook, and wash dishes after the rich dinner. When my parents', my brother's, or my birthday came, Grandma Maria and my mom were chiefs of the kitchen. Father helped cut vegetables for salads and make pelmenee or mantye (meals). Stas and I were expected to clean and serve at the table. We were very tired and hungry by the time the guests arrived.

It is normal in Russia and Uzbekistan to expect gifts for your birthday. It is normal to come to a birthday party to eat, drink, dance and a have a good time with family and friends. My dad used to play the piano, and his parents loved to sing songs. When I was taking piano lessons, it was my duty to entertain our guests by playing my school program polkas, sonatas, and tarantellas. Later, my brother Stas became the entertainer of the family, because he loved to play piano and to be the center of attention.

When I did not get a lot of birthday cards for my twenty-fifth birthday in 1998, I was very upset. I expected people to remember me. A lot of them did not. I expected to get a lot of gifts, but I did not. The most expensive gift I got for my twenty-fifth birthday was from Keith's ex-girlfriend, Dawn Barkett! She sent me a box full of Body Works products from Atlanta. She is a very impressive woman, especially considering how much she did for our wedding! My parents did not send me anything for my birthday except a card. Keith's parents gave me a couple of sweaters, and that was very thoughtful of them. It took me some time to understand that the world did not revolve around me. But in November 1999, I got twenty-two cards from friends and family for my birthday! It was kind of impressive, especially since I had stopped expecting people's attention on my birthdays.

Having a wife from another culture can be frustrating sometimes. Who would not get excited about decorating a house for Halloween? I would not. Who would not care about the 4th of July holiday? Your Russian wife would not.

I like Thanksgiving, when we reunite with Keith's family in Pennsylvania. I made my first pumpkin pie for our Thanksgiving in AZ. When Keith tasted this pie, he had only one question, "Oksana, did you use sugar and eggs with your pumpkin filing?" Of course, I had not. I just made my famous crust from scratch and dumped in a can with pumpkin filling. I had done the same thing before with my apple and cherry pies. This time I did not read the instructions and used the same method. Keith had to dump the filling out of the crust. Yes, then Keith added sugar and eggs, and we cooked "Oksana's pie" again.

Russians do not celebrate Thanksgiving. When they think about pumpkin pie, they don't imagine something sweet. My Mom makes this pie spicy and uses salt on it. Also, Russians do not have a pumpkin pie filling that comes in a can. They buy a pumpkin, peel it by hand, and then shred it. They can cook pumpkin pie any time of the year, because it is a traditional pie for any holiday. When Russians think about turkey, it has nothing to do with Thanksgiving, either.

Most Russians and Uzbeks cannot afford to buy turkey! So when they do buy it, it is for their birthday parties, for their weddings, or for their New Year celebration! For example, my family likes to make pilaf from turkey.

Before coming to the U.S., I had never eaten a green bean casserole before. However, my grandmother bakes croissant rolls for Easter.

What about Christmas? You see, that is another issue entirely! Russians do not mix Christmas and Santa Claus.

People of the former Soviet Union call the Christmas tree a New Year's tree. They buy these trees and put ornaments on them after the twentieth of December. The majority of people in Russia, Ukraine, Uzbekistan, and the other former republics of the Soviet Union do nothing special on the 24th or the 25th of December. These days are regular workdays over there. I had one friend, a psychic and healer, who was celebrating Catholic Christmas and visiting a Catholic church. One day she even took me with her to this church on Christmas Eve, because I wanted to expand my knowledge of the Catholic faith.

The most important night for former Soviet people is the New Year's Eve, when people exchange gifts and kids wait for Santa Claus. Moslems, Christians, and atheists love this night as much as Americans love Christmas! Russians, Uzbeks, Kazaks, Ukrainians, and people from the other republics do not know about the American Santa Claus and his reindeer. They believe that on New Year's Eve they are supposed to get gifts from Father Frost, who is almost like Santa, but he travels with his granddaughter Snow Girl. There are no Christmas stockings, and no Christmas songs. Soviet culture has a lot of New Year's songs, and I still remember some of them.

The Russian Orthodox Church celebrates Christmas on the 7th of January. People do not exchange gifts on this day. My both grandmothers go to the church on this day for the service, make a nice dinner at home.

My brother Stas had to spend New Year's celebration and Christmas at his university in Russia, because the rules say that you have to pass your tests before the vacation, and teens cannot fly home to celebrate the holidays of the year with their families.

When I was a teacher in 1997, all Russian teachers got a day off on the 7 of January. All the Uzbek teachers worked this day at school. They got Muslim day off.

Muslims in Uzbekistan celebrate New Year twice. Their second great celebration happens on the 21 of March. This holiday has a name NAVRUZ. People have a day off in Uzbekistan on that day. Parades, traditional shows take place in the city. It is a very beautiful holiday. I enjoyed going out on this day and eat traditional Uzbek food – pilaf or shish kabob.

In the US I learned about St. Patrick day, Father's day and Mother's day. These holidays are unknown to Russians. Russians celebrate Women's day on the 8th of March and Men's military and navy day on February, 23. I remember that my father always brought flowers, coffee and chocolate to my Mom, his Mom and mother-in-law on March, 8. My mom had small presents for me and her mom and his mom. When I was a school student, our classmates bought to all the girls some small presents. One year I received from classmates a rubber snake, another year it was an elk-bottle cork! One year we received tulips. As students we always brought flowers and chocolates to our favorite teachers. Nobody works on March, 8th. It means that schools celebrate this holiday on the 7th of March. On the 23rd of February, my mom bought gifts for my father and my brother. Sometimes she did not buy anything, but sew new pants or shirts.

I remember getting for my Dad the same thing all the time. It was a shave cream! My Dad could enjoy only practical gifts. Cards and flowers he called a waste of money.

When I was a school student, girls collected money and presented boys with new nice pens one year and a card, another year they bought gramophone records for the boys. Boys are considered to be future soldiers and defenders of the motherland that is why they are congratulated with this day of military and navy, too.

In Uzbekistan, Uzbeks do not celebrate 23rd of February like it was during Soviet era, but they gift their women on the 8th of March.

I never heard of Valentines Day in Tashkent in 1998. In 2004, I received and email from my friend, that Valentines day is so popular now there, that people give each other little valentine cards, not just to loved ones!

Muslims in Uzbekistan celebrate circumcision. In the USA boys get circumcised in hospitals on their second day of life. Russians do not practice it. Actually, Russians believe, that only Jewish and Muslims are supposed to have this procedure done. When I had my business trip to province of Uzbekistan, I was shown a video of the circumcision celebration. The video was taken in a yard, where rams' throat was cut. Animal's blood spilled down the basin. The chef made pilaf from ram's meet for the guests. Two boys, who were 5 and 7 years old, were dressed nicely for the holiday of their maturity. They rode a white horse in the yard, while music was playing and quests were shouting their greetings. Next thing I saw was a room full of kids. Two adults were throwing money on the floor. Kids were picking them up. Then boys were undressed. They were scared. Local surgeon was an old guy in a traditional Uzbek robe with embroidery, circumcised boys fast. They were taken away. Crying part was very short. A video man took pictures of the guests. Guests were sitting on the carpets, leaning on pillows. Traditional Uzbek snack was served before the main meal. People were snacking on walnuts, peanuts, candies, and small cookies. Food was served on table cloths right on the floor. Circumcised part of boy's bodies was cooked in pilaf. Guest, who got this part in their plate, was considered a new family member (something like a God father). Happy parents presented this guest with a new beautiful traditional robe with embroidery. After the meal people were dancing.

I am not sure if Uzbeks from big cities would have such a wild celebration. I heard that some families take their kids to a hospital to be circumcised, and nothing is being cooked from the left over skin. However, this procedure is very important for a boy and his family. Boy receives gifts on the day of celebration, when he is considered to become a man.

I want you to know that in the former Soviet Union, all religions were repressed for a long time. For seventy years, people did not read the Bible because it was outlawed by the communist government. I want you to know that teachers at schools taught me that God is only in the imagination of capitalists, and any religion is just an opiate of the masses.

My parents did not believe in God. When I was three years old, my Grandma Marie baptized me in the Orthodox Church with her niece. My grandma believed in God all her life, but she never read the Bible. She kept her belief in her heart. She is very wise, modest, and kind. Every day before school, she used to tell me, "God bless you!"

I always smiled smugly, because I believed the teacher's words and communist ideals. Every classroom in the early 1980's had a big notice posted that read, *Religion is the opiate of the masses.*

After Perestroika, everything started to change. Schoolbooks started to contain pages from the Bible. When I was a teacher of Russian language and literature, I explained to students about Christianity. After Perestroika, bookstores got new books about different religions like Islam and Christianity. Universities stopped studying Lenin's communist, atheistic books and got new programs about the history of religions and their development and differences. I really loved those lessons.

I started to believe in God when I was seventeen years old. Since that time, I began visiting the Russian Orthodox Church about every two months. Russian Orthodox churches are very different from churches in the U.S. They are very fancy inside. You can enjoy looking at beautiful icons in golden frames, wooden carvings, and iron frames! Different saints' faces are watching over you at the Russian Orthodox churches.

The majority of great icons have candlesticks, and you are supposed to put the church's candles in them. You can buy the church's candles, little and big icons, souvenirs, and Bibles inside the church. It is a tradition to buy candles. You ask God to save the health of your relatives, and you perform a ceremony with the candles. If you have never been at a Russian Orthodox church, you would have to educate yourself and see what is going on inside. You would be impressed.

However, some little problems are awaiting you. There is no place to sit down! Oh, do not even think about complaining! Can you live without benches in a church? Think about it. Interesting, huh?! One day when I was seventeen, I was listening to a liturgy. It was in August, and the church was full of people. There was heat like we have in Arizona, and it made it difficult to breathe. (I caught you! You did not know that in the Soviet Union people are familiar with deserts and 120-degree heat?)

I fainted! Is it embarrassing to faint in public? It is. I remember the next day after this incident that my friend called me and said, "Oksana, yesterday one fledgling idiot fainted inside the church!" Sometimes rumors spread faster than you think. Okay. I hated to stay two hours and listen to the boring ceremony.

A lot of Russians do not understand the Orthodox liturgy very well. Why? That is a very good question. Russian Orthodox churches use the old Slavonic language for the ceremony, for graces, and for songs. Imagine if you were a child of the 20th century and your church did not care about whether you understood their old language or not! That is why some people enter new, smaller Protestant churches like the Adventist church or the Baptist church to understand God better.

One day I went to the church to buy candles and put them in the candlesticks by the icons. Also, I ordered the special graces. Guess. Do you want the preacher to pray for the health of your relatives? Or do you want the preacher to pray about peace for the souls of your dead relatives? Great! I did, too. I paid money for this terrific service because I believed it would work! Usually, I spent fifteen to thirty minutes at the church to do this. In Tashkent, people have only two Russian Orthodox churches, one little Lutheran church, and one Catholic Church. Very few Russians are Catholic or Lutheran.

There is one huge Orthodox Church and one little one at the cemetery Botkino. Both churches have homeless and poor, unemployed people around their property. Are you anxious to know more? In my country, two types of people go to churches: those who beg for money and those who give money. Some poor, homeless people live outside the church. The property of the church is their daily place to ask for handouts. Sometimes beggars are sick, and you can see on their bodies different kinds of eczema, skin cancers, or external tumors or sores. Also, you can have the privilege to pray, "Thank you, God, that I am healthy! Thank you, God, that I have my legs and arms! Thank you, God, that I am not a beggar! Thank you, thank you, thank you, God!!!!"

Poor people always roam around near the churches. Their behavior is quite peculiar. Some of them are very calm, peaceful, serene, and even trance-like. Some are very energetic, because it is their livelihood to be insistent and obnoxious. If you're generous and give some money or food to one beggar, all the others will look in your eyes and say, "Please, give me something! God bless you!" Now what are you going do? Tell me, please! What are you going to say to an old woman or to the little children who have a sincere, inexpressible sadness in their eyes? You see, you cannot help everybody.

When I found out about the unhappy poor people, I started to save my money for visiting the church. One day I bought fifteen to twenty soft buns to give to the beggars. First, my attempt to save the world disappointed me. Before my coming into the church, I presented all the buns to the beggars. After my actions inside the church, the same beggars asked me to give them something again. They had already forgotten my face, and they did not care to remember me! So I made my own rule: *Do not give anything before going into the church.*

Okay. Next time I was very quick to enter the church and relax. I enjoyed the aroma of the incense. I admired the icons' faces and frames. I put candles in the candlesticks. After my routine in the church, I came out and presented the buns to the struggling, hungry people outside of the building. Oh, what a good feeling! I had gifts! They were so thankful! They told me, "God bless you!" and "I hope your ways will be soft and lucky like this bread is soft and tender."

It is a very good feeling when people love you and say nice words to you. However, if they do not love you, you will know it. You will see pouts and even hear some unpleasant words. One day I had no money to buy bread for the poor people. I did not even have money to buy candles or order graces! All I had was some change to buy a bus ticket to get back home. (Do not tell me that I could have walked home. I spent an hour on the bus to get to the church. How could I ever walk back? If you try to imagine Tashkent, think about a big American city with a population of two to three million people. In a city of that size, I could never have gotten to the church in ten to thirty minutes of fast-paced walking!)

Before I got on the bus, a one-legged old man with a red face asked me, "Beautiful, please give me something!"

I looked at his eyelashes and eyebrows that were singed from drunken smoking. It was the same guy that I saw every time I visited the church. I answered, "I have nothing today."

He was upset because he had called me "beautiful" for nothing, and he used offensive language to insult me greatly. Can you imagine visiting the church to talk with God, and somebody does not remember that you had been giving him bread all the time?

My mother and grandmother go to church to light candles and buy graces, but they do not buy bread for the poor. They give some change to the beggars. Sometimes my mom buys some cheap candies or cookies for these people so that they will leave her alone.

In the former Soviet Union, all the Christians in the different republics celebrate Easter. It is different than in the U.S. First, there are no toy rabbits. Second, women cook special bread, which we call "kulich." Kulich has to be cooked in cans of different sizes. The top of it is white, because after baking it, the women spread cream or icing on it and then put wheat or other grains of different colors on top of the icing. The women also paint eggs for Easter. It is a Russian tradition to exchange your eggs and kuliches with friends and neighbors.

Easter is also the day to go to the cemetery to visit the church there and the graves of your dead relatives. Russians usually make a small metallic fence around their relatives' graves. Every year, on Easter, they paint the fence with a silvery color. Also, they make a bench and a table close to their relative's grave. It is a tradition to visit your dead relatives, sit on the bench, eat food, and drink wine or vodka.

I remember very well my last visit to the cemetery before my trip to the U.S. It was Easter of 1997. My grandma went with me. We bought flowers to put on our relatives' graves. We had a lot of little round kuliches to eat and to give to the homeless. We had lunch at our table.

One teenage gypsy girl stopped close to our fence and started to beg, "Please, give me the egg. I am tired of eating bread. Please." So we gave it to her. She said, "Thank you very much! Do not give any food to Uzbeks. They are not Christians like we Russians and Gypsies are." Interesting, huh?

After the visit to our relatives' graves, we went to see the graves of the dead bishops of Tashkent. I had a pail to take water with me to this place. At the cemetery, there was a place where everybody could take water to wash fences or tombstones, or to water flowers. I washed the tombstones of strangers, because I knew that they had special lives, and it was important for me. After my cleaning, I put flowers on each of the four gravestones.

The next thing I did was to order the special grace about peace for souls for my dead relatives and the dead Tashkent bishops. While I was inside the little church, I asked God, the saints, and the bishops, "Please help me. I want to start a family with Richard Keith Leslie. I want to leave Uzbekistan very much and have a family in the U.S. I want to have a Christian spouse who will love me and whom I will adore and admire."

I remember very well the day that I received Keith's first warm and interesting letter with eleven pictures. It was on my twenty-third birthday, the 28th of November, 1996. On my way to work I met the postman, who gave me the letter from the U.S! Also, this day was great because it was the day that Catholics celebrated their Thanksgiving! This was so important to me, like a good sign from God. Can you believe it?

The next day, on the 29th of November, I visited the church to thank God and the angels and to ask for their supervision and help. I stayed close to the icon of Mary and prayed, "Please protect me from making mistakes! I want to create a strong, healthy family with an American man. Can you hear me? Can you help me?"

At that moment, a window opened and the wind shook the candle's flame but did not blow it out. For me, it was a sign from God that He would bless me and help me. I wished I could visit the church more often than I did, but I had no car, and the bus ride took two hours.

When I was a student at the university, I studied six days a week and went to the library a lot. Sunday was the only day of the week that I had to relax and to help my mother with housework. Usually, we went to the theater or to visit friends or relatives. Sometimes I spent Sundays at the library because I had to write a lot of reports about books that I had read. So because the church was so hard to get to, it was not very important to me at that time.

Let me tell you some more about buses. I hate public transport. You cannot imagine how nasty it feels when an uncultured man tries to touch your body or to cut your purse off your shoulder in a full bus or metro train or tram. During my years as a student, I used public transportation, and I hated having a lot of people around me because of the odors of their bodies and of the food they had bought from the markets. I can remember the nasty smell at times when drunken guys vomited on the bus after parties.

There was another reason why I did not visit the church often. I did not have enough money. I could not just go inside without feeding the poor and buying candles. If I did something for God, it was my own sacrifice. I was sure that I could pray and talk with God without the church and its priest. Nobody knows exactly what God wants from us. But remember, even Jesus Christ got angry at the temple and did not always go to a synagogue, but he preached wherever he was. And wherever he was, God was!

One day Keith and I were watching a Christmas opera-ballet. Keith asked me, "Oksana, do you believe that Jesus is the Son of God, and that He died for the sins of the world?"

I kept silent. I believe in God, and you cannot call me an atheist. I also believe in angels. I am sure that Jesus was a great prophet, but I do not like to talk about it with Christians. I did not want to talk to Keith about my true beliefs.

However, he was smart and sneaky. He asked me a different question: "Do you believe in the Virgin Mary?"

I answered right away, "No." Listen, it is normal for Russians, who grew up with the communist and atheistic propaganda, to answer like that.

Keith told me, "If you do not believe that Mary was a virgin, it means that you do not believe that Jesus is the Son of God, and that He died for our sins, and that the only way to Heaven is through Jesus."

Okay, he caught me. We were listening to the voices of the singers in that Christmas show. I was thinking, *Oh, I never saw a real baby instead of a doll in the nativity!* How did they keep him calm? His crying could have turned this performance into hell. I had never seen live camels and sheep on the stage before, either! What if a camel had spit on somebody? Who would clean up the sheep droppings after the show? How much did the theater's janitor make per hour? How much did these singers and dancers make for this show?

On the 24th of December, I went to a new church, Spring of Life, from which I got an invitation to come for the holiday ceremony. I was excited. It was interesting to go and see a new church, whose members met every Sunday in a high school auditorium. So I really went to the school! That location made me feel very comfortable about this new Christian organization, because I am a former teacher. Keith was sick, so he did not go with me. It was my first time in a church in the U.S. alone, the first time I was in a church in 1999, and the first time I was in a school auditorium. However, what else American have to know about our differences?

Americans have to know that Russian people and other nationalities in the former Soviet Union spend their free time reading, and they will never say that Alaska and the U.S. are synonyms. They have plenty of education about American writers, culture, history, and geography. They do not connect the words "Alaska" and "the U.S." When I used to be a 5th grade teacher for the 1996-1997 school year, the school's curriculum included stories of London and Mark Twen. Kids have to study geography for four years in Russian schools. They know more about the U.S. than the U.S. students know about the Soviets. One day our neighbor in Apache Junction, a fourteen-year old boy, asked me, "Does Russia have a president?" Such a nice picture of the American education system!

However, my spouse Keith thinks that I just happened to meet the most ignorant, stubborn, misbehaving kids in the U.S. He cannot believe that I had such bad luck in my first two years. Americans like to connect the words "the Soviet Union" and "Russia." A lot of Americans have no idea that Russia was only a part of the Soviet Union. Each republic has its own climate, not just snowy winter and cold summer. Americans in Arizona used to ask me, "Are you going to miss the snow and frost?" They were amused to learn that Uzbekistan has the same climate as Northern Arizona, except that there are no cacti in Uzbek deserts. It is funny that in the former Soviet Union people know about different states of the U.S. and their population, but a lot of Americans do not know anything about the republics of the former Soviet Union.

I hope my book will be like a discovery for my readers. Don't forget that I used to be a teacher. I love to teach people about my country Uzbekistan and my Russian culture. Please try to imagine what it would be like if every state of the U.S. had its own language, currency, passport control, premises to start a civil war between nations, and its own economical crisis.

Does it sound weird? This happened in the former Soviet Union after Perestroika (reformation, rebuilding of economy and society values). People in the republics got permission to speak out about past years and criticize the ideas of communism. People realized that they had had enough of the Russian dictatorship in their local governments. Well, they got independence, and they did not start any ethnic cleansing.

Can you imagine that your family lives in Florida, but you are living in Arizona? Imagine that you would have to change your state money and use Florida's money. The security issues are interesting, also. I was questioned by customs in Moscow's airport. "Why have you visited Moscow? Where did you stay?"

My friend, Lena Barhanskaya, a teacher of geography, zoology, biology, and botany, was visiting her family in the Republic of Kazakhstan. After she spent a couple weeks in the city Alma Ata, she had to pay a fee to the customs department of Kazak's airport, because she did not have a registration stamp from the local area where she was staying with her family.

Actually, if you were visiting Uzbekistan as a tourist and staying in a hotel, you would get a registration stamp in your passport at the hotel so that you would be a legal tourist. If you were visiting your pen pal in

Uzbekistan, she would have to take you to the local office to register you as her guest.

Okay, relax. Now you can understand the situation in the former Soviet Union a little bit. But imagine if in the U.S. all different races that occupy each state would separate and get independence from one another. Now you can see a terrible picture: Indians live only in Arizona and California; African Americans live only in Georgia, Pennsylvania, Alabama, and Mississippi; Mexicans live only in New Mexico and Texas; Europeans live only in northern states; and Asians live in a different place.

Okay, it is a very bad dream to allow people to make their own communities, because they can decide to start a little civil war, or simply to discriminate. It is good that people in the U.S. live together and each state has its own mixture of different cultures and nationalities. You have to know that before Perestroika, the former Soviet Union had in its republics (Kazakhstan, Tajikistan, Kyrgyzstan, Turkmenistan, Uzbekistan, Byelorussia, Ukraine, Armenia, Azerbaijan, Georgia, Moldavia, Latvia, Lithuania, and Estonia) different nationalities with their own cultures and languages. This is the explanation. The majority of people in Uzbekistan are Uzbeks; the majority of people in Byelorussia are Byelorussians, etc.

Okay, why did I spend time explaining this to you? Well, I found out that for most Americans, other republics of the former Soviet Union don't exist. When I told people that I was from Uzbekistan, they smiled and said, "Oh, Pakistan!" Even people at post offices used to ask me, "Where is this country?"

One day a post office worker brought me a registered letter. We were residents of Mesa at that time. She told us that her friends at the post office had had an argument about my country. She was supposed to ask us who were right. Someone had said that Uzbekistan was in South America. Another worker had said that Uzbekistan was in Africa. Someone else was sure that the country must be by Pakistan and Afghanistan somehow.

We told her that the person who thought that Uzbekistan is close to Pakistan and Afghanistan was correct. Actually, "Stan" means "country" in old Turkish language, if I am not mistaken. So it means that Afghanistan is the country of the Afghan nationality, and Uzbekistan is the country of the Uzbeks.

When I am interested in a country, I go on the Internet.

I would not embarrass myself by asking such questions. That is not all. A couple of times we received phone calls from new phone companies. When we asked them to look up the international rates for Uzbekistan, clerks on the phone were really ignorant and had a difficult time writing the name of this country, and sometimes even hung up on us. They could not find my motherland in their system. It was pathetic to hear disconnect signals instead of rate information. Can you believe that?

If you ever visit the former Soviet Union and tell people that you are from Colorado or Texas, or any American state, they will not ask you the stupid question, "Where is it?" Okay? So I had to tell ignorant Americans that I was from Russia. It is so funny. It is as if citizens of Arizona would say that they are from Alaska, because somebody might not know anything about Arizona.

Actually, I had a rare chance to meet some Americans who were not satisfied by my answer about where I was from. They would ask me, "What part of Russia?" Well, I would tell them more details.

Thank God, Americans love sports. Most of the people I met knew Oksana, the skater from Ukraine. Those people could spell and pronounce my name correctly. This was impressive.

I am Russian, I speak Russian, I can teach Russian, and I can sing Russian songs. However, I was born in Uzbekistan. Uzbekistan is the republic in Central Asia. Most people there are Muslims and speak their native language, Uzbek. I grew up in this culture of mixed communism, Islam, and Orthodox Christianity, plus a lot of regional superstition. I learned to respect other religions. I read the Koran two times in two different Russian translations. I discovered that the Koran calls Christians the brothers of Muslims. The Koran tells the same stories about paradise and hell that the Bible does. The Koran tells the same stories about famous prophets from the Bible. However, the Koran believes that Mary was not a virgin and that her son, Jesus, was a prophet, not God's son.

Still, the Koran does not deny the Bible's basic teaching. The Koran says that Christians and Muslims are brothers, because they worship one God. So many good people die because of their ignorance of the teachings of this book. I knew a lot of Christians in Uzbekistan who had never read the Bible. I knew a lot of Muslims who had never read the Koran. This is very sad. The Koran and the Bible both teach not to steal, lie, kill, or commit suicide.

I wish people could be more open-minded. My motherland now has freedom of religion. I believe this is right. Personally, I respect the Koran, some Muslim traditions of hospitality, and Asian culture. I like Uzbek meals, and Mediterranean foods. I am used to a hot climate. I am used to hearing Russian speech with Uzbek, Armenian, and other foreign accents. I grew up in the capital with two and a half million people. I had Uzbek, Russian, Jewish, and Korean friends. I used to see different races and learn about different traditions, meals, and religions. It is different to be a Russian from a Russian city, than a Russian from Uzbekistan, or Kazakhstan, or Tajikistan, or Armenia. I am very proud of my background. I am happy to know that God gave me a chance to absorb not just Russian culture.

Why did I want to leave my country? I did not feel safe. I was afraid that Uzbekistan might turn out to be a Muslim fundamentalist country, like Iraq or Iran. I was not sure that I would have a future in this kind of system.

Thank God for Uzbek's government work in keeping peace and friendship between the people in Uzbekistan, because my family and friends are all over there, and I do not want to hear about any ethnic cleansing in my motherland. After the Perestroika and the civil war in Tajikistan, a lot of Russians in non-Russian republics did not feel very safe. So Perestroika started a migration process. A lot of people immigrated to better places, since the borders were opened.

Immigrants did not think that we had a future in our collapsed Soviet Union. We did not want to stay and fight for a better economy. We did not want to wait until inflation would stop. We wished to come to a better world like the U.S., Australia, Canada, or Great Britain, and forget about years of socialism, atheism, brain cleansing propaganda, studying Lenin's books, and worshipping Stalin. If Russia would be as close to the U.S. as Mexico, you would have to deal with a lot of Russian illegal immigrants.

One day Keith and I were watching a show about the economy in different countries. We found out from this show that the economy in Russia was even worse than in Mexico. Russia's system was called "mafiocracy." In Uzbekistan, I could buy any antibiotics and medications without a doctor's prescription. My mom, who is a doctor, could always give me advice on what to buy and how to heal myself. In the U.S., I was shocked to find out that birth control pills are available only with a gynecologist's prescription. That is not a problem in Uzbekistan and Russia. A woman does not have to see a doctor to buy her birth control pills. Russians do not have health insurance, so if they do not have money to buy certain kinds of medications (like antibiotics or amino acids), they have to borrow cash from friends and family or die. Keith's mother had lupus for decades. My mom says that in the former Soviet Union, she would never have survived with such a diagnosis.

Personally, I did not want to be in a new generation that would have to learn the Uzbek language, because I was lazy. I had no fire in my soul to build a new system, and suffer with my low teacher's salary. Actually, I never met a man who would want to marry me in Tashkent and provide a stable future for me. However, some Uzbek man offered me to be their well kept mistress right in the middle of a marketplace.

Russians have a tradition to present flowers, but you have to be careful about the number. Only funerals and graves receive even number of flowers. Iris is considered a flower of dead. That is why people do not bring those as birthday gifts. It is common to plant irises around graves and offices. People buy odd number of flowers for birthdays, weddings.

I want to share with you an experience I had with Russian and American relatives. When Russian relatives or friends see that I am overweight, they tell me about it. American relatives, who did not see me for a while, were tactful regarding my changed appearance. If you tell an American that they have a nice outfit, they thank you for the compliment. Russian would tell you how they got it, and how much was it.

We feel that in international marriage people have to learn about each other's cultures from each other, from books or internet. This way no one gets disappointed if sour kraut and pork are not prepared for New Years' Eve or no plans are made for Halloween party, or house is not decorated the right way for Thanksgiving or Christmas.

CHAPTER 7
HOW TO FACE MISFORTUNE.

There is no a certain remedy how to face misfortune. Most important is to help each other in any way possible, except friend's help if offered. Be tough. Clean the house, write a book, see a psychic, do something, so you do not get depressed and scared.

As you remember, Keith and I got married in Atlanta in 1998. Then we moved to Arizona, Phoenix area. I love this state. Views with open spaces and cacti were stunning and wonderful to me. We enjoyed hot climate. That is why we bought a house there in Phoenix area, with yard, in ground pool and waterfall. Building a new house was my biggest desire. Keith preferred to buy a small used house, but I did not want to live with someone else's ghosts! Speaking of ghosts, when I was an 11 year old atheist - teenager, one of schoolmates convinced me that invisible creatures surround us. I remember listening to the sounds of my bedroom, and trying to please my invisible roommate with a cup of milk, placed on the top of my dress closet. I was scared sometimes. I really heard weird sounds like my curtain was moved without any wind in the room. It was time I developed a habit to sleep with a pillow on my head. However, maybe this habit is a product of the fact, that neighbor's bathroom was on the other side of my wall. My atheist dad used to joke about it: "Ghost can live here, I don't mind, if it does not eat much."

Later, when I was 20 years old and a student at the university, I was making money on helping people to get rid of ghosts! I had an assistant, an 11 year old girl Natasha. She could see the ghost's location in the client's homes. I used to destroy them with my mental powers, imagining that fire licks walls. I also was imagining that a huge snake would come out from my third Will charka in the diaphragm area. This invisible snake would eat the ghosts. After the hunt, I would burn several kinds of dried herbs in the client's home to cleanse the place with nature vibrations. I sincere believed that I was very gifted mystic. I read occult books, went to psychic clubs for meetings. When meningitis almost killed me, I felt that God is saving me from the life I was choosing as an occult specialist.

However, it is time to come back to the Arizona story. My first American friend was Pat Durbin. She taught me how to make homemade crust for pies, cream puffs, how to prickle steaks with the fork and other things. Lora Simpson was my second American friend in Arizona. They were our neighbors.

One day my friend Lora Simpson asked me to do her a favor. She told me about her upcoming business trip to California. Laura wanted to take her daughter Alex with her, because she still was nursing. She was concerned about the high cost of getting a baby sitter in California, so she got the idea of taking me with her as her baby sitter.

To me, the deal sounded excellent. I would have a chance to fly to Los Angeles, see the Pacific Ocean and live in a nice hotel at Huntington Beach. It was a chance for me to take a vacation from my life as a homemaker. I told Keith that I honestly wanted to get away from him for three days. I was so excited about my free trip, my free flight, and the chance to spend time with my friend. I told Lora that I would not charge her anything for my baby sitting. We planned that, in return, she would feed our dog and cats when Keith and I went on trips.

Keith was very upset to hear that I was going to leave him for three or four days. He could not imagine how a loving and caring wife could even think about traveling without her spouse. He was surprised to find out that I needed a break. He called me selfish. I wanted to cancel my plans with Laura, but right away he told me that it would be stupid to live by somebody else's decision. Keith worried that I would be raped, robbed, or abused during my trip, so he did not want to let me go.

Well, I had to leave our home on Monday, January 10th, at 5:00 a.m. Keith said to me before I fell asleep, "Good night. If something happens to you on this trip, your family will never forgive me."

Keith woke me up at 2:00 a.m. that morning. He complained of chest pain, nausea, and diarrhea. I got up, of course, and brought him water and a wet washcloth. He was blaming my chicken, which I had cooked for lunch on Sunday. He thought that he had gotten food poisoning from the chicken.

I put my clothes on and offered to drive him to the hospital. He was sitting on the living room floor, and had difficulty getting dressed. I was trying to read in my Russian books about alternative medicine that can cure heart pain, but I could not find anything. I started to massage his fingers, like he does to me when I have a headache, but he did not like that.

I picked up our kitten, Banditka, and told Keith, "Cats are good for hearts. Touch the cat." He could not grab her, because he was in such pain. Now it sounds funny that Keith was having a heart attack while our cat was lying by him, purring loudly.

Keith told me that his heart pain was so strong that he felt burning in his arms and shoulders. When he told me that, it really scared me. I remembered that I had heard a story in my country of somebody who died from a heart attack because help was not provided. This man had gotten the same pains and burning in his arms as Keith.

I told Keith that I wanted to call 911. He said, "Okay, call." I called and asked for help. Paramedics arrived at our place shortly. It was 3:00 a.m. When I was on my way with Keith to a Hospital, I called Laura from my cell phone.

"Lora. Keith is having a heart attack. I am in the ambulance right now. I can not fly with you." The next thing I knew, Lora canceled her flight, too, just to be with me in the hospital and support me during such a terrible situation. When Keith got to the hospital, his heart stopped completely for one minute. He was very clearly in violent agony.

The doctor came up to him with the question, "Did we get a cocainer?"

I yelled back, "No!"

Keith was brought back to life with heart compression and electroshock. I was not able to watch all these details, because the nurses pulled a curtain around his bed. However, I will never forget him dying. It could have happened when I was in California having fun with Lora and little Alex! Keith would never have dialed 911 by himself. It could have happened in the house, if we had not called an ambulance. He would have died in our car, if we had tried to save money and drive ourselves to the hospital.

When the doctors were bringing Keith back to life from hell or heaven, I was sitting and crying. I could not believe that my spouse had almost died.

Keith was moved into the intensive care unit. He was getting lidocaine and heparin intravenously. He was alive.

As soon as he felt better, Keith started to ask the doctors to let him go home. The doctor guaranteed him that he would die at home without this medicine to thin his blood and remove clots. The doctor thought that I could not understand his speech because of my accent. So he talked to Lora about possible damaged heart tissue and bypass surgery.

Lora drove me back home and explained to me everything about Keith's condition. On the way home at 6:00 a.m., I felt heartburn, so Lora gave me some of her mint drops to relax my stomach. Also, we sat down in the middle of her living room and prayed for Keith's health.

I went back home and started to call our family and friends. First, I called my Aunt Lena Rashevskaya. I knew that her metaphysical help was very important. I believe that since she was a healer and a specialist in holistic dynamics, she would be able to help us. She told me not to call my parents until the situation with Keith was clear, because their panic would only make his condition worse.

Next, I called Keith's mom and dad, and left a brief message. His parents were at the hospital, because Keith's mom was getting her catheterization and angioplasty. So then I called his sister and his boss. I cried on the phone to my friends Alina from California and Pat from our subdivision.

Finally I took a bath and tried to relax. I was lonely and upset. My mind replayed Alina's and Pat's information about their relatives, who had gone through bypass surgery. I also remembered a story about Dawn Barkett's dad, who had had a heart attack in Texas and had died in a hospital on the fourth day. I did not want to believe that Keith was so sick.

At 8.30 a.m., his boss came to pick me up to see Keith again. I did not feel like driving, so he really was a support to me. When we arrived at the intensive care unit, I lied to a duty nurse that I had come with Keith's uncle. It was almost true, because this gentleman called Keith his son sometimes. The duty nurse looked at him and instantly knew he was Keith's boss. Her voice said confidently, "No computers for Keith." Well, the boss was Keith's first visitor.

Three days later, Keith received several visits from his boss and his boss's family, some co-workers, and our neighbors, Don and Pat Durbin. Keith's family called me at home and at the hospital. He really felt their support and prayers. He made everybody think about their own heart history, diet, and physical condition.

To be honest, I did not know that I could stay in the hospital with Keith outside of regular visiting hours. I did not know that he expected me to stay or that he needed me. I believed that in American hospitals everything was taken care of. Why did he need me, if he had nurses to serve him? So his first night in the hospital he spent alone, without my support, love, and care. I can not imagine how terrible he felt. I slept at home, cleaned the house, fed the pets, watered the plants, and sent e-mails about Keith's condition to our friends in Atlanta, Hawaii, and Australia. I called to the pool company, to tell them about Keith's heart attack and about our filter, which had been making weird noises since Sunday. I believed that this pool filter had to be cleaned and fixed as soon as possible. It was like a symbol of Keith's heart. I wanted to fix his heart by fixing our pool filter.

I came to visit my husband at 9:30 a.m. and brought him some things he needed. I left him that afternoon, when he fell asleep. I went to change car oil, because we had not done it for months. I decided that changing the oil might help Keith's condition in some way. Maybe that doesn't make sense to Keith or to my readers, but I was sure that I had to do something to save him.

After getting the oil changed, I went to the Motor Vehicle Division in Apache Junction. I was trying to get myself a new ID. I was so scared to drive around without it. Of course, I was not able to get an ID that day, because I did not have a valid ID from Immigration Services. To the Motor Vehicle Division, I was an illegal non-immigrant. Sure, they tried to act like they cared about my situation, but they couldn't do anything to help me. I left there with a great hatred for the MVD, Immigration Services, and all other Americans. My Work Authorization card expired. I did not know that I had to apply for its renewal three months ago before the expiration date. I thought that INS system automatically would send me an appointment letter.

After three hours of driving around, I came back to see Keith again. This time I had comfortable clothes on, and I was ready to spend the night at the hospital with him in the chair next to his bed. It was his second day at the Hospital, but this night he was moved from intensive care to a regular heart monitoring department on the fourth floor.

It was my first night in an American hospital. It was terrible. A nurse had to wake Keith up every hour to check his blood pressure. I am a light sleeper, so I heard the duty nurse every time she came in. Poor Keith did not ever have a chance to really rest! I forgot my solution for contact lenses. It was my first night at a hospital as a visitor. I was not ready at all.

He let me go home to feed our pets and take a bath at 4:45 a.m. the next morning. I was back at the hospital at 7:00 a.m. That day I helped wash him in the shower. I know that I was irritating him all the time. Everything I did or said was stressing him out. He said that he had a heart attack and I had a brain attack. That is why the first few days I felt as if I needed to go do something else to get my mind off of Keith and the hospital. When I went home to clean the house, I accidentally lost Keith's keys and my passport, and it took me two hours to find them.

On his fourth day, he had an angiogram. Keith was scheduled for angioplasty catheterization at a Phoenix hospital two weeks later. It seemed ridiculous to me that the doctors had to do two surgeries, if they could have done one on the same day. Maybe I am wrong, but to me, it sounds like hospitals tried to get more money from the insurance company.

The night after the angioplasty in the Phoenix hospital, when Keith got the stent in his left anterior descendent, nobody came to check on him. He was bleeding in his groin area and his wrist, where the IV needle had been pulled out. I slept very well, because nobody really came into his room. He could not get comfortable, and was very tired and upset. It was my second time to be his nurse at the hospital, and I was doing really well. I did not irritate Keith at all that night.

When he went to see his doctor in Mesa, he prescribed three months of disability for Keith. We told him that Keith did not need to be on disability for such a long time. I personally told the doctor, "Keith works from home, and he loves his job very much. He will have more stress from not working, and having to clean up his IRA's."

The doctor tried to look smart and helpful as he said, "Any job is stressful. He does not need stress during these first three critical months. He can go to the Social Security office and apply for short term disability, and for food stamps."

We trusted the doctor's knowledge and went to the Social Security office in Mesa. We left there very sad. It was the first day of February 2000. A clerk at the office told us that we needed an appointment to apply for benefits on February 24th. However, the same clerk told us that Social Security does not have three months' disability benefits unless an individual is disabled from working for at least one year. Even if you get approved, you can't get your benefits sooner than six months after your appointment.

Keith also could not qualify for food stamps, because his wife was not a citizen, or a legal permanent resident. Why am I not a permanent resident yet? There are too many immigrants in Arizona, and that is why I have to wait for three years to get my green card. I know Russians in Georgia and Michigan who got their green cards faster.

I was very upset and angry that we could not get food stamps because of my status. I felt like I was worthless, that my spouse was the only one in the country who cared about my existence.

This is so ironic! The same day that we found out all this garbage from the doctor and the government, Keith and I had an appointment with our new dentist, Dr. S. The dentist asked us about our jobs. Keith said that he loved his job as a programmer. I answered that I did not have to work. I liked how that sounded. I did not have to work, okay?

When the fact that I might have to get a job occurred to me, I became stressed, angry, and scared. I was sure that nobody would want to hire me with my university education from Uzbekistan. I was afraid of rejection by society. This is how I will finish my chapter about my travel to California. I did not get to see Los Angeles, but I saw three American hospitals and bruises on Keith's legs. I got to learn some medical terms like *bypass surgery*, *stent*, *angiogram*, *IV*, *angioplasty*, and *balloon*. I learned which items a hospitalized spouse will need in his room the first day to feel comfortable.

Most important of all, I had the chance to see how much our friends and family cared about his health and life.

Now I wish to share some ironic events which took place after Keith's heart attack.

I got a phone call from a telemarketer. She offered us a trip to a Sedona resort. I was nice and explained to her that my spouse had just had a heart attack, and he was in the hospital. The lady swallowed this information like it was nothing and asked me, "Well, are you not going to go, then?"

After I took Keith home from the hospital, we got a phone call from another telemarketer, but this time he told me about our brave police, and tried to get "a $25 or $30 donation for police officers." I explained to him that my spouse just got home from the hospital and that he was not working now, and I didn't have a job either. We could not afford to give any donations, even to our brave police officers. The gentlemen on the phone listened to me, and then said, "Well, maybe you can give $10."

In Uzbekistan and Russia people do not get calls from telemarketers, because there are no credit cards to apply for and there are no credit cards to use to buy products over a phone. I know people who have no phone lines at their homes at all.

When Keith was brought back from his temporary death, I was allowed to see him. I told him, "It is your entire fault. You always like to say how old you are."

Keith had the strength to be sarcastic, and said, "Oksana, your bridge to a better life almost died. It would have been so ironic if you had to go back to Tashkent!"

Actually, he was right. While I was filling out some paperwork at Immigration, I asked them what would happen to me if my spouse died. I was told that I would not be able to get my green card if my spouse could not come for the interview. I would then be deported back to my country, even if I had gotten pregnant and had a child.

While Keith was in the hospital, several events were taking place at the same time. On January 10th, his mom had an angioplasty surgery, our lovely Uncle Larry was sick in the hospital with heart and lung problems. Two Uncle Jacks were in hospitals in Chicago and Florida. My dad spent thirteen days in a hospital in Tashkent with viral hepatitis. It sounds like a family thing. Yes, if it rains, it pours. My cousin died from botulism in Tashkent in January of 2000 when he was only twenty-six years old. It seemed clear to me that in the beginning of the new century we were all working out some problems and karma with sicknesses and death.

At first, I was trying to smile wide and pretend that I was okay. However, Keith saw that I needed a vacation from all that stress. He was insisting to send me back in Tashkent in February or March. Later, we figured out that I needed to get a job to help us out financially while Keith was not working.

Well, I applied to Basha's, Food City, and Domino's Pizza. Those places were hiring at that time. No one called me back. I was very frustrated that I, "Princess," couldn't get a job as a cashier or even as a produce stocker in the U.S. I stopped by one fast food restaurant and talked to a manager about my situation. It was Keith's advice that I tell my story.

I was hired! I was so happy that I got my first real job in America without anybody's help or references. I did not care much about the low salary. I wanted to work and learn to fit into society. I wanted to prove to myself that I could do my best, and grow.

Now I want to tell you what most of my Russian friends and family think about my job.

"Oh, how can she go to work in such a place with her university education and writer's talents?" It is true. I had thought the same thing about my friend Galina, who was a waitress in Atlanta with her university degree as an architect. It took me more than a year in the U.S. to understand the system of education, jobs, and references. It also took me more than a year to not be embarrassed about working as a normal human being without an American education. Yes, I had too much pride. I was too proud to work until I had to. I used to brag in my letters about my life in America, surrounded by 6 phones, two computers, and three living room sofas. My letters before Keith's heart attack were about our cats and a dog, about our camping and trips to Salt River, Canyon Lake. After Keith's heart attack I was writing about my new job and what I was learning there.

Now I really smile wide, because my spouse is alive, we were able to keep our house. I was not deported back to Tashkent. I got to learn how to be a team member on minimum wage. I am very thankful to God for all these things.

One day Keith was sitting on the sofa. It was March 9th, right after I took him home from the hospital after he got his appendix removed. He could not believe that he had been rushed to a hospital by ambulance twice in two months. The first time was with his heart attack, and the second time was with appendicitis. He was still "enjoying" his short-term disability.

He said, "Why did it all happen to me?"

My answer was clear. "All events happen to make our book more interesting, Baby. Can you imagine how many things I can write about us now?" I am not sure if he liked my answer or not, but I liked it.

If Keith would not suffer a heart attack, I would never look for a job at a restaurant. However, I do not regret that I had to go work at the fast food place. I learned a lot about people and about the fast food system.

First, I want to write about the people on the other side of the sales counter: the customers. To me, customers come in only two categories: there are intelligent customers or ignorant customers. Ignorant customers spill drinks and walk away as if nothing happened. Intelligent customers who spill drinks tell a cashier and apologize to the workers for the accident.

Ignorant customers believe that they are better than everyone else. They get upset easily and are rude to the staff if a service error takes place. The packing person can forget to put biscuits or side items with the order. So what? We are all human, and we all make mistakes. Intelligent customers know that from common sense. Experienced, intelligent customers check all the items of their order before they leave the sales counter. Ignorant customers make a big deal out of a mistake and yell and scream.

Ignorant customers do not greet the restaurant staff. Yes, we have to greet our customers and be nice. We say, "How are you doing today?"

117

I personally love to hear an answer, even if it sounds as if the customer doesn't really care. Ignorant customers right away say, "I want such and such." Intelligent customers answer the cashier's question first, and even ask the same back.

Intelligent customers teach their kids to take their food scraps and paper plates to a trash can. Ignorant customers tell their kids to leave their trays with leftovers and trash on the tables. They think it is our job to clean up after their kids. (No, it is not! You are at a fast food restaurant, and I am not your waitress, dummy!)

After working at the fast food restaurant, I learned how to respect clerks and cashiers everywhere. You know, I have realized that life seems much better when you learn how to wish people a great day, a wonderful weekend, or a nice evening. I have also realized that to the intelligent customers, I am a real person in a uniform. To the ignorant customers, I am just like trash or like their servant.

One day Keith took me to McDonald's for breakfast. After our meal, I stuck a sandwich wrapper in our empty paper cups to save some space in the restaurant's trashcan, and I cleaned the crumbs from our table. Keith was impressed that I had started to care about other people's work. My job at the fast food restaurant changed me from being an ignorant, uncaring, rude customer to an intelligent customer and person. I learned how to say "sir" and "ma'am" not just to our customers, but also to other people I meet.

You would not believe how much I hated the politeness of American cashiers, store assistants, and receptionists during my first months in the U.S. I felt that it was all just American hypocrisy. Russians save smiles for friends and family. In Uzbekistan, where I was raised, walking with a smile was an invitation to interested men to start a conversation. In Uzbekistan smiling to strange people is considered a flirt. It took me some time to learn how to smile to everybody without a fear to be understood wrong. Since working at the fast food restaurant, I changed my mind. Naturally, people are good, and we all want to be happy with our jobs and with those who surround us. That is why all those service people really greet us. They want to serve us better and to hear us respond. I did not know that before I became one of them.

To be honest, I didn't like to serve customers at the fast food restaurant. I am going to explain why, right? First of all, I have a strong Russian accent. Intelligent customers like to ask me, "Where are you from? How did you get into the U.S? Where did you meet your spouse?" My answer was the same for everybody: "I am from Russia." Experienced, intelligent customers like to show their intelligence by asking, "What part of Russia?" They are ready to hear something like Ukraine, Georgia, Siberia, or Armenia. They get very confused to hear me say *Uzbekistan.*

It used to upset me and make me think, *Oh, another ignorant American.* For some time, I felt as if all Uzbek citizens and their heritage (the history about ancient Sogdiana and Silk Road, palaces of Samarkand and Bukhara, and the emperor Tamerlan) meant nothing to the majority of Americans. Later, I decided that Americans would learn about Uzbekistan from my book, if they did not learn about it in college.

Anyway, Uzbekistan got its independence in 1991. It has cities which are 1500, 2000 years old. Cities of Uzbekistan existed before first Russian cities had been built! I had an opportunity to visit some of those ancient cities like Samarkand, Khiva, and Bukhara. I still remember the air of medieval burial vaults, and Arabic letters on walls telling stories about beauties and their children, khans and shah's remains resting there.

The history is captivating to me. I think that Uzbekistan and Russia are the best places to visit and learn history. However, I am not a travel agent to advertise any tours. Let's get back to the fast food restaurant.

Ignorant customers are not interested in my history and do not understand my accent, or they act like they do not. They look at me as if I am some kind of second-class idiot. They ask the cashier, "What did she say?" I can hear in the tone of their "she," that they mean me.

One day two ladies were ordering some sandwiches. Only one lady asked for a sandwich with no sauce. The other kept silent after she ordered her sandwich. We did not realize that the other lady wanted her sandwich without sauce, as well. After I made the sandwiches, the ladies went to our lobby to eat. Very soon, I faced an angry, disappointed customer who wanted her tender roast sandwich without sauce. At first I thought that her friend had gotten the order with no sauce by mistake, and so I tried to explain what happened. It was a mistake to argue with an angry customer. The lady almost threw her unwrapped, partly eaten food at me. "Just give me another one!" she yelled.

I felt terrible. I was thinking, Oh, here I am with seven years of education in music school, a master's degree of education, teaching experience, and published articles and miniature books in Russian, making a sandwich for an angry lady who probably does not even know the difference between Russia and Uzbekistan. I felt like I had more education and knowledge than any of my co-workers and most of my customers, and it was like being behind prison bars. However, who needs my knowledge of early Slavonic language, some Latin, some Macedonian I was studying in Tashkent?! Let's feed people!

Keith's heart attack made me leave my nice housewife's position and get the first job I could get. I remember my first day at the fast food restaurant! It was Valentine's Day in the year 2000, and Keith picked me up after work with a bouquet of wonderful roses. Of course, he charged the, since we did not have cash to fool around with.

HOW DO YOU LIKE THE STATES? - Well, people ask me this question a lot. Yes, I like it a lot, but there have been times when I've hated it. The red tape in this country is incredible.

Keith signed a contract to get my fiancée visa, stating that he would be my sponsor. We were told to wait for my green card for three years in Arizona. Each year, I had to buy a new work authorization card. That meant that I had to get in line at 4:00 or 5:00 a.m. at the INS office and then pay almost $100 for the card. I had to buy it even if I did not work, just to be able to get my ID. So every time I renewed my work authorization card, I would also renew my driver's license.

When Keith had to stay at home for three months on disability, he could not get Social Security, because three months disability was not enough to qualify for it. We even found out that a person who is disabled for a year or more can start to collect Social Security only after six months. Come on, wonderful American laws; is that how people should be taken care of?

That is not the end of the story. We could not even get food stamps, because Keith was fortunate enough to have married a foreign woman who did not have her green card yet and had not worked for the necessary amount of time. Did you get that? An American citizen got screwed by American laws all because of his choice of a bride! Congratulations!

How do you think I felt about the States after finding out the stinky truth from the Mesa Social Security office? I could not believe that I could feel so insecure in this wonderful country! I could not believe that my spouse, an American citizen, could be so vulnerable!

However, when people ask me how I like the States, I answer, "I am very happy with my marriage and my life. However, America is not that great. Do you know any perfect country? Me neither."

I did not care about jobs and my future in the U.S. before Keith's health problems. Our life now had surely made me care about them now. That was why we did everything we could to send me to Central Arizona

College and to get my master's degree evaluated at an independent agency in Phoenix.

I did not see myself working my way up to a manager of the fast food restaurant, because I did not like the business. One day a dirty looking customer tried to be sarcastic with me. "You look intelligent. Can I have some butter?" he said.

I was insulted. Maybe his question sounds like a compliment to you, but it did not sound like one to me. Who has to be intelligent to know the difference between butter and honey? I gave the man some butter and told him, "Yes, I am intelligent. I have a degree from a Russian university. (I did not want to talk about Uzbekistan.) I used to teach Russian language and literature in a school."

He got excited and told me about his brother, who worked in one of the Apache Junction schools. A few days later, his brother showed up at the fast food restaurant. Let's call him David. He wanted to learn Russian. He tried to speak some Russian to me.

Before my work at the fast food restaurant, I hated to be with anyone in my kitchen at home. I learned to work at the fast food restaurant's kitchen with less space and a bunch of other team members. I learned how to clean my work counter right away, and I transferred this habit to my home. Keith noticed! I started to wear my husband's apron in my kitchen, because it got to be my habit to protect my uniform in the restaurant's back area. I got these good habits from working at the fast food restaurant!

I learned a lot about people, too. Now I will talk about my co-workers.

In the morning, I used to ask my co-workers about their school and life. I realized that most of the people I questioned had zero curiosity about me or my life. They would never ask me back, "Why do you want to know? Is it different in Russian schools? How long are lessons in Russian schools?" It was weird to me. I thought, *Oh, American teenagers do not know anything and do not care about anything. How can I hope to teach them Russian in their schools?*

I wrote a long letter to my family and friends about the system in American schools. My correspondents were shocked to know that some high schools in the U.S. count the work hours of the students as credits. Of course, students will work instead of read! Sometimes I want to be dramatic and tell people, "When I was a teenager, I was reading a lot of interesting Russian and American books!"

121

However, American teenagers can say, "We help our parents to pay bills! We save money for our college! We learn to be independent. We do not have time to read books!"

Russians study the works of London, Twain, and Hemingway in school. When I was growing up, I was very excited about reading James F. Cooper's books about the whites and the Indians. I loved to read mysteries, mystical stories by Edgar Allen Poe, and science fiction works by Ray Bradbury and Isaac Asimov.

What kind of Russian literature do American students study in their schools? Okay. I am just surprised about this difference in our education. If Americans feel so threatened by the Russians, why do they not try to study more about them in school? That is what the Russians have done. It is very good to know about your enemy.

Let's take another example. Most Russians know about American cinematography, actors, and political leaders. However, most of the Americans I have met know about only three things in Russia: snow, communism and Siberia. Some people have told me that people in Russia stand in line for two hours to buy toilet paper. This is very old information. Russia has a lot of products now, including your sugar-free Orbit gum and Snickers chocolate bars. Russians know what Americans like to eat. Do you know what Russians like to eat? If you are familiar with the word "borsch," do not think that you have won this game. I happen to dislike borsch. My brother can only eat it with sour cream. Well, I still do not understand how Russia can be the biggest country in the world and be the least known, especially after the fall of the Iron Curtain.

At my job we had an assistant manager I'll call W. He was the first guy with an earring I had ever met who did not irritate me. He also impressed me with his knowledge about Russia. He was one of the rare people who know more than how to fry chicken at the fast food restaurant!

I heard some bad things about my managers at the restaurant from former and current employees. I did not let this affect my own opinion, though. Personally, I think that I was very lucky with my management. They were very helpful and understanding with me, especially W. I knew that he could calm down anyone at the restaurant, because he was mellow and wise. He was the one who showed me how to make mashed potatoes and sandwiches. He was an example of a good, hard-working American man.

Sometimes when I get mad with Americans, I try to remember the people at the restaurant whom I really liked. I had a lot of fun with our day shift cook, R. At first, I thought that he hated his job, because sometimes he would call chicken strips "disgusting." When we would sell a lot of fried chicken, R. would get mad, because that meant that he had to cook more!

But most of the time, R. was in a great mood. We were always joking and talking while I was dishing mashed potatoes and he was marinating his chicken strips or washing trays. One day R. asked me, "Oksana, you make mashed potatoes all the time from water and powder. Can you make mashed potatoes from scratch?"

I said, "Yes, of course. I take potatoes and scratch them." Now this is my favorite professional joke, when I talk about the fast food restaurant.

When Keith was sick, this job was our only income. I was taking things at work too seriously. I just could not say the common American expression, "I do not care." There were lots of days when I left my work very unhappy because of uncaring people, customers or co-workers.

I used to pick up chickens that had been dropped on the floor and take them home for my dog and cats.

There was one team member whom I will call "the Veterinarian." He never cared to ask me, "Oksana, why do you work so many hours? Why do you need this chicken?" I would have told him that I was trapped by circumstances. I would have told him that I could not afford to buy my dog Science Diet, as I used to. My spouse was not making any money. I almost lost him this year. I hated working at the fast food restaurant, because it was humiliating. I needed to feed my pets!

No, Veterinarian never asked me anything. He was just judging me every time he had a chance. He was sure that I was a stupid Russian who did not know about the latest pet nutrition. His first question to me was, "Do you eat this food after it's been on the floor?" After he got my answer, he would tell me as often as he could, "You are killing your dog. Your dog will get fat and die from a heart attack."

Veterinarian did not have any idea about what kind of dog I had. He did not know that my pets were young, hyper animals. The lab would run in our yard and swim in the pool. If you had a lab, you would know that they are as active as puppies for the first three years. Fat would not stay on their bodies for that reason! Our kittens were chasing each other so often that fat would not stay on their bodies, either.

Veterinarian thought that he was being smart. No, he was ignorant, uncaring, and condescending. However, I have to forgive him. He is a good American boy who loves pets and tries to protect someone else's pets from abuse by their owners. (How nice, let's smile twice.)

My job at fast food place taught me a lot of new words. At first, I did not know, what "pop-tray" meant, one customer was asking me to get. I had no idea, that "pop" and "soda" was the same thing! At my job I had to listen and learn new words. Sometimes my head was spinning.

I bet, people's heads are spinning when they can not understand someone's accent. I would like to share one story with you.

One day when we were already living in our house, Keith called an electrician, John, to come do some work. Actually, Keith has his electrician degree, but he did not want to crawl up into the attic. The skinny teenager John could do the job much easier.

After the job was done, we were all sitting in our yard and talking about life. John asked Keith when I left to get drinks, "Does Oksana get upset when I do not understand her accent?"

Keith told him that I hate it when people do not understand me. Also, he told him my secret about "feet on fire." They decided to test me. Keith told John to ask me something by using words I would not know for sure, and to see my reaction.

"Oksana, how do you like my shoddy job?" John had picked a great word.

Instead of asking the meaning of this word, I agreed with him, and said, "Yes."

Keith was glad. "I know my wife!"

John was curious and asked me, "Why didn't you ask me what I said, if you did not understand?"

I was honest with him, "I really didn't care what you said. I have friends who use new words with me, I learn from them. At work I had to learn new words, because I cared and wanted to know. Lots of Americans do not care what I am trying to tell them, and they ask me to repeat my phrase again and again and again. That is why I am selfish. I listen to only what I care about or whom I care about."

John was shocked. "You know, Oksana, that this is rude."

I told him that I was very honest. You see, my reader, sometimes the truth is rude, especially if it comes from me.

I am not too proud of not being a good listener. Two days before my dad died, I was on the phone with him. His voice was weak and quiet. I could not hear him. His speech was long. I did not understand, and I did not want to make him repeat it. I hate it when someone asks me to repeat words or my whole speech.

So when he asked me, "Did you hear me?" I answered, "Yes, I did."

I thought that I would be able to talk to him a lot, because I had my plane ticket! In a week I could see him, hug him, kiss him, and talk to him! Dad died two days after our conversation. The oncologist's prognosis was wrong! His three months had turned into three weeks! We did not get a chance to talk again, and I will never know what he told me so quietly.

I am crying while I am writing this story, because it hurts me to realize how wrong and uncaring I was. I did not care what he said, because I was sure that I would have time to spend with him later. I feel guilty and stupid that I did not take the opportunity to listen to him and understand him. I did not take the chance to know what my dad wanted to share with me. I did not hear his last words to me, because I did not want to make him repeat anything! It is not funny, but my feet were on fire, and I cannot forgive myself for not listening!

OKSANA'S DIARY – MAY, 3, 2000

Today I am leaving the U.S. All day I was cleaning the house, our back yard, the refrigerator, and the glass shower door. Our American friends and family called me to wish me a safe trip. Everybody was asking me the same questions about Russian traditions after someone passes away. It caused me to come up with the idea of writing about it in my book. My e-mails from Tashkent will be the chapters about it.

My passport expired on my 25th birthday. Actually, in Russia and in Uzbekistan, people used to get their passports three times: on their 16th, 25th, and 40th birthdays. I celebrated my 25th birthday in the U.S., and that is why my Uzbek passport expired. To get a new ID to travel overseas, I had to contact the Uzbek consulate in New York.

They were very helpful, and when I sent them the $25 fee and my old passport, they sent me the certificate of citizenship so that I could return to my motherland. This certificate will help me enter Uzbekistan, but I still have to get a new passport. This is not much trouble. However, I will also have to get a special visa from the Department of Foreign Inner Business.

Everybody has a passport in Uzbekistan, but it does not mean that everybody can travel easily. Whoever wants to travel has to apply for permission to leave the country. If you are a criminal, you are not supposed to get this visa and leave when you want.

I am leaving with a lot of fears. I do not know if two months is going to be long enough to get my paperwork done. How difficult will it be, and how long is it going to take to get a new passport? Is it possible to add my spouse's last name to my maiden name without a lot of hassle? I have to keep my maiden name, because my advance parole to reenter the U.S., my certificate of citizenship, and my plane tickets were given in my maiden name.

So instead of being happy to see my family and to support my mom, I am paranoid about the strange Uzbek clerks whom I might have to bribe to speed up the processing of the paperwork.

I had a lot of dreams that I was in Tashkent trying to call Keith, but nobody was answering the phone. I had those dreams before Keith's heart attack. I was afraid that now that I was in Tashkent, something would happen to him. Now I am trying to think that if God wants to take Keith away from me, he can do it any time. If Keith has to die somehow, God will not ask for my permission or my presence. Anyway, Keith could have died from his heart attack or from his inflamed appendix while I was home, but he didn't.

People kept telling me that bad things usually happen in threes. What? Something else is going to happen to Keith? Oh, maybe Dad's death was the third bad thing.

I am afraid for Keith's health, especially since he won't have me spying on him or supervising him like a nurse for two months. I am also afraid that my family will judge or criticize me. I gained weight in the U.S., and my family and friends kept telling me about it in their letters. So I cannot wait to hear their precious compliments again.

I am taking some gifts with me. I cannot wait to see my family's reaction. Is it going to be enough? Would they appreciate our gifts? I took some bottles of ranch and bleu cheese dressing, so they can try them out instead of sour cream or mayonnaise. I also bought some BBQ sauce to cook meat for my family. My dad had read in a book one time that ginger can clean the intestines and is very good for your stomach. He had asked me to bring some ginger. I bought some ginger powder, ginger candies from Trader Joe's and also some ginger tea. Now the rest of my family can try the ginger that my dad dreamed about. I bought a couple of cans of marinated artichoke hearts to expand the food horizons of my family. Before I came to the U.S., I had never seen or tasted artichokes, I had only read about them in French literature. So to me this vegetable was a royal food.

Discount Cards and party shops made a lot of money off me, because I also bought twenty-two refrigerator magnets. Twenty were thermometers with Arizona symbols. When I was leaving Uzbekistan in April of 1998, there were not any magnets for refrigerators. So I wanted to bring those cute little souvenirs from Arizona and from America. For my mom, I got a special magnet saying, *A mother's love is never-ending.* For my dad, I bought a special mirror-magnet saying, the *best dad in the world belongs to me.*

Now I am wondering to whom I will present his magnet? Should I give it to my mom or to dad's parents? Yes, he never had a special magnet for the refrigerator in his whole life.

I bought some maple syrup as an example of American food for my family, because they had read about maple syrup only in English books. Actually, from English books I learned a long time ago about oatmeal, eggs, and bacon for breakfast. I had a chance to enjoy those foods when came to the USA. Funny, I was going to buy ten jars of peanut butter, but my dad found out for me that this product exists in Tashkent and costs only fifty cents a jar, and that is three times cheaper than in the U.S.

I wanted to let my family know what dried papaya is, and I bought several nice cheap packages in Trader Joe's. I took some diet tea and Slim Fast for my mom to try. I got a bottle of English gin, which my family had never tried before. Now we will all be able to drink it in memory of my father and in his honor. I got a can of coffee for my mom. They have coffee in Uzbekistan, do not get me wrong. I wanted to spoil them with hazelnut cinnamon flavored coffee. I had intended to buy chestnuts, hazelnuts, and mangoes, but I already had a lot to carry. I bought some clothes and toys for my family members and some jewelry for my mom and brother.

Keith took me to the mall and bought me some nice new black clothes and shoes that said, *Made in the U.S* on them. I have clothes for two summer months in Tashkent. I also have a lot of patience to share with everybody. I wanted to tell Keith, "Hey, do not even think about dying while I am gone, because I would not be able to fly back for your funeral, because I would not have my passport and visa ready."

I did not tell him that, but I was very scared for him. After my mom lost my dad, human life seemed so fragile to me. It is funny, but I am not afraid that something bad can happen to me, too. All those black thoughts are just because I had a hard year.

God, help me. I am leaving my spouse, my house, my pets, my job, and my American family and friends. I am very scared about my trip. Help me, please. Give me strength.

OKSANA'S DIARY – MAY,4, 2000

Today is the fourth of May. I flew for thirteen hours from Los Angeles to Seoul, Korea. I love flying. There are always new foods to try. It is like a Christmas surprise. I love to eat, and I am an explorer. I am proud to tell people that I have eaten snake, horse, bear, and dog. I think that I will gladly try most different foods, but do not give me chocolate-covered cockroaches or crickets. I hate insects.

I enjoyed the service on Asiana Airlines. But when I had to clear the customs in Los Angeles, I had a little problem. A representative of Asiana Airlines took plenty of time to make sure that my Certificate of Return was not some kind of false document. So she had to run and ask a superior and show them my piece of paper. The poor girl was definitely confused.

When I was standing in line to get on board, I got to talk to some people. One woman from China asked me, "Where are you from?" I told her that I was from Uzbekistan. I was sure that if you lived in Asia, you would know your neighbors. The Chinese girl had another question, "Is that in Europe?"

I said, "No. Uzbekistan is in Central Asia."

She asked, "Are you sure?"

I was mad. Why do people have to be so stupid? The great Silk Road led from China through Central Asia. I am angry with myself that I have difficulty accepting people's ignorance. We are all ignorant in different ways, but some common facts should be studied in schools, and should be known by everyone.

One day I discovered why Russians are more educated than Americans. They have more time to read. Most of them do not have computers to play around.

Russians in Russia, Uzbekistan, Armenia, Ukraine, Kazakhstan, and other republics do not have a credit system like the Americans have. They can buy only what they can pay cash for (TV, furniture, car, clothes). Americans work and put their expenses on credit cards and take out loans.

Russians work and save money if they can. Russians usually do not work more than eight hours a day, because nobody will pay them overtime for it. For Americans, it is no big deal to work ten to twelve hours a day or to have two jobs. Americans stay so busy just to get more luxuries in their lives that they do not have much time to read books.

I do not want to insult the Americans in the U.S. that are readers, especially the people who are reading my book. When I saw American bookstores, I was impressed how many books and book buyers there were. Another difference I noticed between Russians and Americans was that Russians love to read foreign literature, but Americans prefer modern American authors.

Americans work harder because they know that if they work hard they will get promotions and raises. When the principal at the school where I worked wanted to have a meeting after school hours, the teachers would not get paid for staying overtime or for coming in to the meeting on the weekend. There are no clock-in or clock-out registers in Uzbekistan or Russia yet!

I cannot believe how people can wait for eleven hours at the airport for the next flight!?! I am bored and tired of sitting.

KEITH'S NOTES – MAY 2000

I woke up to the phone ringing. Suddenly I remembered that I had heard the phone ringing before. Was I dreaming? I thought, *No, it is real and it was just as real the night before when it rang just after I fell asleep.*

Oksana must have gotten the phone. It was our mom from Uzbekistan. She was calling to say that our dad was gone. Oksana wept and told me the news. I was really shocked. I had no idea that he was so far along. It is truly amazing to me that this man could have endured all this pain just for the sake of his family. He was quite a man. I wish that we had known. I wish there was something that we could have done!

I felt helpless, so I called on God. I thought, Okay, let me imagine him with God. Hmm, I hope they are all up there right now playing a symphony, and maybe I can join right in one day and play beside all the saints, Jesus, the Holy Spirit, and our Father. Amen. Excuse me if you are not United Methodist in basic belief. Fill in your own prayer above. Excuse me again if I happen to think of some of my losses.

Before I get too teary-eyed, I had better continue. I have worked three and seen five days since his death now. It is midnight on the 3rd of May. Oksana is on her way to Tashkent, via Los Angeles and Seoul. I miss her already. She is my everything right now in life. I love her more all the time, and I respect and admire her. She can make me smile, and she never leaves me bored, unless she is writing. In those moments, I feel as if I were a widower, but only for a short time. I usually rudely interrupt her with a quiet hug or a tap on the shoulder, or maybe even a playful nudge with some complaints. Definitely, she will hear lots of complaints. Oksana and I are trying to see how she can handle money.

CHAPTER 8
TRIP TO TASHKENT 2000.
SEPARATION CAN HELP
APPRECIATE EACH OTHER.

This chapter contains only emails which educate readers regarding Russian and Uzbek cultures, and how separation is good for you.

Dear Keith!

It is good that I do not have a lot of Uzbek money now, because right now I am still learning about their prices. Galina's mother was at my dad's funeral and took some pictures of him in the casket. So we will have those pictures, but I did not take them to be developed yet.

I have so much to tell you. I think about you a lot. In the U.S., I used to think about getting gifts for my family, and here I think about getting gifts for you.

I am running around getting some paperwork done. I have to get some money from my dad's jobs.

Now I have to write e-mail to the Uzbek Embassy in new York and beg them to send my expired passport to Tashkent. My Certificate of Return is almost nothing for local clerks.

Imagine! I have to wash my bras and underwear by hand every day.

I will wait for your phone call Monday. Your spoiled rotten, Russian wife from Uzbekistan loves you. Thanks a lot for sending me to visit and support my family here. Good-bye. Have a nice weekend. Say hello to your parents and our friends.

I kiss your eyelashes.

From oksana@tseu.silk.org Tue May 16 10:14:34 2000 Date: Tue, 16 May 2000 10:14:31 +0500 (TSK):

Hi, Honey Baby! Keithulyonochek!
I want to tell you briefly about last weekend. I went to my grandparents' house. Grandma Nina cries a lot and judges my mom. It is as if everyone is looking for someone to blame. At my grandparents' house, I did some ironing and washed the doors.
If before my arrival to Tashkent I thought that my relatives would not be impressed with our American gifts, I feel differently now. My relatives were so depressed about my dad's passing away that they did not care about our gifts, their sizes, or their prices. My family is in shock. Our gifts cannot bring my dad back to them or warm up their hearts. My mom does not wear makeup, and does not try to use my makeup or nail polish. My family understands that you care about them, but they think that your greatest gift to them was allowing me to come and support them. They pray for your health and say hello to you, Keith.

From oksana@tseu.silk.org Tue May 16 10:56:17 2000 Date: Tue, 16 May 2000 10:56:17 +0500 (TSK):

It has been two years since I left Tashkent, the capital of Uzbekistan, my motherland. Now I can see a lot of changes. All cities' garbage places are different. Before, those places were ugly and stinky, and the trash containers did not have lids. Now I saw giant green trash trucks like the American ones, which take trash from city neighborhoods. All the garbage containers look nice and clean, have lids, and are surrounded by fences.
However, the city still needs a bunch more trash receptacles. One day I left my parents' home with a piece of cotton dipped in nail polish remover. I was walking to the bus stop and cleaning my nails. I did not see any trashcans there. I took a bus and went to the photo studio, and I still did not see any trashcans inside the studio or at the whole plaza. People litter everywhere. Finally, I brought my cotton ball home again.
I was delighted to see how all the flea markets had been rebuilt. They have roofs and high walls with Asiatic design. Tourists would think that they were seeing modern Muslim museums and palaces. Most of the bus stations now have benches, roofs, and small shops selling bottled drinks,

cigarettes, and newspapers. It is really weird to see otherwise nice bus stops with a bunch of litter around because there are no trashcans. Honestly, I believe that someone must be working on it, so when we both come back to see Tashkent, hopefully it will be much better.

You know, in Tashkent, like in Moscow or New York, you do not need a car to own around. The public transportation system has greatly improved. There are lots of new buses that can take me from my parents' subdivision to any part of the city. While I was taking buses, I had time to look through the bus windows. Billboards in the city have commercials in three languages: Russian, Uzbek, and English. I was surprised to read the English words: pizza, hot dogs, bakery, Good Will, Lucky Strike, Welcome to the shop, Kodak express, cheeseburgers, supermarket, seafood restaurant, ice cream, and fried chicken. I cannot wait to make some videos of these signs. Uzbek language can be written in two alphabets. I could read some Uzbek signs in Cyrillic and some in Latin. It was really weird. I also saw paper towels, cereal, and Kleenex. I did not know that Uzbek markets had those things now.

My mom was so nice; she bought her "spoiled rotten, American daughter" some travel-size Kleenex and garbage bags. Those things are luxuries here, and my mom never buys them for herself. Let me give you an example. Imagine that your monthly salary after taxes was $8000. You pay $2000 for your house bills. You do not have to worry about car insurance, health insurance, or credit cards in Tashkent. You pay cash for everything. After you pay your bills, you have $6000 left. You can buy yourself one bottle of hair spray for $1000, one bottle of air freshener for $1000, one chocolate for $350 and one hot dog for $150. You have to save at least $2000 for your daily transportation (buses or subway), because you do not have a car. You have to remember that a loaf of bread costs $45, two pounds of the cheapest meat are $700, and two pounds of cheap cheese go for $1200. Would you rather spend $222 for a one-minute call to another country, or buy 25 garbage bags for $250?

My Uncle Andrey did some research for me and my American friends. An American man with a minimum wage of $900 per month after taxes could afford 900 pounds of the cheapest American meat. An Uzbek citizen with his minimum wage of 4000 (Uzbek money) can buy only ten pounds of the cheapest Uzbek meat. Yes, prices here are much lower than in the U.S., but salaries are disproportionately lower. Several years ago, prices in Uzbekistan were lower than prices in Russia on most groceries, but now *things have changed. Uzbekistan is facing an economic crisis and is trying to survive.*

From oksana@tseu.silk.org Thu May 18 10:01:31 2000 Date: Thu, 18 May 2000 10:01:30 +0500 (TSK):

Hello, sladkiy zolotoy Keith!

I received from my Mom my Dad's summer green shirt. A safety pin was pinned in the pocket. I was amazed to find it. It meant only one thing. My Dad grew more superstition then he was. Safety pins are considered good amulets against bad eye, against curse. In Uzbekistan local women put special bead bracelets on their kids against curse. Those are beads are black with little white spots. They are sold at flea and produce markets. Russians do not wear those. It is Uzbek's superstition. Uzbeks also like to hang a dried herb named issrik by their houses to prevent bad luck and ghosts from entering the home.

I want to tell you a joke. You can share it with all our American friends and family members. Do you remember our new DVD "Wild, Wild West?" I have seen lots of advertisements for this movie in Uzbekistan, and the videocassette is on sale. Two words have been translated into Russian, but the word "West" has not been translated. One day my mom took me to our local flea market. I started to explain to her about the meaning of "Wild West" in English. The person who was selling the videocassette became really upset. He started to argue with me and said that "West" was the name of one of the movie's heroes. It was so funny to hear that! The whole city had been fooled by the wrong translation. The whole city thinks that "Wild, Wild West" is about a crazy hero named West!

Today I was riding the bus to my Internet place. One girl was reading the Bible. One man started to talk with her and argue. He said, "There are lots of books that are more interesting than the Bible." She was arguing with him, and he was talking back to her. People around them in the bus kept silent and kept smiling at each other. All the people on the bus came from different religious backgrounds, and some had none at all.

Please say hello to your co-workers and our guests. The more I live here, the more I miss our American freedom, service, and you. People ask me here how I like living in the U.S. I tell them that I got lucky because I have a very good spouse who loves me, and whom I love a lot.

My mom says every day that I have to lose weight, but that doesn't bother me. She has been telling me that since I was 15 and my weight was 130 pounds.

Good-bye. Oksana. I miss you.

From oksana@tseu.silk.org Thu May 18 10:43:18 2000 Date: Thu, 18 May 2000 10:43:17 +0500 (TSK):

I think that my dad's last days were brightened with dreams and plans about meeting with Stas and me this summer. He was excited that I was coming to spend time with him. My Uncle Andrey, my dad's first cousin, had been living with my parents for some months. He had been helping my mom to do repairs in their apartment. When my dad needed pain relief injections, Uncle Andrey was his nurse. My mom bought all the necessary medications, since in Uzbekistan and Russia, like in Mexico and Canada, a wide variety of drugs like antibiotics available over a counter.

My dad kept working up until the last week before his death. That was the only week during which he had consistent pains after every small meal. My mom told me that Dad would watch her and Andrey eating and say, "You are fortunate, happy people. You can eat whatever you want."

When I repeat those words over and over again in my mind, I put a higher value on life. We can dream of being rich and make plans to realize our ideas about happiness. But my dad gave us an understanding of true happiness in life: being healthy. Happiness is being able to eat and not suffer from stomach pain.

Also, my dad could not wait to get a "new nurse". He had been complaining to my mom about Uncle Andrey's appetite for some time. My dad could not stand to watch how much food his first cousin could eat. My mom kept telling him, "Slavik, soon Oksanochka will be here. She will take care of you, and Andrey will leave us."

My mom said that for the last week my dad had pains in his back and belly. Dad was sure that he was suffering from an intestinal hernia, but my mom knew the scary truth. He had cancer of the intestinal lymph gland, which was growing fast and creating a blockage in Dad's intestine. My mom believes that the cancer's roots took over his liver, spine, and prostate in a very short period of time. Dad did not have bowel movements for some days.

He felt as if his whole body stank from the cancer. Dad was asking to be washed by my mom or his cousin, since he was too weak to do it

135

himself. Hot baths helped relieve Dad's pain, but they were also speeding up his death. My mom blames herself for not telling my dad the truth.

Uncle Andrey told us, "If I knew that I would die soon from cancer or something like this, I would first kill all my enemies and rob a bank to help my relatives financially. I do not believe in God and Heaven. I will finish my days the way I want to. A lot of people who are sick with cancer commit suicide. It is not a good thing to tell them the truth."

Uncle Andrey told me that he and my dad had gone to the Russian Orthodox Church on that last Thursday for the service and communion. We believe it was my dad's first and last communion ever. The next day after the communion was Friday, the 28th of April. My dad faced worse pain. My mom decided to go to the policlinic on Saturday morning to get morphine. She was going to tell Dad the truth about his diagnosis and prognosis.

She remembers this Saturday morning very well. Dad was sitting in the armchair in the living room. Mom asked him, "Should I maybe take a vacation to spend time with you?" He answered, "No, you have to work and make money to buy food. I will be all right."

Later, Uncle Andrey told me the story of my dad's last hours. He was conscious when he started to vomit up bile. Uncle Andrey did not have time to wash the floor before Grandma Nina came. She had been told on Friday that her son was getting worse, and that is why she had come to visit. She had to ride a tram for an hour to her son's place. My dad was lying on his bed in the master bedroom. He recognized his mom, kissed her cheek, and tried to talk. His last words were, "Give me. Give me."

Dad was in a coma from 1:00 p.m. until 5:00 p.m. Uncle Andrey told us that Grandma Nina tried to warm his hands with her scarf and breathe. My mom came back from her work early, at 2:00 p.m. after Andrey's phone call. My dad's last convulsion had been witnessed only by his mom Nina and my mom Luda.

After this, his mom left. Everybody was amazed by her behavior. Her excuse was, "I am a sick old woman, and it is too late. I have to take a tram and go home." When Dad was in a coma, my mom had sent Grandma Mariya and Andrey to buy new shoes for my dad.

Uncle Andrey and my Grandma Mariya washed Dad's body. In Uzbek-Muslim tradition, the deceased person must be washed only by his spouse or the person of the same gender. My grandmother Mariya washed deceased bodied before, so she knew the tradition. My mom dressed him up in all new clothes and shoes. This is a tradition to bury a person in new shoes and favorite clothes. So he was dressed in his new white shirt, new black shoes, and his favorite gray suit for the burial. Everybody says that he went to Heaven, because he died on the day before Orthodox Easter. Amen.

From oksana@tseu.silk.org Tue May 23 16:15:53 2000 Date: Tue, 23 May 2000 16:15:53 +0500 (TSK):

Hello, Keith! How are you?

I would be great, if you were here with me. Well, I am just fine.

This Saturday, my dad's parents, my mom, and I went to the cemetery. My mom and Grandma Nina were sobbing on my dad's grave. Grandma Nina told my mom everything she was upset about. I left them alone and stayed with Grandpa Sasha. Grandma Nina was sure that if she had been my dad's nurse, he would still be alive. My mom had to remind her that after his hepatitis, Grandma Nina had not let him come to visit her for some time, because she was so afraid of getting sick, too. So it was a ridiculous argument that they both needed to have.

On Monday, I found out from Grandma Nina that Grandpa Sasha had gotten angry with her for her behavior, and she would not say anything bad about my mom to me or to my mom.

After the cemetery, my mom took me shopping to show me how the Uzbek markets had changed. I was really surprised to see cashiers and assistants in uniform with nametags! I was glad to see lots of Uzbek, Russian and European products. One store even had a gift-wrapping department. I saw Uzbek and Turkish rose (red) gold, and American and Italian yellow and white gold. I even saw American Zippo lighters! One of them was exactly the kind that we had given to Uncle Andrey. The price of this lighter was $21! We paid $15 for it in Arizona!

Uncle Andrey has started to irritate me. He tells me one story, my mom or Grandma Nina has another one for me. He was complaining to me that he wants to start growing fish tank weeds, and that he only needs $7 to start his business. He told my mom that he needs $100 to start his business. I am not going to help him financially, because he just wants to take advantage of me.

My mom bought some very comfortable sandals and some shampoo for my Grandma Nina, and I took those gifts to her on Monday. She was pleased and impressed. Do you want to know how Grandma Nina eats our gift of bleu cheese dressing? She puts it on a piece of bread and eats it like bread with cheese. She loves it that way, but she did not like it on salad.

Grandma Mariya lives with us, because her pension is just enough to pay her bills. She is our cook and dishwasher, our comforter and listener. She takes good care of us. My mom works six days a week. She is very proud of her job. I wash floors, vacuum carpets, and do not argue.

Good-bye. I will try to write you again soon. I love you.

From oksana@tseu.silk.org Wed May 24 11:46:20 2000 Date: Wed, 24 May 2000 11:46:18 +0500 (TSK):

Hello, Keithulyonochek!

I got your e-mail. Thanks for your news. I want to tell you about things here. Every day I wear black pants and a black shirt – tradition for family members after the death of a loved one. My Grandma Nina gave us a crystal ashtray and a set of six nice plates plus one serving dish, and an Uzbek cookbook in Russian and English. Now I can let you read the recipe and decide if you would like me to cook such a surprise or not.

From oksana@tseu.silk.org Wed May 24 12:26:41 2000 Date: Wed, 24 May 2000 12:26:39 +0500 (TSK):

Hello! I want to share some news about Tashkent with you. There are lots of beautiful hotels and banks made with black glass. These buildings have between ten and sixteen floors and look really nice in the center of the city. I really admire the new fountains and nice new bus stops in Tashkent. Most of the bus stops have roofs, benches, and garbage cans. Soon a new subway line will be built. The public transportation system has made excellent and impressive progress. Most buses and trams look nice and new, but they do not have air conditioners.

The majority of people are dressed nice. People prefer to wear long dresses and pants. Miniskirts and shorts are popular only among kids and teens. Men like to wear slacks, not shorts or jeans. Uzbek people have not changed their taste in the two years since I've been gone. Uzbek women still like to wear red gold earrings with rubies and necklaces with river pearls. The wealthier Uzbek men and women like to smile and show their golden teeth. That is one of the interesting facets of the Uzbek nation.

A new Korean factory in Tashkent makes cars. The city's roads are full of Tico and Nexia compact cars and Daewoo minivans. I have not seen one truck yet, but I saw a couple of Jeeps, which are quite rare here.

It seems that people in Tashkent buy their drivers' licenses when they buy their cars. Everyone drives poorly, and people like to honk their horns a lot. Their horns are supposed to tell pedestrians something like, "What nice legs!" or "Move out of the way!" Other drivers use their horns to say something like, "Hurry up."

Tashkent got a new youth theatre called "Aladdin." It looks nice, but I have not gone inside yet to see anything. I found some stores where customers could buy American movies in Russian and in English in both SECAM and PAL systems. I saw Men in Black, Titanic, and several other great American movies in English on sale, for $3.00 for each videocassette.

In Tashkent several years ago, there was a lake called Rohat. Now it has been changed into Tashkent's first new golf club for royalty. Tashkent has a lot of billiard clubs, as well. I discovered for myself that the city's public bathrooms had been rebuilt and look nice. However, you have to pay a cashier to use the bathroom. Also, you have to ask that cashier for some toilet paper, because none of the stalls has any.

I went to check prices in the electronics store. I was surprised to see that microwaves are more expensive than a multi-system VCR. Multi-system VCRs, which can read American NTSC and soviet PAL and SECAM systems, cost between $80 and $100. Microwaves cost $125 or more.

My American jewelry looks cheap, because most people in Uzbekistan wear pink gold. One day I tried new Uzbek ice cream and really loved it. I was even proud that the Tashkent dairy factory has such great new technology to make tasty ice cream. One cone cost only twenty cents. However, remember that minimum wage here is only $10 a month.

Now I want to share with you a story about how I wanted to send a small package to my friend Aliya in Turtkul (province city in Uzbekistan). I came to a small postal office to send it and found out that I could not do it without a passport. A passport has a stamp with an address on it, and this address is supposed to match the address on the package.

The next time, I came to the post office at 4:45 p.m. with my mom's passport. The same postal clerk recognized me, but again she would not take my package. She said, "We do not take money from customers after 4:00 p.m. We close our scale and cashier's machine at that time." I asked her, "If your office is supposed to be open until 6:00 p.m., what do you do until closing time?" The clerk told me that the only thing people can do between four and six is check their mailboxes. The postal clerk also told me, "You can leave your package here, and come back tomorrow with money and the passport." That sounded so funny to me. She was afraid of being robbed of my money after 4:00 p.m., but she was not afraid of losing my package.

When I came to send the package the next morning, the same postal clerk recognized me and did her job. First, she checked that my package did not have any bombs, and after checking all the items she wrapped the box. At the end, she did not even look at my mom's passport, and I left.

Now I want to finish my e-mail. This Internet center is in the Economic University. I have my e-mail account at this place. To check my e-mails and to write to you, I can have as much time as I want. The only problem I have is that I have to ride a bus for forty minutes to get over here, that's all.

From oksana@tseu.silk.org Fri May 26 11:27:31 2000 Date: Fri, 26 May 2000 11:27:30 +0500 (TSK):

Hello, baby!
I agree that my English is bad. I make a lot of mistakes. You should see my circumstances! All the keyboards have plastic covers. It is very difficult to type. Why the covers? So people will not break the keys. The Internet services will be closed on Monday (Memorial Day), because this place is run by Americans
My mom took me out yesterday. She bought me shish kabob. She also took me to a special clinic to check my vision. She paid fifty cents. In the U.S., a doctor would charge me around $50 for such fast service. She still tells me that I have to lose weight and not to eat a lot, etc. However, that does not irritate me.
Good-bye. I miss you a lot. Oksana

From oksana@tseu.silk.org Fri May 26 11:46:06 2000 Date: Fri, 26 May 2000 11:46:05 +0500 (TSK):

Hello, Keith!
I am surprised to see how nicely people dress in Tashkent. Uncle Andrey says that most people here are milking their sponsors (parents,

boyfriend) for financial help. Most people, in his opinion, have a couple of nice outfits, but an empty refrigerator. That is because people in Uzbekistan love to show off.

Uncle Andrey spent last night with us. He is helping us to prepare the 40th day of the funeral feast. He bought several cases of bottled mineral water (an Uzbek special soda without a sweet taste). My mom gives him money to go to different stores to buy drinks. He does not ride a bus. My dad gave him his old bicycle, and Andrey rides it everywhere he goes in the city. I bet his legs are very strong. He always repairs his bike's old tires, because it would cost $5 to buy new wheels. Do you think we should give him such a gift? My mom gave him money for cigarettes. He hates the idea of working for a salary, and that is why he likes to go fishing and feed himself this way. He says hello to you, Keith. He thinks one day he will take us fishing where you do not need any license.

Good-bye. Say hello to your parents and family. I love you. Oksana

From oksana@tseu.silk.org Fri May 26 12:14:58 2000 Date: Fri, 26 May 2000 12:14:58 +0500 (TSK):

When my dad died, he wasn't taken to a morgue or a funeral home. My mom explained to me that only people with strange or unknown causes of death have to be taken to a morgue for an autopsy. All murder victims have to be examined for sure. My dad's diagnosis was known by my family and his doctors. That is why he was kept at home for two days before the funeral, and buried on the third day. Uzbeks, like all Muslims, bury their deceased before sunset. When I was 17, my classmate Dinara died from kidney failure. Her mother called the teacher, and teacher informed us, her classmates. Several students, our teacher and I were standing by the entrance of the room, where she was laying on the floor. She was wrapped in white cloth. All mirrors in the apartment were covered with cloths.

In Muslim world, women do not ride to a cemetery to mourn. That is why we came to say our good byes to her home. Bodies are placed directly on the ground in the grave. No tombstones and writing are allowed by Islam. No funeral feasts like Russians perform. I like this Muslim tradition, that unnecessary funeral expenses should be avoided. In Russian world, people expect to be called and invited to come and eat and drink in memory of deceased person. Some people would arrive without an invitation.

Uzbek relatives and friends of the grieving family would provide them food for three days. I like this tradition, it is very caring one.

My mom had to go to the local clinic on Sunday morning to get a temporary death certificate. Only with this document could my grandparents buy a casket and order a catafalque at the city's Black Tulip Mortuary.

My dad's brother Valera ordered a bus for the funeral. Why? People had to follow the catafalque to the cemetery in the bus, because they do not have cars.

Orthodox Christian tradition requires relatives of the dead person to never leave the dead body alone. For my dad's body, the mourning guards were his wife, his mother-in-law, Andrey, and his second aunt. His parents and brother were busy with funeral arrangements. My mom's cousins and aunts were busy buying lots of water, vodka, wine, and food. My mom gave them money for this shopping, cash that she had saved. They added some of their own money, too.

On Sunday and Monday, neighbors and friends came to see my dad's body in the casket. It was a regular viewing in accordance with Russian Orthodox tradition. Just imagine! My mom had to buy formaldehyde and invite the specialist to take care of my dad's body. Unfortunately, my parents never had an air conditioner in their home. The specialist had to work hard to fight death's decay from the summer heat. It had been 100 degrees outside those days.

The day of the funeral was the 1st of May. My mom's first cousins Luda and Vera were cooking different foods for the funeral banquet. My dad's Uzbek friend Gulyem cooked pilaf outside in a huge pan. My mom borrowed plates and spoons from family members and neighbors. There is another Orthodox Christian tradition about forks. For 40 days after the death, forks are not supposed to be used, especially for the funeral feast.

It probably sounds weird to Americans to have a dead body lying in the casket in the living room while food is being prepared in the kitchen. Orthodox Christians (Russians, Armenians, and Georgians) have to be very strong to stick with their burial traditions. Our relatives who were cooking could not go to the Botkino Cemetery, because they were busy preparing this banquet for the guests. It is the accepted funeral custom to eat and drink in honor of the dead. Some people bring money and flowers, but some do not. In the U.S., family members pay money to mortuaries, but the Russians spend most of the money to feed their guests.

On the day of the funeral, there was no hot water! Our neighbors were helping in the kitchen to wash dishes with cold water. They were using big pans to heat up water on the range. Dry mustard was used as a degreaser for lots of plates and dishes.

After the death, relatives have to organize a feast on the 9th and 40th days for family members and friends. Russians believe that the late, lamented human soul roams for forty days among the living. I believe that, too.

From oksana@tseu.silk.org Thu Jun 1 11:37:17 2000 Date: Thu, 1 Jun 2000 11:37:16 +0500 (TSK):

Dear honey baby!

Sometimes I feel that I want to write English songs about you and my love for you. I love you so much. I cannot wait to see you again, make you coffee, and walk with you and our dog Shok.

My vision is now -6.25 in one eye, and the other eye is -6.50. I am going to get new glasses here and maybe new contacts. There are a lot of places here that sell American contact lenses. One pair of Bausch and Lomb contacts costs $10, and there are no charges for exams.

Did I tell you that I lost my contact here? Thank God I was smart enough to take a second pair of my contacts with me.

Today I had breakfast with Babulya Mariya's thin pancakes and maple syrup, which I had brought from the U.S. My mom did not like this syrup. I will not eat anything for the rest of the day, because my stomach has to be empty for tomorrow's procedure.

I will be able to write to you again only after the 7th of June. We all have a lot of preparation to make to feed at least 70 people (relatives and my dad's best friends) on the 7th of June. It will be the 40th day after Dad's death.

This Sunday morning I will leave Mom's place early. Uncle Andrey, Stas, and I will go to pay for my dad's marble headstone and put it on his grave at the cemetery. I will make a video for you.

Good-bye for now.

From oksana@tseu.silk.org Thu Jun 1 11:57:23 2000 Date: Thu, 1 Jun 2000 11:57:23 +0500 (TSK):

Hello, Keithulyonochek!

You are wrong. I do not portray my American life in the same way that my mom does. Actually, my friend Nuriya said that after reading my letters about the U.S., she realized that just to get into the U.S. should not be her goal. She says that I helped her to see the truth. People have to work

143

hard in any country to be wealthy. When people ask me about America, I tell them that money do not grow on trees there. I tell them that I know Americans who have never left their state or who have never flown on an airplane. So I do tell them about my job, and I tell them my super joke about scratch potatoes.

Today I was riding a bus, and my red silk shirt got torn by a nail. I have no idea how it happened, but now I have a hole in my sleeve. Every time I ride a bus, I remember your words about "stepping stones." You were talking about some jobs in the U.S. In public transportation, I feel that my feet are the stepping stones for other people. Most of the time, people do not apologize, and they act like nothing happened.

Igor, my vanity publisher, gave me a book to read. I have already finished reading it. The name of the book is Hotel California, by Russian author Natalie Medvedeva. She was a model in the U.S. during the 70's. Her book is full of facts about how difficult life was as a new young supermodel in Los Angeles, after growing up in Moscow. I enjoyed reading this book. I am surprised that this book, which was published in 1992, is not more popular among Russian readers, especially people who think that the U.S. is a paradise.

I did not like that this book contained a lot of swearing (in Russian and English), and the author hated Americans and "Americhka" (the U.S). I could feel the author's hate and irritation, but I did not share her attitude.

When I think about the U.S., I think about you, our love, our house, our family and friends, our pets, and our great Arizona cacti.

Good-bye. I miss you. Your Oksanichka

From oksana@tseu.silk.org Thu Jun 1 12:05:49 2000 Date: Thu, 1 Jun 2000 12:05:48 +0500 (TSK):

Dear Keith!

I do not feel ashamed about my job at the fast food restaurant! I learned so much! I learned English, a new specialty, and to appreciate you more! When my mom gives me weird looks that mean, "Do not talk about your job in the U.S.," I do it anyway, just to be an independent thinker. I told her that I would publish books in Russian and in English about my life in the U.S., and I would share my experiences with my readers. It's not like I was something to be ashamed of, like a prostitute or a stripper. However, I see that some prostitutes are not ashamed of their occupation, either.

Stas told me that he was not proud of me for my "mashed potato" job. Uncle Andrey said, "An extra specialty is always a plus. I would even clean toilets, if my salary was good. I do not work, because I cannot find a job with a good enough salary. When I was making repairs for the government court, I was buying all of the necessary construction supplies for it. The court never paid me, and that is why the business failed. I do not want to work for government organizations anymore. Private businesses do not need me, since they like to hire their relatives and friends. That is why I would rather be a criminal than work."

From oksana@tseu.silk.org Fri Jun 9 11:25:40 2000 Date: Fri, 9 Jun 2000 11:25:39 +0500 (TSK):

Before the 7th of June, the day of the last funeral feast in my dad's honor, we made a lot of preparations. We spent several days taking the bus to do shopping. We could not buy everything at once, because I could not drive my dad's standard transmission car, and my American driver's license was not valid without a passport (my only Uzbek ID, which I do not have yet). So we had to go shopping again and again. We had to buy several kilograms of meat, tomatoes, cabbage, and bell peppers to make stuffed vegetables. We bought four big fat hens to cook in a big pan. Grandma Mariya spent time making homemade noodles.

So on the 7th of June, we had chicken soup for the souls and stomachs of our guests. On the table we had five kinds of kielbasas and two kinds of cheese, and they were sliced and arranged nicely on plates. We had fresh and pickled tomatoes, cucumbers, eggplant salad, Russian potato salad, and mushroom pies. We also had crystal bowls full of fresh cherries and apricots, and china plates full of cookies, sweets, and pie slices. We served vodka, wine, water, and lemonade for our guests. We filled our bathtub with cold water to chill the drinks, because coolers and ice are still new and expensive here. Most people were drinking wine and Tashkent mineral water. Dad's parents gave us cherries and apples from their garden, and we cooked a big pan of compote. The cool compote was a very tasty refreshing and cheap drink.

For two days, our kitchen was as hot as Hell from using the oven and the range. The kitchen walls got so hot that pieces of tile came off! We borrowed a table from neighbors. We used two long boards as benches for the table in the living room, and we used chairs for the table in the dining room. Russians, Uzbeks do not eat from paper plates and do not walk around during meals. That is why we had to make sure that we borrowed enough plates, spoons, glasses, and pans.

People were invited for 2:00 p.m., 4:00 p.m., and 6:00 p.m. Every time, after the guests left, we had to clean the tables, wash the plates, and dishes, serve new drinks and everything! It was a lot of work! We did not have a great desire to talk with friends and family, because we were so tired and nervous. We could not spend time with our guests, because they knew that they had to leave soon and let the other people come to eat, remember and honor my dad.

This time we fed seventy people. My mom's cousins helped us again to cook and serve. My mom spent $85 for the funeral banquet. She did not ask me for anything during all this time. My mom read a book about Russian Orthodox traditions, and she said that it is supposed to be like that. Russians have to do these things to help the late, lamented soul to be free and to leave this world peacefully.

When the guests left, after 9:00 p.m., my mom, her mom Maria, and I cleaned the house. I washed the floors and all the small greasy pans. Grandma washed all the big pans in the bathtub, because they would not fit in the kitchen sink. Mom washed the small plates and glasses. Stas returned borrowed items to neighbors. His friend helped him. We went to sleep very late but very happy. The burial feat was over!

The next morning we could not get up for a long time. My mom said, "Your dad should not be upset with us. He always liked to visit all the funeral feasts and eat a good meal. Our guests had a good feast. We prepared foods that dad liked to eat. His spirit should be happy. Amen."

From oksana@tseu.silk.org Fri Jun 9 12:18:46 2000 Date: Fri, 9 Jun 2000 12:18:45 +0500 (TSK):

Hi, honey baby!

My mom continues to impress me. She bought us our first audiocassette with songs in Uzbek and Russian by different singers and groups of Uzbekistan. She also bought a roll of film for her picture camera. She spent $10 for my new black sandals with small heels. (The brown ones you chose for me in Mesa got messed up). I liked them so much that I hated to throw them away. At first, I wanted to bring them back to the U.S. to show you how I can wear out new shoes in one month of walking. However, I do not like the idea of paying money for the extra weight of dirty shoes.

My mom told me the story about my dad's last hope. His friend, whose nickname was "Ogurets" (cucumber), gave him an article about a new miracle treatment for cancer invented by a Russian named Shevchenko. My dad mixed 30 ml. of vodka and 30 ml. of sunflower oil, shook the mixture up, and took a sip twenty minutes before his meal, just like the recipe in the article had said. The article included different people's stories about how they survived the 4th stage of cancer by drinking this miracle oil-vodka mixture three times a day (7:00 a.m., 2:00 p.m. and 9:00 p.m.).

My mom gave me this article to read. It was interesting to learn something new about fighting cancer. The person who takes this mixture has to exclude any other alcoholic drinks from his diet. Patients are supposed to drink this mixture for ten days, and then take a rest for five days. After the second course of treatment, the patient has to have a 2-week break. In short, I read some letters from cancer survivors who survived by using this treatment.

My dad, who never minded drinking any nasty fluids just to get healthier, felt better for only three days after beginning to take the new medicine. My mom tried to keep his hopes up, but he soon realized that the mixture did not work. How can my mom say that Dad did not know his diagnosis? If he read the article "Treatment of Cancer," he should have known about his condition.

His friend Ogurets had surgery, and he was drinking this mixture himself. He believes that it saved his life. He thinks that my dad started to drink it too late. I saw Ogurets at the funeral feast on the 9th day after Dad's death. He looks healthy, as if nothing had ever happened to him!

Oh, more news about us! My mom took Stas and me out! She spent $2.00 and fed us with shish kabob. This was before we found out that I am not supposed to eat it. Later, she spent the same amount of money to buy Stas a new Rich toothbrush. (Stas had been very impressed with my Oral B toothbrush.) Of course, my mom could have bought him another cheaper toothbrush, but Stas would never use it. He is very picky.

From oksana@tseu.silk.org Fri Jun 9 12:24:54 2000 Date: Fri, 9 Jun 2000 12:24:52 +0500 (TSK):

My mom took me to the hospital to have my stomach checked. The hospital has marble floors in the corridors, on the stairs, and in all the rooms. It looks really nice. I had to lie down for my endoscope procedure. I wasn't given any medication. A doctor stuck a tube down my throat. It felt *very nasty and made me gag. My mom held me down and was promising me a quick end to the procedure.*

Soon my mom knew what kind of condition my stomach had. The GI doctor told her and even let her look inside my stomach through the tube with the camera. Later I went home and you called!

After my conversation with you, I had to go to a shoe repair store. I had a little bit of cash with me as a deposit. I wrote my name on the shoe soles. I explained to a busy, dirty cobbler what kind of material my mom wanted to use as heels for her shoes. The shoemaker told me the price, took the deposit, and wrote the difference on one of the shoe soles. He did not give me any receipt, because this small place does not use any paperwork with their business. I think this is one smart way to fool the government and avoid taxes.

From oksana@tseu.silk.org Tue Jun 13 10:21:18 2000 Date: Tue, 13 Jun 2000 10:20:58 +0500 (TSK):

Keith. Yes, I will share with you what I did for my family. Since my Grandma Mariya slaves as our cook and dishwasher, I made her a special gift. I paid her bills (water, gas, and property tax) for eight months. It only cost me about $25. Now she can have extra money for her medication. Now my mom can save money on this deal, because she used to give money to my grandmother to pay these bills. If Grandma Mariya lived alone, her pension would be enough to pay the bills and buy bread. She cannot go and get a job because she would lose half of her pension. Grandpa Sasha works and gets a full pension because he is a war veteran.

Also, I bought special gifts for my mom and Stas. I bought him contact lenses. His vision is -3.0 now. I know that he was going to make my mom buy him contacts anyway, so I helped her. He is very happy now. I think that if I had not brought him any gifts, and only bought him the contacts, he would be happy. I bought contacts for myself, too. With the new contacts, I can see much better.

Bye.

From oksana@tseu.silk.org Tue Jun 13 10:31:42 2000 Date: Tue, 13 Jun 2000 10:31:38 +0500 (TSK):

On the 5th of May 2000, I took my mom and brother out to eat shish kabob. We ordered chicken, hamburger, ram, cow, and liver shish kabob.

One special shish kabob looked very white and different. We asked, "What is this?" The answer was weird: "This is called the 'light bulb.'" We said, "The cook must be kidding." The cook told us, "No, we call this shish kabob the 'light bulb.' Pardon my language, but this kabob was made from ram balls."

We ordered it and were excited to try something new. But our mom refused to eat ram "treasures." Stas said, "Imagine that this is a whale's heart. Can you eat a whale's heart, Mom?" She could not imagine that, either!

From oksana@tseu.silk.org Tue Jun 13 10:42:09 2000 Date: Tue, 13 Jun 2000 10:42:02 +0500 (TSK):

Since I have been back here, I have heard a lot of anger from my Uncle Andrey toward the U.S. and Americans. He likes to say, "All Americans are dummies. We should shoot them all." That sounds so weird to me. He judges Americans by their politics. From Russian news he gets the "Soviet" opinion about American political actions and decisions, and he takes these things too personally.

For a while, I listened to his opinions in silence. I was thinking that young Russian ladies want to leave Uzbekistan, Russia, and guys like Uncle Andrey. That is why he hates Americans. He is a single, lonely, unhappy, unemployed loser.

On the 40th day after Dad's death, I was just too tired to be patient with Uncle Andrey anymore. When he started to say bad things about my new homeland to some of my friends and me, I stopped him. I said, "You are wrong. I have met a lot of intelligent Americans. None of my friends or Keith's friends is a dummy. Keith's relatives and co-workers are very smart and helpful people. I see how Keith's sister Kim Haring and my friend Pat Durbin try very hard to give their kids the best education possible. You cannot even imagine how hard most Americans have to work. They have no time to spend with their kids to make them smarter. You watch American thrillers on TV. You never saw a good, American, family channel on TV with no swearing, violence, or politics. How can you talk about bombing the U.S. where Keith and I live? My American relatives do not talk about bombing Uzbekistan or Russia! When you talk about shooting Americans, it makes me mad, because to me Americans are the people who have helped me the most. When I think about Americans, I think about my spouse, his family, and our friends. They do not talk about shooting

149

anybody. There are lots of Americans who do not have a job or do not want to work at all just like you do. If Americans would only meet you, they would think that all Russians hate the U.S. and that they all are lazy and embittered just like you are!"

He got upset and left.

From oksana@tseu.silk.org Tue Jun 13 11:19:03 2000 Date: Tue, 13 Jun 2000 11:19:01 +0500 (TSK):

Keith! This is not the end of the story. Stas met Uncle Andrey outside, when he was leaving on his old bicycle. Stas asked me at home, "Did you have a fight with Uncle Andrey?" I said, "Yes, how did you know?" Stas said, "Oh, he left and told me that he does not need new wheels for his bicycle, does not need that crumb from you."

I was still angry, so I said, "I am tired of listening to his stupid and groundless conclusions! He has never met one single American. How can he talk about all of them so badly, like he lost his house, his job, and his family because of them?"

Stas was calm. "Oh, Oksana. Relax! He is your blood relative. We are your blood relatives, not the Americans."

I got mad with Stas and shouted, "You know, in the two years when I had problems and depression in the U.S. when Keith was sick, I got help and support from my American family and friends. I did not get any help from you or Uncle Andrey! I only got your letters saying how much you needed my financial help, and how Uncle Andrey "the loser" lives!"

Stas replied calmly, "I am just trying to be an independent thinker."

I almost yelled, "No. You took Uncle Andrey's side. I do not appreciate your independent thinking. You have to hug me right now, before I really get mad."

He did. He kissed me and hugged me. I was sneaky and spanked his butt. Maybe I was happy to know that Uncle Andrey does not want wheels any more, so I do not have to spend my American money on him.

From oksana@tseu.silk.org Fri Jun 16 15:16:28 2000 Date: Fri, 16 Jun 2000 15:16:23 +0500 (TSK):

Honey baby!

I got tears in my eyes when I read your e-mail about Uncle Andrey. I was so upset with him. You said such nice things to me. He told Uncle

Valera and Grandma Nina that he would never visit my mom's home again. He did not say anything about our discussion! He said that we called him lazy and other bad words and that we told him to leave us at midnight. I found that out from Uncle Valera. I had to call Uncle Valera and get all the news about what Uncle Andrey told him.

I had to explain to him all the details about our argument. Uncle Valera said that to hate a whole nation or race is political ignorance and stupidity. My friend Larisa Melkumyan said that Uncle Andrey's behavior was disrespectful to me, because I chose the U.S., and I have a new family there now.

I told Uncle Valera, "When Uncle Andrey was talking about shooting all Americans, I was thinking about Keith's relatives. I saw my sister-in-law, Bridgett, and her innocent kids. One time she sent money to my mom by hiding it in a package. Why would he want to shoot my American sister-in-law? In the U.S., there are a lot of kids like your little daughter Olga, who do not know about Chechnya, Kosovo, or any of the American and Russian political arguments. So that is why I was upset with Uncle Andrey."

Uncle Valera told me that he was glad that I had called him and told him everything. Thanks again for being understanding, Keith.

Oksana.

From oksana@tseu.silk.org Fri Jun 16 15:43:48 2000 Date: Fri, 16 Jun 2000 15:43:47 +0500 (TSK):

My dad was buried in the same grave with his Grandpa Zahar (a Ukrainian), who died in his eighties from cancer of the esophagus. Uncle Valera explained to me that the gravediggers had to take out the gravestones before digging. Great-grandpa's casket had been destroyed over time. There was no longer a casket with Zahar's bones in it. Thirty years had done their job. It was just a hole with wood chips on the bottom. My dad now sleeps there, too.

Two weeks after my father's funeral, Uncle Andrey, Uncle Valera, and Grandpa Sasha went to the cemetery. They had sand, cement, water, and a shovel. They put back the gravestones and covered the fresh dirt with those stones.

I wanted to buy a gravestone for my dad, but the place had one already with Zahar's name and picture. So I ordered Dad's portrait and biographic notes on the gray marble which was surrounded by a black metal frame.

151

On the 4th of June, my brother Stas, Uncle Andrey, and I went to the Botkino Cemetery again. My order was ready. Stas dug a hole in the ground on the right side of Zahar's gravestone. The frame with the picture was cemented in the hole. I made a video of our work.

In the evening, Stas went to sleep with Mom on Dad's bed, where Dad had closed his eyes forever. I think Stas has just realized that his father is gone. Several days ago, Stas would say, "Dad is on a business trip." Now, after the work on his grave, Stas has finally let his emotions out. He sobbed into his pillow, and Mom was crying, too. I was writing this chapter.

I want to say that this grave has a special meaning for my Grandpa Sasha (Alexander). That is because it is the same grave in which his dad Zahar and his son Vyacheslav (Slava, my dad) were buried. My Grandpa Alexander is seventy-five years old. I do not know what he thinks about life. He keeps silent, and no one sees tears in his eyes. He never liked to talk or to write. Maybe if he liked to talk like his wife Nina, or write like me, he would have a way to express his sorrow, but he doesn't. He has lost a lot of weight. He still goes to work as an auditor in the Ministry of Geology.

Is that the right ending for this story? No, it is not.

On the 2nd of June, I got the diagnosis regarding my stomach. I have a hypertrophied gastritis, erosion in my stomach. Now, since I know my family's cancer history, I must be strong and stop my overeating cravings. I have a choice. My dad did not have it. He was brave and hated to complain about his stomach pains three years ago when his ulcers led to cancer. I read in one book, "People eat to live, they do not live to eat." I am just starting to think this way.

From oksana@tseu.silk.org Fri Jun 16 16:18:04 2000 Date: Fri, 16 Jun 2000 16:18:03 +0500 (TSK):

Keithchik!

People ask me about you. They say, "What is he doing without you, Oksana?" I tell them how great you are. We are impressed to hear about your irrigation system! They cannot even dream about such a system in their yards! I tell them that you bought and planted roses! My family and friends are impressed to hear that a computer programmer can do yard and housework. I am proud of you. I love you and I miss you. I want to come back and be a better wife to you.

Your Zaika

From oksana@tseu.silk.org Tue Jun 27 10:34:59 2000 Date: Tue, 27 Jun 2000 10:34:59 +0500 (TSK):

Hello!

Uncle Valera had a housewarming party, and it was very cool. Uncle Valera invited all his relatives. Uncle Andrey was there, too. We just exchanged greetings and were trying not to look at each other. He told Uncle Valera and Grandma Nina that I am ungrateful. He told them that five years ago, when I was twenty years old, he had spoiled my friends (Lena and Aliya) and me all summer long! He said that he had fed us and his house had been like a resort for us.

I am sure that he wanted to tell them that I did not help him financially that year as he expected, because I do not remember what a great time we had together. I told Uncle Valera and Grandma Nina that my friends' visits to his place were like a charity thing. Imagine, honey. We were bringing all the food we needed (even tea and sugar), soap, detergent, and gifts! We were washing his clothes by hand and boiling them in a big pan. He did not have a mashing machine! We were renting videos to watch with him. Every time we visited him, we brought a gift. We bought him a T-shirt, some summer sandals, bedding suits for him and for his daughter Larisa, and audiocassettes for his tape recorder. We took lots of pictures, and I even paid for those and gave them to him!

During that summer, I worked as a housekeeper for my friend, Luda Arkadievna, and I was spending most of my money for our trips with friends to Uncle Andrey's house. We liked to watch his VCR, because it was something new for us. Now all my friends who visited him five years ago have their own VCRs. If he hadn't had a VCR at that time, we would not have gone to his dirty little house, which we helped him and Larisa to clean. Also, I was his personal manicure and pedicure girl that summer. My other friends gave him massages, so he was very spoiled. We were always bringing food and cooking meals. He was our best buddy!

Now he invites Stas to his place. Stas has visited Uncle Andrey here twice already with his friends and food. They went fishing in the closest river. You will see that soon Uncle Andrey will tell everybody that he spoiled and fed Stas and his friends all summer long.

I feel angry with Uncle Andrey, not for his anti-American ideas, but for his lies about my friends and me.

Good-bye.

From oksana@tseu.silk.org Tue Jun 27 10:42:34 2000 Date: Tue, 27 Jun 2000 10:42:23 +0500 (TSK):

Honey baby!

Stas and I went to make videos of the closest grocery market. People were waving at us because they thought that I was making a video for TV.

I videotaped the meat market with hanging meat that never gets packaged like in the U.S. It still has the brains, tongues, livers, and hearts of the animals. It all looks juicy, bloody, fresh, and innocent.

When we finished our videotaping, we met a woman from the local police, who was wondering why we were making the videos. I was really nice, and I told her that I was a citizen of Uzbekistan, and that I was making videos of Tashkent's most popular places for my spouse in the U.S. I said, "When my husband gets a chance to see Tashkent, he will want to visit the city with me next year! Tashkent has a lot of beautiful places that will surprise and impress our American friends and family."

She smiled and left us alone. I thought she was very nice and understanding. However, I was shaking after my short conversation with this lady.

Good-bye.

From oksana@tseu.silk.org Tue Jun 27 11:19:57 2000 Date: Tue, 27 Jun 2000 11:19:48 +0500 (TSK):

Keith, I want to share more news with you about how I spoil my family. I invited my mom, my Grandma Mariya, and Stas to a Russian theatre of drama. Stas did not want to go, so we invited my mom's friend Alexandra.

The performance was called "Jokes in a Country." It was cool. I laughed louder than anybody else. One young man wanted to get married, but no one would take him seriously. He wanted to make all his family members come together so he could introduce his pregnant girlfriend to them. So he made an anonymous phone call to his father and said that his brother had died. So, all the brothers with their wives came to the funeral. The hero, Timofey, who had not really died, found out the bad news about himself from his mom. He asked her not to tell anybody about this stupid joke and acted as if he were dead in the casket. He said that he wanted to find out if his wife loved him or not. She cried and said, "I hope it is just a joke or the doctor's mistake! Maybe he is just asleep, because that can happen to people. When we first got married, I would tell him that I did not love him. I started to love him when we had our first child. I would tell him how much I missed him when he was not at home. I need you, Timofey."

It touched my heart. I want to tell you, Keith. You do not need to play dead or sick to hear that I need you and that I love you very much. I want to come back and prove it to you again and again

After the performance, we were all in a great mood. I invited them all out to eat. Grandma Mariya said that she had not gone to the theatre since my departure. She had not eaten out for years! I bought two bottles of champagne, two salads, and chicken shish kabob. At the end, I bought one rose (25 cents each) for my mom and one for Alexandra. I spent $10 for the meal, including tips! They were all happy. We were drinking to our nice evening, to your health, and to everybody's health.

From oksana@tseu.silk.org Tue Jun 27 11:30:58 2000 Date: Tue, 27 Jun 2000 11:30:39 +0500 (TSK):

I took Stas out for breakfast, and it cost me $1.00. I wanted to let him try Uzbek cheeseburgers and Uzbek toast. I wanted to try the toast, too. I took a bite of his cheeseburger and gave him a piece of my toast. We were drinking tea. I can tell you now, that the Uzbek method of making toast and sandwiches is different, and I would call it a parody of American fast food.

My mom told me two stories this summer.

One day a freelance seller came to my mom's office at the hospital and tried to sell her some expensive makeup. When she refused to buy it, the seller said condescendingly to her, "Oh, I forgot that doctors do not make enough money to buy such expensive makeup."

My mom felt humiliated, but she found the answer, "I do not need to buy any makeup. My daughter sends it to me from the U.S."

It was the truth, but it was also a lie. I do not send her everything she needs. She was embarrassed to say that at that time she could not afford to buy some powder for her face from him. Americans are more candid. They can say, "I do not care." Americans are not embarrassed to admit that something is too expensive for them to buy. Lots of Russians I know would lie about their financial situation.

Another story is about earrings. My mom bought herself a pair of gold earrings with cubic zirconium in them. Her co-worker exclaimed,

"Oh, what a nice pair of diamond earrings! I bet your daughter brought you those from America!" My mom did not want to disappoint her friend and agreed with this statement. She fibbed again. Why? It is all about competition: whose daughter is better, whose clothes are nicer, and whose appearance is neater.

From oksana@tseu.silk.org Tue Jun 27 11:47:12 2000 Date: Tue, 27 Jun 2000 11:46:37 +0500 (TSK):

Grandma Mariya has two sisters, Vera and Lida. Her sister Vera had broken her leg and is not able to leave her house. She is a widow in her late 70ties. God did not bless her with children. She helped to raise her nephews. Vera means Belief in Russian.

We tried to tell her about our visit, but she did not answer the phone for two weeks. So we came without an invitation and without her expecting us. I brought some chocolate candies, bread, and kielbasa. She was happy to see us and glad that we had brought food with us.

Vera wanted to prepare some tea. We realized that she ran out of matches. Grandma Mariya ran to the closest grocery store to get some. When she came back, we still couldn't make tea because the house was temporarily out of gas! Vera did not have any drinks in refrigerator. It was almost empty.

I walked to the store and bought some bottled water and "fanta" soda for us. When I got back, we had lunch.

When our visit was over, the natural gas was on again, but we refused to drink tea. It was too hot for tea anyway. Vera's house had no air conditioning. To make things clear for you, summer in Uzbekistan is almost like summer in Arizona. Now I am happy that I made this one important visit. Vera said to tell you hello. She said, "Oksana is a horse with balls, and her handsome Keith is a gift."

Good-bye, gift!

From oksana@tseu.silk.org Tue Jun 27 12:04:31 2000 Date: Tue, 27 Jun 2000 12:04:29 +0500 (TSK):

Do you remember that we got my purse strap fixed in Mesa for $12? My purse strap broke again here in Tashkent, but I paid only fifty cents to get it fixed. I wear black pants all the time. I do not feel like wearing shorts in Tashkent.

My mom has stopped pushing me to get a permanent and to change my hair color. She trimmed my split ends, and I am happy.

I did not lose weight. I walk a lot. I pay fifty cents to take a taxi sometimes. My feet feel better after the surgery on my inflamed corns. I took five laser treatments for only fifty cents each.

When I go grocery shopping, I spend minimum $10. I spoil my family with good meat, salami, and fish.

From oksana@tseu.silk.org Fri Jun 30 13:41:02 2000 Date: Fri, 30 Jun 2000 13:40:59 +0500 (TSK):

Hello, dear Keith!

This is my last e-mail to you. I think that I was in Tashkent at the right time. This Internet office will be closed on the 6th of July for a month. I liked all your short e-mails.

This morning I spent time with my grandparents. I made videos and did interviews with them. They told me about their parents, their childhood, and about participating in World War II.

I am doing pretty well. I think about you most of the time, and I cannot wait to be with you. You are the fire on my butt. I love you and kiss you, and I want to wrap myself around you. Oksana

Separation helped us to realize that despite Keith's and mine misunderstandings and disagreements; we miss each other very much. I believe that to go on a vacation alone can be good for a couple as a test.

I am back and very happy! Keith is alive, and he even had gotten lots of yard work done while I was gone! He had moved the furniture around in the living room and bedroom with the help of his friend Rob. The house looked clean and organized.

I think that those two months that I spent in Tashkent made us appreciate each other more. I had all those fears in Tashkent, and now I am back. Keith was happy to see me! He admitted that he had fears, too. He was afraid that I would not come back, and that I would have lots of trouble changing my passport. We even canceled our satellite service from Direct TV, because we did not have time for movies or world news.

Keith, of course, got the collection of currency from my country. I had bought twenty audiocassettes with Russian and Uzbek musical groups at $1.00 a piece. I gave four of them to my friends in the U.S.

I brought back twelve videocassettes that had cost $2.00 each. Keith and I had some wonderful times watching Russian cartoons and music clips. I had taken several videos of my family and of Tashkent on the small 8mm videocassettes.

Before leaving Uzbekistan, I had to take all my videocassettes to the customs at the international airport. High security is something new in my country. The entrance to the airport was only open to people with passports. I had mine, so I entered. I signed a journal stating that I had brought my videocassettes for customs review. Each videocassette had my last name on it. I left them all in a plastic bag. All those cassettes were 16mm size. Customs told me that they did not have the equipment to watch 8mm videocassettes. That sounded funny to me. The security in Tashkent was high enough to have police officers (militia) at each subway station and at the airport, but airport customs did not have the right equipment for 8mm videocassettes.

In a week, it was time for me to fly to the U.S. Well, I went to check in my luggage, and then I went upstairs to pick up my plastic bag with the videocassettes. I signed a form saying that I got all my cassettes back, but I had no idea if anything was missing or stolen. Well, I left my motherland without two of the videocassettes which I had really wanted to show Keith. When my mom went to the airport customs to ask for my missing cassettes, she was told something like this, "Oksana signed that she got it all." My mom told me that I had missed my opportunity to retrieve my tapes.

Keith and I went to Central Arizona College to take some tests. We were excited to become classmates in an Art Appreciation class and to become "college sweethearts."

It was great to be home! I felt at home, as soon as I entered the Los Angeles Airport! I took a free cart to pick up my heavy luggage. To me, it was a symbol of welcome to the U.S. When I went to Tashkent, I could not get a luggage cart for free. I did not have any Uzbek money with which to pay the local airport guy. I gave him a U.S. dollar. He quickly hid it and gave me a cart. I did not receive any change in Uzbek bills. He was supposed to, because I had paid three times more than I should have for the cart.

Keith told me that one day he would like to move to Tashkent. I told him, "I do not like that idea." Americans can be victims of the crime there. Locals will try to rip you off. I missed the American service and the American credit system. People are rude at the markets and in buses there. They bump each other and walk on your feet, and they do not apologize most of the time, because they did not even feel that they had done something wrong.

On the other hand, people on buses in Tashkent are very quick to give up their seats for elderly or pregnant passengers and mothers with babies. It was not like this in Moscow.

Anyway, I do not want to live in Uzbekistan. After I am used to the service, freedom, and luxuries of the middle class in the U.S., I cannot ever give them up just to be close to my family. I am home! I love my Keith, and I want to stay with him in the U.S. Thank God, I have love in my life.

After my trip to Tashkent and my successful return, Keith and I enjoyed our time together. We would spend every evening by the pool having drinks, watching the floating candles, and talking. We would lie on our new lounge chairs, which Keith had bought for our yard while I was gone.

I admired the new look of the yard. Keith had done a lot of work. He had put in a sprinkler system and sod all by himself, and he planted a bunch of shrubs, verbenas, and Chinese hibiscus. We would lie and look up into the sky. It sounds so simple!

However, I miss this time. I thought that our marriage had gone to a new level. We did not have time for movies or world news. We were busy with each other. I believe that our love and strength had been tested a lot by Keith's heart attack, his appendectomy, my minimum wage job, and our time away from each other.

CHAPTER 9
TEACH YOUR SPOUSE
INDEPENDENCE.

We had planned to start a family after my trip. We became students at Central Arizona College, and our lives were becoming more interesting and busy. We thought that all the bad luck of the year 2000 had been left behind.

However, honeymoons always have to end.

August 2000 started with another funeral. Keith's favorite uncle, Larry Nolder, passed away. We flew to Florida for the funeral. We did not care that we did not have any money. We put our expenses on our credit cards. (Russians, Uzbeks can not buy tickets with credit cards.) We wanted to see Uncle Larry and thank him for the all the joy he had brought to our wedding, to our honeymoon in June 1998, and to our life.

When we got back, we had more bad news. Keith's routine blood tests revealed that he had hepatitis C. We do not know how he got it. He was in the hospital in January and March, and he had a dentist appointment in February. His blood tests during those hospitalizations did not have any high levels of liver enzymes, which are a positive indication of hepatitis.

First, Keith notified his boss and colleagues about his diagnosis. Next, his boss asked him to resign with no explanation.

Here I want to tell you a very interesting story about friendship and trust. In July, Keith reminded his boss that his contract was over and he wanted a raise. The boss complained that their company did not have enough money. Keith asked for the severance package in case the company would decide to fire him.

The boss looked at him sincerely and said, "Keith, we will never fire you. You are like a son to me."

The next thing we knew, Keith had to leave right after he had finished with some difficult part of the computer program for the company. When I came by one day to pick up Keith's books, the office was locked from the inside. Either his poor colleagues were scared, or the boss had ordered them to lock me out. The secretary had to ask permission from her co-workers to unlock the door for me.

I cannot believe that Keith considered these people his friends. He had made me buy lots of souvenirs for them in Tashkent, because he cared about his little team. It was his idea to share a cake and my Russian candies with them one day. Did they share anything with him? No. They were only showing disrespect for a person who should have been like a "senior" programmer to them and who had been in this business for sixteen years!

Another thing I will never understand is how some of these people could call themselves Mormons. Since then, I have hated Mormons, and I do not want to deal with them. My opinion is that the company was getting rid of their expensive key players and hiring less experienced programmers. Later we found out that Keith's shares, which actually kept him from getting a raise for two years, were worth nothing if he left the company.

Nice work, dear Mormon friends and other traitors. I thought that situations like that could only happen in corrupted Russian or Uzbek society. Keith felt that he had been stabbed in the back. His "friends" and his "father" had left him without a job or a paycheck.

We had to close our second IRA account just to pay our bills. We also had to borrow $1200 from Dawn Barkett to help pay bills. We had to drop our college courses and move to Texas, because there were more job opportunities in this state for C/C++ programmers and database designers.

On the day that Keith left Phoenix, I had a miscarriage.

"Swallow this, Keith. That is exactly what you need after your heart attack, appendectomy, your relatives' funerals, and your new diagnosis."

August 2000 ended for us like another disaster.

My Mom thought that bad luck stroked our happiness because I sent too many pictures of our new house and pool to all me family and friends. So, they were jealous and their thoughts affected our American existence.

My friend psychic says that people's jealousy is like a vacuum. It sucks your luck out.

I read a feng shui book on the subject. I learned that our house had bad design according to this Oriental décor teaching. First, the house was built on a dead end street, which creates bad energy circulation. Second, Keith planted a huge cactus in front of the door! Feng shui teaches that front door entrance should not be blocked by anything especially by a cactus! Third, our prosperity and health areas in the house were located in both bathrooms! No wonder our live got all messed up!

OKSANA'S DIARY – SEPTEMBER, 12, 2000

I feel that with Keith, I have learned so much because of the circumstances. My other Russian friends have not moved at all or just a little distance and they have no idea what it means to move, to change locations, friends, and climates. It is such an adventure. Now I know how to sell a junk car without a title that had been registered in Atlanta. I learned a lot about selling and renting a house. I am working on scheduling my flight with the dog, hiring movers, setting up a weekly pool service and taking care of other business. I feel so proud of myself that I can be so helpful to Keith and learn so much. Sometimes it is nice to be a weak lady, but I like to think of myself as a very strong person who takes care of business, no matter what.

My mom and all my grandparents are upset about this move. To them, I should be having a baby and getting an American education. They believe that Keith should have a nice job in Arizona, and enjoy his house and the pool. My family writes me,

We do not understand.

Will we like Dallas? I should, because they have a Six Flags! I love amusement parks, and I missed them in Phoenix! Keith feels important at his new job. He never felt appreciated at his last position. So we decided that Dallas could be much better for our financial situation and for Keith's career. I want my husband to come home from work happy and satisfied that he had saved some lives, done some projects, discovered new ways to solve problems, and was understood by his boss and colleagues.

At first, I was scared to move. I did not want to pack, or worry, or unpack my treasures. I did not have any desire to drop my college classes and learn the new highways in Texas. I know that to move to a different state where you do not have family and friends is like being born again and starting all over. I had a chance to keep Keith from accepting the job in Dallas, but I did not stop him. I probably wanted to live someplace close to Six Flags.

OKSANA'S DIARY – SEPTEMBER 14, 2000

Today I was independent and self-confident again. I got my moving estimates and plane tickets. I did not know that round trips were cheaper than one-way trips. So I bought a round trip ticket, and it saved me $400.

I found out that only two airlines take large pets like Bill Clinton's dog. I mean that my dog looks like his, but even better. Now I know that those airlines do not take pets in cargo if the outside temperature is higher than 85 degrees. That meant that I had to pick an early flight. Also I have to make sure that I am early enough to drop my dog off at cargo registration. If I am late, the cargo section will be filled, and I will feel stupid and lost in the airport with heavy luggage, a kennel, a dog, and non-refundable tickets at 6:00 a.m.

Today I charged the battery for the lawn mower and cut the grass. Of course, I would prefer to think that I am a city girl and not supposed to cut the grass. However, I do not have the desire or the money to pay somebody to do it for me. Anyway, if Keith would give me money to hire someone to cut the grass, I would send the money to my family in Tashkent, and cut the grass myself.

MY FIRST INDEPENDENT CAR WASH

When Keith went to Dallas for another job, I tried to be a big shot and pay for a car wash. Usually, I did it myself every couple OF weeks. It never was a big deal to me, because I was never lazy about washing the car by hand. However, this time I paid $4.00 to have it done. In fifteen minutes, I had to go get my money back, because my car never got rinsed! I was sitting in my Plymouth waiting about fifteen minutes for a rinsing after soap and water had been poured over my vehicle.

Did you get it? I left the service station with soap all over my car! I think stuff like this can happen only to me.

MY FIRST GARAGE SALE

Keith left me to be the independent sales manager of our junk. However, when I was preparing notes with ads about our yard sale, I wrote, *No Junk.* I had only four boxes with my ads on them to place around our Sunrise Canyon subdivision.

It was a hot night on September 8, 2000. I was ready to place my last ad on the corner of Valley and Southern. Suddenly, I noticed that someone was following me in a car. It is always too dark in Sunrise Canyon. You cannot see anything easily at night, because lots of streets in Apache Junction do not have streetlights, and they look really scary and unpredictable.

I made a fast decision. It would be stupid to stop the car and get out with my box. I did not have any desire to be a victim. So I turned on the first street I saw without using my signal. I was driving slowly and watching the same car behind mine. Then the car that was following me turned on its police lights and commanded me to stop.

You just do not know how happy I was at that moment, illuminated by the colorful police car lights! Sometimes people hate or fear police officers, but I was thrilled to see a person of the law instead of a maniac.

The officer came up to my car and asked me, "Are you lost?" He looked well-groomed and fit.

I explained to him that he had scared me and told him why I had been driving around in Sunrise Canyon. He shone his flashlight into my back seat to make sure that it did not have any cadavers or heroin.

I did not have my driver's license with me. I think it was my first time to leave my wallet at home and be stopped by the police. He checked my registration card and used his radio to find out about this "white female with no license." He told me that I had not signaled when I had made my frightened turn. He recognized my Russian accent and let me go without a ticket. The officer told me to keep my record as clean as it is now.

Well, I felt a slight shaking in my knees after all that, but I had a pretty good first experience talking to the police.

The next day I had my garage sale as I had planned. I sold some furniture and some clothes that Keith had outgrown. My friend Pat was my right hand and explained to people who did not understand my accent about my goods, like the motorcycle and a damaged car with a new engine. She took my place several times when I had to go inside the house and show people my cats, Jasmine and Banditka.

That same day, I got rid of my cats and their favorite houses, chairs to scratch, kitty litter boxes, kitty food, litter, and treats. I did not want a penny for my cats and their property. I was just happy to find new homes for them.

I had gotten so tired of cats! At first, Jasmine had an eating disorder. She always had to have her bowl full of food. Otherwise, she would be hungry and overeat and vomit.

On the other hand, Banditka was a real bandit. She had a hard time holding her dumps in, and she used to poop before she made it to the kitty litter box. Oh, I had to pick up her poops from the floor around the litter box a lot! She was a very messy cat.

Also, she made me believe that Keith was peeing in our bed! I was blaming my spouse, okay? I made him believe that he had some kind of disorder. One night I witnessed her peeing on my white down comforter while Keith was sleeping like a baby. I realized then that Banditka had been peeing on my nice green rugs in the master bathroom, and on my cleaning rags in the garage. One day I got so tired from doing laundry that I packed up my nice green rugs and my comforter.

People told me that Banditka would stop marking her territory like this after being spayed! Do you know what? She did not stop behaving as a little dirty bandit after I paid $100 to get her fixed. I gave up. After I took away her favorite things to mark, she stopped doing it. I was thinking that this cat was ready to change.

But on September 6th, 2000, she started to poop in her kitty litter box and continued on my terracotta master bedroom tile! She wiped her little butt on it right in front of me! I was so mad! I told myself that day, "No more cats!" Thanks to God, to Pat, and to the garage sale, I got rid of the cats!

I was surprised that most of my stuff sold in about one hour between 7:00 a.m. and 8:00 a.m. One couple had very fine jewelry. The gentleman had a hat with a dozen silver pins on it. I told him how impressed I was. I had met a man who makes jewelry! He gave me a small plastic angel pin. He actually gives away those angels to people who notice his charming, outstanding hat.

So my first yard sale was successful and interesting.

MY FIRST INDEPENDENT MOVING

When I say *my first independent moving,* I mean that Keith was not around to arrange anything. I got movers to come and load their twenty-four-foot truck with my stuff. They had to come at 2:00 p.m. on the 21st of September.

However, my movers didn't arrive until 4:30 to start their work. There were only two guys, who could not fit all my stuff in their truck until 10:00 p.m. The three of us became very frustrated, but their boss Larry solved the problem. He came at 10:30 with two more guys and unloaded the truck completely.

When I saw that, I got so upset that I could not watch them do their job anymore. I started to vacuum the house and clean the refrigerator and bathrooms. I had planned to do all the cleaning with my friend's supplies after the movers left, but my plans failed. The movers didn't leave until 1:00 a.m. on the 22nd of September. They actually fit everything in their truck and my car, which they had to tow behind.

The problem was that the truck was two feet shorter than the twenty-six-foot truck the company had promised to provide us with. My boxes had not been counted, I had not gotten any tags, and I was really worried.

Anyway, I am happy to tell you that none of my electronics or furniture were stolen or damaged. All of my china and Keith's alcohol collection made it safely to Texas.

However, the license plate and the light on Keith's motorcycle were broken. We did not get any refunds, because of my stupidity. I had signed the contract without reading it. The moving contract says that I agreed that the moving company only had to pay for any damage that was under sixty cents per pound. I had no idea that before moving, I should have had a full inventory of our belongings with prices ready in case something big or small got broken.

I am trying to tell you to pay attention to what you sign. Do not fool yourself.

So my first independent moving experience went more smoothly than I expected it to, but I still feel that I was kind of ripped off.

MY FIRST INDEPENDENT FLIGHT WITH MY DOG

When the movers left, I had two more hours to get ready for my flight. I did not have much choice in airlines, because only a couple of them take large dogs on their planes. My travel agent told me that I had to buy a kennel for Shok. I got a health certificate from the vet about Shok's shots and condition.

A private shuttle picked me up at 3:00 a.m. on the 22nd of September. When I got to the airport, a clerk (a brand new employee) from the airline I had chosen would not let me get registered. She told me that the kennel I had was too small, and it was not comfortable enough for the dog. However, I could not get a heavier kennel, because its weight including the dog could not exceed one hundred pounds.

She very helpfully told me to take my sleepy lab with his cage and my luggage, get a taxi, and go to any Pet Smart to buy another kennel. I asked her, "Can I buy the right type of kennel from cargo?"

She very confidently answered (she was a witch), "No, we do not sell kennels." (She was an ignorant witch).

I almost had a panic attack, okay? I could hear a weird noise in my ears, and my vision was becoming blurry. I was trying to hold onto the counter to keep from falling. I was in a situation where there was no smart advice and no help. I had not slept all night, and I had a dog that had taken two magic pills to keep him from getting excited. I was stressed.

I walked to a phone and called Keith. I was sure that he was the one who could tell me what to do. He was always telling me what to do before.

Keith told me not to listen to the clerk and to get a cab, go to the cargo section and buy a kennel from them. So I did. The people in the cargo department had more knowledge than the clerk did. A guy named Bob told me that he would make the trip painless for me. We put Shok in a nice plastic kennel that looked like a house and had absorbent padding. They folded my metal kennel and packed it as part of my luggage. They sent Shok as a parcel. So cargo took him and took care of him the right way. Bob arranged a free shuttle for me, which took me back to the airport. I got registered on another flight and paid for my dog and for the kennel. Keith met me in Dallas.

We picked Shok up as a parcel, and he had done great on the flight. His kennel was clean. The next time I have to take Shok on a flight, I will go straight to the cargo section with my dog and deal with an experienced person.

By the way, I sent this chapter with more details to the above-mentioned airline whose clerk had caused me trouble. I got a letter from them with an apology and a $100 voucher for future travel with them.

Well, it was still my second year in the US. Keith and I reunited in Dallas.

The most important thing is the law about drivers' licenses in Texas.

In Arizona, I could not get my driver's license for more than a year, because I did not have a green card yet. I applied for a green card in September 1998 at the Arizona INS. The law states that you have to wait for three years. During those years, I had to pay $100 each year to INS to renew my work authorization card as well as a fee to MVD to renew my driver's license.

Moving to Dallas had a reward. I got my driver's license for six years. That meant that it did not matter that my work authorization will expire. I still had permission to drive! God, Thank you that we moved to Dallas, the city with smart laws!

We were married for two years, and I still was scared. What a foreign wife can be scared about?

At first, I was afraid that Keith would change his mind and send me back to Tashkent. I tried very hard not to let that happen. I was afraid to tell him my opinion about a lot of things or argue with him for that reason.

When we got married, I did not have much confidence in my relationship with Keith. I felt threatened a lot that if I did not appease him or did not spoil him, he would divorce me. At that time I was probably stressed with all the new things I had to learn about the U.S., and on top of that, I did not know how deep and generous his love for me was. Every time he told me how very messy I was and that I could not clean very well, I felt threatened that he would divorce me because I was not the perfect homemaker.

For our first two years of marriage, I would wake him up for work, make coffee and bring it to his bathroom and even prepare his clothes to wear. When we moved to Texas, I stopped doing all that. I stopped because I realized that coffee is not good for his heart, and that he doesn't love me just for the coffee or for spoiling him in the mornings. However, I still make his lunch and enjoy doing it.

I was afraid and am still nervous when I think about how Keith almost died. I am afraid to have to take care of myself or to be alone in this strange country. I know that I am strong, but I prefer to be weak and hide behind my spouse's back from trouble.

I am always worrying about my family in Tashkent. I wish my mom and her mom would come to live with us. Keith wants that, too. It is hard to live so far away from them. When it is morning here, they are getting ready to go to sleep. When someone dies over there, there is no way for me to get there in time for the funeral because of the eighteen-hour flight.

As a foreigner, I was afraid to apply for jobs, because I was sure that I would be turned down. However, I came to Texas on the 22nd of September, and I got a job on the 2nd of October as a preschool teacher! Keith helped me a lot to get to this point in my life. He was always telling me that I could get a better job, fit into society, and make friends.

I met one Russian lady, who lived for three years in the USA. She does not drive, has no idea about their bills and finances. When she wanted to get a job at local child care, her husband said: "NO." During these three years she was depressed a lot, went to a psychiatric clinic three times. She does not know how to write a check, and does not even understand American movies very well. I wonder what would happen to this lady, if her American husband would have had heart attack like mine. She would not be able to give him the support he needs like driving to a rehabilitation center, for example, and make sure all bills are paid in time.

Keith did not keep me misinformed. We talk about finances a lot. He even let me listen to his business phone conversations. For example, he wanted me to listen how to talk to a credit card company, to do a balance transfer by phone. I listened to his phone conversations with State Farm agents, movers, telemarketers, job interviewees. I already wrote earlier, that Keith taught me how to drive, manage accounts on line and save on stamps, how to plug washer and dryer...He wanted me to be somewhat independent, so he can count on me to help him. He also said: "When I am not around, you will know what to do."

CHAPTER 10
WHEN PEOPLE MISJUDGE YOU.

When I graduated from high school, I knew only one thing for sure: I wanted to become a writer. I had no desire to be a journalist! That is why, following my friend's advice, I decided to become a linguist. I was learning to be a "philologist," and my degree had to be a degree of philology in Russian language and literature. During my student life, I used to spend most of my free time in the library, taking students' orders for compositions. I had my own business without a license. I just typed some ads saying:

If you do not have time to do some of your papers in subjects like history of art, history of religion, foreign, Uzbek, and Russian literature (modern and ancient), children's psychology, ancient and modern methods of teaching, logic, etc., call this number to order your paper. Orders are confidential.

I had a lot of phone calls. The majority of my clients were women with infants who were unable to complete the required reading that their professors wanted them to do.

My passion to read and write made my hobby turn out to be a pretty good seasonal income. I even hired some smart friends to help do the job, if I had too many orders. I would meet a client someplace at a subway station or at the university, deliver the order, and collect twenty percent of my friend's earnings. That is less than Uzbek's government taxes, which are forty to forty-five percent. Sometimes I took an order, but the client somehow failed to show up and pay. I never felt that I had spent the time for nothing, because I was getting more educated by writing all these papers.

I never would have read some of the novels (for example, Homer's poems, Nabokov's novels, etc.) if I had not received an order to write a composition for a course or a diploma paper for graduation on this literature.

Some professors knew that someone was doing "ghostwriting" for their students. I even saw some ads in the newspaper saying that teachers wanted to write some papers for busy students.

When I was a student, my mind automatically would separate other students into three categories. There were potential clients who ordered papers, business-minded students who took orders for papers, and "independents," who neither bought nor sold their works.

I started to do my business when I was a third-year student. My smart younger brother in Russia's university started this business while he was a first-year student. He is an ace in a totally different area from literature and language. He has clients who need help in economics, English, calculus, and physics. Stas is good at tutoring.

Even if you heard about Perestroika, when the Soviet Union collapsed, you probably never heard that Uzbekistan proclaimed its independence in 1991. So lots of things started to change. Since the republic had a new migration of Russians and Jews to Russia and other countries (the U.S., Australia, Canada, etc.), the schools became very short of teachers. So when I got my diploma, it said that I was a teacher of Russian language and literature. My friend graduated from the same department of the university five years ago, her diploma read, *Russian linguist.* She works now in the Russian city of Omsk as a librarian. When I graduated, the university's authorities proclaimed that I would not get my diploma unless I got a job at a public school. I had no choice. I did not want to be a teacher. I was afraid of the students.

I remember that my first week at the school was in August of 1996. I spent that week painting walls in the building! In August, the schools do not teach anything yet. The first day of school is the first or second day of September.

I became used to being a teacher. I would never have left the school if the pay had been good enough. While I was teaching, I still took orders for papers sometimes from university students. Probably, I was satisfying my desire to write.

So, I got my degree in Education without choosing it and without any desire to be a public teacher. I could not choose courses, or time for my education.

You see how sometimes things can be totally out of control.

MY WORK AT CHILD CARE

If we had not moved to Texas, I would never have tried to get a job at the child care facility.

At first I was sure that I would have never been hired at such a place. While we were in Arizona, we took care of some important business. We found an International agency in Phoenix which evaluated foreign diplomas. We had to pay a fee for their work, but that was how we got a new face for my Uzbek diploma. The grades in my Uzbek diploma were seen as numbers, not letters like America uses. In Russian-Uzbek style, I had all "5" and "4," but in American custom they were all "A" and "B."

Straight "A" students, who never got "4" for any exams, get "red diploma" and gold medal. I heard that the medal is really gold plated silver. It is a great honor to graduate high school, or university with red diploma and gold medal. It means a lot – scholarships. If a high school student has a gold medal, he does not have to pass any tests to enter any college or university.

When we moved to Texas, the closest place to us was a child care facility. It was Keith's idea and advice for me to apply for a job there. I tried. My evaluated diploma made me one of the highest paid teachers. The assistant manager, who had interviewed me, was making less money per hour than I was.

Why didn't I try to become a public school teacher? I did not know the area, and I did not want to drive far from my apartment. I do not have an American teacher's certificate. I did not feel confident with my English.

What was amazing to me at child care?

1. Children had to sleep in little cots, fully clothed, in the same room where they also played. In Uzbekistan, every classroom was separated from one another and was divided into two sections. One section was where the toys and tables for activities and meals were kept. The second section was where the good, strong, metal beds were kept. Kids would undress and take naps in their underwear. Teachers at child care facilities in my country never had to move any cots or beds.

2. I worked for at the child care facility where we did not have a janitor. In Uzbek child care, cleaning would be the work of a teacher's assistant or a janitor. It was frustrating to me in the beginning to put on gloves at the end of my day to clean toilets and sinks, vacuum, and wash floors.

However, I got into cleaning so much, I enjoyed it! My spouse joked with his coworker, saying that his wife was nesting at her job instead of her home place.

3. At the American child care facility, lunch was served at 11:00 a.m. and children drank milk every day for lunch. In Russia or Uzbekistan, lunch had been served at 1:00 p.m. When my brother and I were growing up, we had milk, sweet tea, or fruit compote for lunch at Tashkent's child care facility. Uzbek and Russian cooks made food from scratch in their kitchens. They did not have cans of soup like American child care facilities do. In American child care, children only receive only one plate of food, and sometimes a small bowl of soup. Russian and Uzbek child care served a bowl of soup as the first item of the lunch, and then a plate of something else, such as mashed potatoes and meat cutlets. Russians believe that the American "dry" diet without soup is unhealthy, and I still hear the same thing from my family a lot.

In the beginning, I felt like my job at child care was like hell. At that time, I thought I had made the wrong decision about working with kids. I did not like the kids and my work. To me, all the kids seemed like little stinky animals. I wanted to quit, but to give up seemed to be the weak thing to do. It would mean that the kids had won the game. Later, I understood that these feelings were because of my irritability during my first month of pregnancy.

How did you feel when you were in your first trimester?

So I stayed at my job, learned how to be patient, and how to be a better mother. I learned many new words such as *cots, enrichments, corporal punishment, puzzles, time-out, potty training, freeze dance, open art project, construction paper,* etc. These are words my spouse, his family, and our friends had never used in their speech with me before – or if they had, I had forgotten them. I even learned how to use a laminator! Working at the child care facility was a great learning and teaching period of time for me.

I got used to my job very soon. I liked to have lunch there and then go home for a two-hour break. I became a fitness instructor for the kids because I enjoyed being the center of attention and a dancer. It was much easier to exercise there because I have a hard time forcing myself to exercise or go to the gym while I'm at home. I had this need to bring my favorite CD's to class, teach the children how to follow motion directions, feel the rhythm of the music, look at me, and repeat what I was doing.

Now I have to tell you a story I can never forget. I had a girl in my class named Dina (the name has been changed). She was one of the cutest and smartest girls, and was so attached to me. When I was not there, she would cry all day long. I loved the girl with all my heart, and she was the one who would sit on my lap and whom I would listen to the most.

One day her mom complained to the principal about how she wished I would communicate more with her. So I did. I explained to her that her sweet daughter Dina required too much attention. Since I had more than fifteen children in the classroom, it was hard for me to give it to her. I asked Dina's mother to tell me why her daughter was so spoiled with attention. Excuse me, but what is wrong with the phrase "spoiled with attention?" Had she ever gone to a child care facility before?

The answer I received was that Dina had attended a private school before coming to the child care facility. There had been no more than seven children in her class there, and so it was easy for each child to receive enough attention. However, the school had not made it financially and was forced to close.

I hoped that my conversation with Dina's mother would have helped out the situation. I thought Dina's mother would have talked to her daughter and explained that things are different now, and that she should not cry for her Miss Oksana.

When the lady left me that day, she left calmly and did not look upset. However, the next thing I knew was that Dina's mother was a hypocrite and a liar. She had told the principal that I had called her daughter a "spoiled brat!" When I found this out, I was in deep shock for a week. I knew only one thing. The word "brat" was not in my vocabulary.

One day, I was explaining how to play dominoes to my best student Dina. She could not understand it, which was frustrating to me. I made the mistake of saying, "Do not be stupid. Think again!" She started crying, which did not surprise me. She was my sensitive little student!

When I looked up the words "stupid" and "silly" in the English-Russian dictionary, it gave me the same Russian definition. The word "stupid" sounds harsher, and that is why I used it. Later the principal opened up my eyes and told me that the word "stupid" is a mean variant of the word "silly" and that teachers are not supposed to use that word with children. I feel bad that I insulted little sweet girl. I was sure, that my choice of words was right. I was prompting Dina this way to pay attention to the game rules.

Dina's mother became angry with me for that. However, she made up a story about how she witnessed me calling her student "stupid" in front of all the other children. She called the child care headquarters and complained about the "verbal abuse" Dina had received. She made them pay her for six weeks of tuition, even though she had only paid for four weeks.

I cannot believe how some people can make money by manipulating the truth. I was afraid I was going to be fired which I did not want to happen because I enjoyed my job, my colleagues, and my understanding boss. I just hated the idea of losing my job as a result of someone's fibbing.

I ended up not being terminated because of someone's fibbing, but because of my own honesty and stupidity. I printed the rough draft of this chapter and gave it to my boss to read. She had many years of experience, and had earned my trust. I felt that she had a right to see her name in this chapter before it was published.

I expected her to tell me what she did not like in the chapter and what could hurt her company. I gave her a printed e-mail from my editor, a professional in the field, which read: *You don't have to have permission from a company to write about them. If you say false things about the company, and if the false things could hurt them, and if you do it maliciously, then they can sue you for libel. If you want to change the name of the company, we can make up a name instead. We can also change all names. Just let me know.*

This e-mail should have made my boss confident about my editor-mentor relationship. It did not. She sent my rough draft to the corporate office because she wanted to protect herself and the company. Corporate management decided to terminate me because of the things I had done in the past, such as using a loud voice and using exercises as a punishment (pushups and squats). The corporate management did not even get anything I had written about Dina. This chapter was not clear enough for their brains, since they were scared for the business's image. They hung this ugly word *brat* in my file: *reference to a child as a spoiled brat.*

I was asked to not use the real company name because of all of the things that could hurt the business if I did. I was not going to write anything about using my special "drill-sergeant" voice to build up a discipline or about using pushups as a punishment. Headquarters was upset that a person like me, who probably should get a job at a boot camp, was taking care of children in a child care facility.

I agree that my terminators were right about some things. Some readers and parents will not be too happy to read about their kids seeming like "stinky little animals" to a teacher, or about my feelings during my first month at the child care facility. It was my first pregnancy month!

The corporate office terminated me because of my "violation of the child discipline policy." They did not realize that their decision was based on things that I had done in the past, for a very short period of time, and that these things were promptly corrected by me and my managers.

My honesty in letting my manager read my rough draft set me free from that job. I would have had a hard time quitting myself because I had become attached to the facility, children, and my daily routine. I even ignored my chronic cold and flu symptoms, which I was receiving from the children who were coughing in my face as I tied their shoes. For the five months of working with children, I survived by using nasal spray! During those five months, I was on antibiotics three times, all because of my work!

Some of my clothes were ruined because of spilled drinks or paint. When you have your own baby, this does not sound disgusting or frustrating. But when you deal with a bunch of other people's children, it is a different story. Who would pay for my ruined clothes and poor health? I do not think that the child care facility would.

I have learned several things from these situations. First, if a child loves you, it does not mean that his/her parents will love you also. Secondly, it does not matter how great and competent your boss seems; he or she will be taking care of themselves and their company, not you. Third, there are always people who will manipulate what you say, even if you try to control your words. Fourth, most people have to learn to appreciate the truth and honesty, not lollipop fiction or fairy tales.

My third year in the US was 2001. It was my third year of adjustment to this planet – America.

Do you know what it's like to live with a spouse who has been diagnosed with hepatitis C?

To me, it was not fear that I would get the virus from Keith. His diagnosis did not stop me from being intimate. I faced a fear for Keith's life. We read some books about this decease, and we talked to some people. We learned that most people die from liver failure caused by the virus. So I could just watch Keith die slowly. . .

It is horrible to expect your partner's life to end, to know all about it. Even if you are ready, you are not ready. The fear eats at you inside. I could feel it. I was telling myself that if Keith did not live long, I would enjoy our baby, my little Keithchik.

Keith started the treatment after a liver biopsy and new blood tests in January 2001. Few people can fight the virus; most have to live with it, watching their diet.

The treatment includes three shots per week and six pills per day (for Keith's weight). The cost to our insurance company is almost $1400 a month. We had to pay only $25 per month. My soul wants to bless people who invented health insurance and who work in this field. I cannot imagine how we would pay for this treatment without them.

The first injection made Keith sick with a fever. He was shivering all night, and I was trying to warm him up. We were afraid that those symptoms would continue, but they did not. They come and go, like a "surprise party" from the virus. You never know when it will hit you. Medication can make people depressed, violent, and suicidal. It brings to Keith all symptoms of fever and worsens his neck pains, and it keeps him awake at nights.

The medication, Rebetron, can cause anemia and heart failure in hepatitis C patients. Keith had a heart attack, and those side effects made me worry a lot.

He is a person who came back from death, but it did not change him a lot. He did not quit smoking. He does not exercise, and he still does not like to eat fruit. However, he is not drinking as much as he used to, and I got him to take two pills of vitamins and a glass of juice every morning.

We do not know what the final outcome will be, but we have hope. With my pregnancy, my fear became loose and weak. I joked with Keith about his disease.

"I am pregnant. I feel nausea, and I am tired and irritated. You are not pregnant, but you are irritated, tired a lot, and have nausea, too."

God blessed me with my pregnancy. Keith said that I am having an easier pregnancy than other women he knew and talked to about their condition. Thanks, God. God gives me strength to be strong when Keith is fighting for his life and future.

MY GREEN CARD APPOINTMENT

It was the first of February 2001. I was sick with a 102.6° fever, a cold, and a cough. Keith checked the mail after he got home from work. One letter was from the Dallas INS! It said that I had an appointment at

8:00 a.m. on the 6th of February, and it told me what papers I should bring with me.

The appointment for a green card is very important for every immigrant. It means several things. First of all, getting a green card is getting a permanent resident status. Until I get my green card, I am just a non-immigrant who has to buy a work authorization card every year!

If I have to travel overseas, I have to apply for a travel document which allows me to come back into the U.S. It takes two to three months and $100 to get this document. If you have an emergency, such as a relative's death, you can get it immediately from INS, but only after standing in line for about two to six hours. With a green card, I can travel without any problems!

Lots of foreign permanent residents can file a new application to become an American citizen. Some unhappy foreign wives would divorce their abusive, unloved American husbands after getting their green cards. So as you can see now, the green card is something all foreigners apply for, wait for, and pay for.

To get a permanent resident status, I had to apply for my green card in September 1998, in Arizona. I was told that in this area I would have to wait three years to get my first interview. When I moved to Texas, I had to write to the Arizona INS and ask them to send my paperwork to the Dallas INS. That was in January 2001!

When people say that everything is bigger in Texas, I have to add that everything is also faster in Texas! I had thought that I would have to wait for my interview in Texas until September 2001. However, I got my interview sooner!

I had to bring certain important papers with me. Some of the papers were my IDs, my marriage certificate, and a letter from my work. Keith had to be with me, too! He had to bring his ID and an Affidavit of Support (his and our taxes for three years) as proof that I would have his financial support.

We had to have proof that we actually live together as husband and wife. Such proof can consist of leasing documents, bank statements, tax papers, or security titles. We had both our names on all these documents as proof that we live together. INS wants to make sure that the "American husband and foreign wife" situation is not a temporary relationship just to get another immigrant into the country. That is why INS gave us a very short time to get the papers together before the interview. If we had lived apart, and if Keith was some kind of con-man, we would not have been able to have all this paperwork with both our names done in a couple of days.

I had to go to a special INS medical center in Addison on the 2nd of February, to get my medical tests done. INS requires all immigrants to have all their immunizations before getting their permanent resident status. I did not get my immunizations because it could have been harmful to my fetus. I had my first sonogram pictures with me as evidence of my pregnancy for the medical center staff.

When Keith and I came for the interview, one of the first questions was, "Do you have children?" Children are real proof for the INS officers that you have a stable relationship. Keith joked, "Hmm, we have a third of one so far." We showed our sonogram pictures to the officers and told them that the due date was in July 2001.

That was enough for them, and we were never asked to show our bank statements and other papers with our names on them. The INS officers only cared about our ID's, the Affidavit of Support, and my medical records. Since my medical records were not complete because of the lack of immunizations, my application could not be processed.

Why did I need immunizations? The American INS does not trust foreign immunization records or medicine, and that is why every applicant for a green card has to get immunized in the U.S.

We were told that I did not have to come to the INS anymore, but I could not get my green card soon. I would have to wait for my delivery, and then go back to the INS medical center for immunizations. After three days, I would be able to get my new completed medical records in a sealed envelope. Then I would have to send it to INS with my baby's birth certificate. Only after this would my file be closed, and I could get my green card in the mail. It sounded like I will maybe be able to get it by autumn.

MY FIGHT FOR THE GREEN CARD

I was a fool again thinking that I would finally have my greencard without red tape and tears. I did not. When Jessef was born on July 11, 2001, I went to a clinic in Addison which does immunizations. I had to pay again for the health check up and for the shots, which cost us about $100.00.

I mailed my immunization records to INS in Dallas. I also included Jessef's birth certificate. By the end of August, I got a letter from the

INS president stating that my greencard was denied. The reason…any additional paperwork has to be sent in 120 days after the interview. That was impossible to do in my case, because I was still pregnant during the 120 day grace period.

Therefore, when my immunization records were received, my file already was automatically closed by the system. So, in order to re-open it and to be reviewed, I owed INS money. At that time I did not have any extra money in our checking account. I had just paid all the bills plus our medical bills. I wrote a letter to INS with an explanation of what had happened. I did not get an answer. I kept writing letters to this place every month. When I finally wrote a check for $110.00 to INS, my file was re-opened and reviewed.

I received a cold letter from the same president of Dallas's INS stating that I would get my greencard in 12 months. However, I received it in three weeks.

It is valid for 10 years. I can reapply for another greencard or apply for citizenship. I would like to become a citizen one day because I would like to consider one of the secure government jobs. You have to be a citizen to get that kind of job.

So, I got my greencard (permanent resident status) after living in the USA for almost 4 years.

I feel that I was treated unfairly by INS. Just think. I saved my husband's life three times. I gave birth to an American citizen. I am respectful of American laws. However, I had to fight for my visa, while terrorists had no problems with their visas and flew plains into the buildings on September 11, 2001.

When people misjudge me, I get upset, take it personal, complain to Keith and everybody I know by phone and email, and try to get over it. I will be the one without a sleep all night, suffering and reliving hurtful events. It hurts more, than you are a foreigner, the one who speaks with an accent and the one who does not understand what is going on one hundred per cent. When people misjudge you, learn from it, try to fix what is fixable, and do not mess with INS.

CHAPTER 11
FRIENDS AND STRANGERS HELP TO SURVIVE IN INTERNATIONAL MARRIAGE. HOW TO LIVE WITH A HEPATITIS C PATIENT.

Every chapter of this book has some story on Russian superstition. This one should have one, as well. Russians do not have BABY SHOWERS. They believe that gifts can bring bad luck, a death to a newborn, if presented before the birth. Asians, among whom I grew up, would not take a newborn shopping or to a restaurant with them. For forty days, only closest family members can see baby's face. It is because people believe that jealous and "bad" eyes might curse a newborn. If these superstitions were true, most American newborns would be dead, since their parents have baby showers, take their week old baby shopping, to church or to a restaurant...

July of 2001 brought us joys and sorrows.

My in-laws drove all the way from Pennsylvania to help us when the baby arrived.

Keith was getting weaker every day. He was missing more days of work.

Sometimes he slept 18 hours in a row without eating, using the toilet, or smoking. Sometimes he could sleep for two days. We had asked his doctor to prescribe sleeping pills. Well, Keith started taking Ambien. Ambien and Rebetron (the medication for hepatitis C) did not work together very well.

181

Keith would fall asleep, when he would wake up two hours later in the middle of the night, take more Ambien.

I asked my obstetrician to help me. Jessef was past due. I did not want to wait until the 19th of July to have labor induced. I was afraid that Keith's parents would have to go back home and would only be able to spend a little time to help me. My doctor rescheduled my hospitalization to July 11th. Keith and his parents spent the entire day at the hospital. I had been on a hospital bed with an IV to start the contractions since 7:00 a.m. Jessef was born at 7:00 P.M.

Keith cut the umbilical cord. Mom and Dad took some modest video shots of the event. Their sixth grandchild was born!

When Jessef was 7 days old, Keith ended up in the same hospital. He could hardly move the day before his hospitalization. Dad and I took him to see his doctor and to have some blood tests done.

Keith's sister, Kim, and her daughter, Jessica, arrived from Ohio for two days to help. So, the two of them and Mom were baby-sitting. Thanks to God for the inventors of baby-formula! I did not have enough milk and Jessef was refusing to take my breast. Formula saved us.

The blood tests showed that Keith's blood cells were down to a count of 100. His doctor called and told me to bring my husband for hospitalization immediately. It was the third time I had to call 911 during my three years in the USA. Keith had a high fever and was delirious. He did not remember how I dressed him or how he was taken to a hospital. If I had not called the doctor and if I had not insisted on going for blood tests, his parents would have been attending their oldest son's funeral right there in North Dallas. Keith was too nauseated, delirious and exhausted to think straight. And, as during his heart attack and emergency appendectomy, he did not want to see the doctors and drag himself to the hospital.

On July 18, Keith was in ICU. Later he was transferred to a regular room. I was home when Keith called me and complained. He could barely talk. He was hot and weak. I flew to the hospital to find him lying in bed without any medication or water. Nurses were in a meeting.

The nurse who had brought him to the room had turned the heat to the highest level when he asked her to warm up the room. I could not breathe in the room because it was so hot.

Some people tell me that I am pushy and disrespectful. However, it can be very helpful. I won't let people push me or my husband around. I was walking back and forth from the nurse's station to Keith's room, getting on people's backs and nerves, raising my voice, calling the doctor.

I got them to move Keith to the isolation unit and to start his antibiotics, like his doctor said. I had no idea that in America I would have to be so pushy to get people to do their job.

People had to enter his room with masks. Fresh fruit was not allowed. Why? Keith's immune system was so weak that at that time any virus could kill him. Keith spent 5 days in the isolation unit.

I felt like I was falling apart between hospital visits, learning how to take care of my newborn, and pumping myself in order to produce milk. I knew that one day Jessef would learn how to drink my milk and I would get his solid immune system once and forever.

Well, to make a long story short, Keith came home. I called his work and found out how to apply for short term disability benefits. Obviously, Keith could not work even part-time while this medication was taking over his system. In the beginning he could. Rebetron had such side affects on my husband that he almost died.

When Keith's parents arrived in Carrollton, TX, in 2001, they found one small United Methodist Church with the beautiful name ALDERSGATE. They went for a service and met Pastor Victor Casad. They talked to him about baptizing their grandson at Aldersgate church. However, the baptism was cancelled due to Keith's sickness. The first day Keith ended up in the hospital Vic was there to talk to him.

So, Keith's parents left and I was left alone with my sick husband and my newborn. I was eager to get my son baptized. So I went to Aldersgate and spoke to Rev. Casad. He told me that their church baptizes only children of church members. He was going to baptize Jessef as a favor to his colleague, my father-in-law. I said that I would become a member so he could baptize my son. I strongly believed that it was a very important ritual.

I had to step on my pride and beliefs to become a member of the church. You see, in my head church was associated with narrow religious views, narrow people and donating money. That is why I felt that I was not honest with myself. However, I did it. It was for my son's sake. Keith and I wanted to baptize him and raise him as a Christian in a good church community. However, before Jessef was born we had not yet found one. I remember visiting Baptist, Unitarian churches and "Unity" Church in Dallas. Keith did not like even the idea of me joining one of these places. He wanted to go to a United Methodist church.

Jessef was baptized on August, 19, 2001. I was his only family member to be at Aldersgate. Keith could not get up. He was too sick. He was taking three shots a week and three pills a day again. Months later, every time someone at the church would be baptized, I would witness those events with tears and happiness. I was thrilled to see how many relatives, family and friends could attend the baptism ceremony. I felt sorry for myself that I was alone, even that I was married to my American dream.

During this time I read two books which helped my sanity: "Why bad things happen to good people" and "Do not sweat the small stuff".

While on medication, not just Keith's general condition was changed. His attitude towards me was also changed. He was irritable, picking at me for everything I did. He was talking about crazy things like divorce, sending me back to Tashkent. It was time of many conflicts. I cried and prayed. Sunday church services were as escape for me from the person he had become. I was considering leaving him and going to a women's shelter. On the other hand, I was praying to God to give me more strength and patience. Deep inside, I knew that this was not the man I married. He would change one day when his health was back. I could not bear the idea that I would leave him because I could hardly stand him. He would forget to pay the bills; he would fall and hurt himself. I did not wish to be a traitor. I did not wish to find an easy way out. I did not want to start my life over as a single Mom with a suitcase. I also still had a memory of my own sickness, which almost took my life in 1995. I had mumps, and as a secondary infection, meningitis encephalitis. I was weak, was fed with IV's, and got sick a lot. I remember how irritable I was. Noises, light, smells were triggers and drove me crazy. So, I can admit, that in my short life I already stood with one foot in a grave. I was 21 years old; I did not graduate my university yet. These memories helped me to stay by Keith, too.

I made a decision that I would never leave this man in such a painful situation. Church members called me frequently. I was called to attend different events and meetings. So I joined the United Methodist Women of the Aldersgate United Methodist Church. I joined a Sunday class called "Kaleidoscope". It gave me more time away from my honey-bunny, which was not funny.

One day Mary Brooks Casad asked me why I didn't attend Wednesday's dinners for socializing. I answered: "We have to watch our cash. We do not go out at all." The next week the director of children's ministries, Liz Moen, came up to me with an offer: "Oksana, how about you come at 6:00 p.m. on Wednesdays to eat dinner and take a plate for Keith. When everybody goes to their classes, you can volunteer in the nursery." I was thrilled. I had two more hours away from Keith. He had two more hours of less irritation in his miserable life. He loved when I came back with the dinner for him. He called me "my provider" on those nice evenings.

The church was my escape place. I realize that I was wrong about churches! I met people who were caring, nice, generous, thoughtful, and educated. I learned more about the Bible. Vic Casad explained to me the difference between Baptist and Methodist beliefs. I realized that I am on the Methodist side. Why? I never believed that if someone had a different religion than me it means they will go to hell. I always felt that God was at work in Buddhism, Islam, etc... One day Victor Casad said during the service: "You will not make it into heaven because you are a Muslim. You will not make it into heaven because you are a Baptist. You will not make it into heaven because you are Methodist. It does not matter which church you attend. What matters is that, if you cannot love and forgive people around you, you are not making it." At that point I wanted to love my husband no matter what.

Sometime ago I never felt comfortable seeing church members gathering donations.

First, I thought these people were getting paid for doing this. Second, I did not know the input that the church has in other people's lives. I was slowly discovering for myself what a great organization the church is with the help of Aldersgaters.

People were coming to Wednesday nights not just to study the Bible. One class was teaching how to play guitar, another was teaching how to work in a woodshop. Even "stained glass class" was there! I was amazed to see how many volunteers come to participate in the HABITAT FOR HUMANITY mission. Of course, prior to this, I did not know about such a mission. I found out about FAMILY PLACE there also. Our United Methodist Women's group was supporting this women's shelter. One day I donated a lot of my clothes, a queen-size bed and mattress, baby-crib, and toys to this organization because I learned that some missions are impossible without donations.

FAMILY PLACE is a safe place to go for abused women and their children. If the abuser is an American citizen, sometimes he can threaten his foreign wife to send her back or to report her to Immigration offices. This was that person is in control, but not any more, since you are reading this book. If wife has police reports handy, when she leaves for Family Place, (she can call any police department, and they would pick her up and take her there to safety), report her spouse to Immigration, and get her green card without staying in abusive marriage.

SEC. 1513. PROTECTION FOR CERTAIN CRIME VICTIMS INCLUDING VICTIMS OF CRIMES AGAINST WOMEN.

(a) FINDINGS AND PURPOSE-

(1) FINDINGS- Congress makes the following findings:

(A) Immigrant women and children are often targeted to be victims of crimes committed against them in the United States, including rape, torture, kidnapping, trafficking, incest, domestic violence, sexual assault, female genital mutilation, forced prostitution, involuntary servitude, being held hostage or being criminally restrained.

(B) All women and children who are victims of these crimes committed against them in the United States must be able to report these crimes to law enforcement and fully participate in the investigation of the crimes committed against them and the prosecution of the perpetrators of such crimes.

(2) PURPOSE-

(A) The purpose of this section is to create a new nonimmigrant visa classification that will strengthen the ability of law enforcement agencies to detect, investigate, and prosecute cases of domestic violence, sexual assault, trafficking of aliens, and other crimes described in section 101(a)(15)(U)(iii) of the Immigration and Nationality Act committed against aliens, while offering protection to victims of such offenses in keeping with the humanitarian interests of the United States. This visa will encourage law enforcement officials to better serve immigrant crime victims and to prosecute crimes committed against aliens.

(B) Creating a new nonimmigrant visa classification will facilitate the reporting of crimes to law enforcement officials by trafficked, exploited, victimized, and abused aliens who are not in lawful immigration status. It also gives law enforcement officials a means to regularize the status of cooperating individuals during investigations or prosecutions. Providing temporary legal status to aliens who have been severely victimized by criminal activity also comports with the humanitarian interests of the United States.

(http://www.shusterman.com/hr3244.html)

Domestic violence hotline is 1 800 799 7233.

One day Keith and I were struck by a financial problem. He had to be on his medication one more month but the insurance did not want to pay his benefits. We could have our credit history ruined in the blink of an eye. We had to come up with the payment for the house in Arizona because we did not have renters yet. I was complaining to Vic Casad about our troubles and he allowed me to place an ad in the church: "Everything is for sale". We did not sell most of our stuff. However, after the Sunday worship Liz Moen came up to me and gave me an $1800 check. She said: "This should help you to pay the bills. This is a gift from our church to you, Oksana. You do not have to pay it back. If you ever can help someone else, please, do." I was so amazed and thrilled that I did not have anything smart to answer. I had no idea that churches would financially help people in need. When I came home with the check, Keith could not believe it. He had been an active member of churches before. He had been donating more than 10% of his salary. He had even written some computer programs for free for the churches. However, when he was in need and unemployed, his church had never supported him. This is why he stopped attending church.

One day Vic Casad gave me an envelope with a card and a $100.00 bill. It was an anonymous letter. The giver did not wish to be known! That had never happened in my life. I just could not believe how God brought all those wonderful people into my life!

That is not all. One day during social talk at Wednesday dinner, I was telling Mary Brooks Casad about my Mom. I had not seen her for two years. She had never been in the USA and had never met Keith. Jessef was already more than six months old and she had never seen her first and only grandson. I offered a deal: Aldersgaters would organize my Mom's trip to TEXAS and then Aldersgaters could visit my Mom's place in Uzbekistan. They could stay for free in my Mom's apartment and save on hotels. It was December, 2001, when I made such a proposition to Mary. In March she told me that things are cooking. The tickets were bought in the USA and we sent them to Tashkent. My Mom arrived in May and stayed for a month.

Church members organized a pot luck party to honor my Mom. She got to try American foods and meet my friends. My Mom was surprised to see a mansion, where lives a man, who is interested in World War 2 between Russians and Germans. Doug collects war uniforms, tank and airplane models. After the pot luck party my Mom told me, *"Everything was delicious. I do not understand why we told that American food taste like garbage."*

One couple from Kaleidoscope class invited my Mom and me for lunch to their house. Eve, who showed her craft work my Mom, impressed her deeply. My Mom had this opinion, that Americans are lazy and do not know how to hold a needle. Eve showed my Mom her embroidery, sewing work, art paintings. Terry impressed us with his electrical and plumbing jobs around the house. My Mom thought that only Russians do home remodeling without professional help. Meeting Terry and Eve was an eye-opening experience for her.

Terry and Eve organized an excursion to an American hospital for us the same day. My Mom was astonished as a doctor by American hospitals, computerized systems and modern equipment.

Because of Aldersgaters effort to bring my Mom here, she got to see Dallas, Baltimore, Pennsylvania. For the first time she could experience seafood, steaks, Chinese food, CHUCKY CHEESE, McDonalds, American ice creams. Most of all she enjoyed to eat yogurt and cereal, which she can not afford in Tashkent. I was very happy to spoil her. I had a break, because of her help with the baby!

So, I finally learned why donations are so important. Donations help pay pastors and staff salaries, church maintenance and bring about mission works. Money can save lives. Money can make people happy.

My forth year in the US was filled with the joy of my Mom's arrival. However, it was a bad year for Keith. Keith was laid off as soon as he went back to work. He felt betrayed and lonely. That is why he did not make a huge effort to find a job in Texas. How to live with a hepatitis C patient? Well, like you did before, but with more patience and support. Make sure, you have hobbies and friends, maybe a child to care for, so spouse's disease does not bring your inner light down.

We decided to move to Pennsylvania by the end of the lease if some local job offer did not come up. We were blessed to have a severance package, unemployment benefits, and the support of our church. Barbara Shuman was delivering food boxes to us because we were on the list of "needy" people. The food boxes had fruits, vegetables, chicken, hot dogs, pasta, and rice. Aldersgate United Methodist Church was delivering food boxes once a month to all people who needed help. I had no idea about such a church mission before. I was happy that I was touched by it. Once again, I was witnessing how God opens up people's hearts and works through them. However, we could not sit at home waiting for hand outs forever. I was looking for a job!

I delivered pizza for seven days and quit. I decided to try a serving job. An Italian restaurant hired me. I was very happy to have something to do and to learn new skills while Keith was a stay-at-home dad. This job taught me to be more considerate of other servers who wait on me and have other tables to wait on, too.

I was taught that, while I serve a table, I have to build a relationship with my guests so they will come to eat again because I have made a good impression. So I was coming up to the tables with a special greeting: "Hi! My name is Oksana. I am the only Russian here. That makes you eligible for a Russian joke tonight!"

"I do not know any Russian jokes!" I heard from a lot of people. It was so funny. I think that if Publishers Clearing House would send them a letter saying that they were eligible for a million dollar prize, no one would think that they would have to give this prize to Publishers Clearing House.

Usually I would carry a wine bottle to offer a free sample to my guests. One time a lady interrupted my speech by saying: "I do not want any wine!" Of course, I did not talk to her after that rude start.

I would tell people my joke: "An American, a Russian and a German ended up on an island after their ship had crashed. They found a genie in the bottle. The genie came out and granted one wish to each guy. The American wished for a house in Chicago, a million dollars in gold and a supermodel wife. Well, he disappeared from the island and got everything he wanted in Chicago. The German asked for everything the same except he wanted the house in Frankfurt. He disappeared also. The Russian was thinking and thinking and then said: "I want three cases of vodka and those three guys back on the island." Most people understood the joke and had fun. I had one table with six teenagers from high school. One girl asked me: "WHY? Why did he wish that?" They did not get the joke. It was weird. I noticed that, if the table did not get the joke, they did not leave me any tips or just a little bit…less than 10%.

While working in the restaurant I learned how some customers abuse their waitress. For example, they want countless free drink refills, free salad or soup refills. I could be going to the kitchen so many times for a ticket of just $6. Some people leave a tip by looking at the price, not by how much work they caused me.

It is hard to be a waitress from another country. I had to learn not just how things work at the restaurant. I had to learn new words like *swordfish, farfale pasta, and mussels.* Most guests do not understand that

I may be very busy. They want to know where my accent is from, what kind of country Uzbekistan is. I like to talk to people if I only have one or two tables. However, it is hard to provide good service and answer all the questions. Some people felt that they had to tell me joke in return. It was not in my plans. I used to time my jokes and entertainment. I had to pretend that I cared to hear their jokes. It was so amazing that all the jokes I heard were plain or dirty. They made me sick and it was a waste of my time. Most of my customers did not raise their tips because I provided great service, entertainment or wasted time listening to their crap.

I tried to be funny and joke with my guests. When one lady said how much she loved the salad, I mentioned to her: "I had to come in at 5:00 in the morning to chop up the lettuce!" The lady joked back: "Oh, so that is why I found nails in my salad. Do you want them back?" Sometimes people denied my offer of the refills and said: "No, I am good." I would use my joke: "I did not ask if you are good or bad? I asked if you needed more bread." Sometimes I would ask people to try Black Russian or White Russian cocktails. One lady told me that she would like to order Sex on the Beach. She asked me, also: "What do you think about Sex on the Beach?" I said: "Oh, I just had a baby a year ago. I do not care about sex on the beach, sex in the park, or sex in the garage…"

When I had time, I would ask people a question: "If you guess what my occupation back in the Soviet Union was, you will get a free Russian joke to go." I would give them three hints: "I was 22 years old. It has nothing to do with customer service or the restaurant business. I would like to get the same job here, but it is hard and a rare profession." Most people guessed that I was a bartender, stripper, a police officer, a spy, an actress, a singer, or a comedian. Some people guessed right. I was a teacher of Russian language and literature! So, they got my free Russian joke to go: "A Russian scientists created a new kind of watermelon. They combined the genes of a watermelon and cockroaches. So when you cut into the new kind of watermelon the seeds run away all by themselves!" I felt good entertaining people, like maybe I should be a comedian.

One day I had only one table. It was a slow afternoon. I was talkative and nice, but my guest told me that I talked too much. I told her that I had been working two months at that restaurant and she was the first to tell me that. I believe some other people felt the same way, too. However, they did not let me know that. I did not feel like an unappreciated piece of crap every day after serving tables. Thank God most Americans have some manners and respect for others. I call it: "CULTURE".

I learned that it does not matter who you are. One day you have a house with an in ground swimming pool and a waterfall, a master's degree and a hope for the best job offer. The next day you can be taking people's orders and answering endless questions: "Where are you from? How did you get here? What is your special for today?"

What is our special for today? Our special for today is another moving! I was getting ready to live in forth state in 2002!

Keith and I were packing to move in with his parents. We had made a decision that Jessef should know his family. So we would live up North. Keith would have to look for a job in Pennsylvania or Maryland.

This time we decided to put our nice pine and oak furniture in a consignment shop. We figured that it did not make sense to rent a big truck, pay for movers and keep our furniture maybe all winter long at some storage unit in Pennsylvania. So I called a consignment shop and they sent a truck with two guys to load our stuff.

We donated bookshelves, file cabinets, plants and sofas. Two of the sofas were LA-Z-BOYS. In November, 2002, I did not care anymore about all this nice stuff. I felt that we could downsize so that it would be cheaper. I could always buy Wal-Mart's carton shelves. They are light to move and you do not have to worry that your child will get a boo-boo from it. We kept our electronics, cheap desks and our biggest treasure—the king size mattress. We sold our old Plymouth and a motorcycle.

I went to a Russian store to get some goods to share with the Leslie's at our Thanksgiving reunion later. I also bought some Global PAPA international phone cards which are the cheapest way to call Russia, Uzbekistan and all over the World. I can only get them at the International, Russian, or European food markets. This way for five dollars I can to Tashkent for 29 minutes! Later, I found out, that there are websites which sell international phone cards. I like www.Uniontelecard.com. I bought a card for 10 dollars, which let me talk with Tashkent for 2 hours!

I rented a 15 foot long truck. I thought that after all our sales and donations it would be a perfect fit. I did not ask for anybody's advice. Keith trusted me on making these decisions. He was loading the truck with an appliance dolly when we came to a conclusion: we needed a bigger truck! All those boxes with books, the washer and dryer, clothes, kitchen items…we had no choice but get a trailer to pull behind the truck. This meant one sad thing…I would have to drive the SUV behind the truck.

Well, Keith did not want to wait for our property to be checked. We just cleaned it as best we could and left Carrollton by midnight on November

21st. I was following Keith's truck. It was a dark, cool night. My Isuzu was filled with boxed food items. Jessef was asleep. I put his car seat in the front seat so I could see him better and hold his hand sometimes. I was very sleepy and exhausted. I thought that Keith was stubborn when he decided to make it to Little Rock that night after all the hard work we both had done! Anyway, I did not insist on stopping at a hotel. I kept following him.

When I woke up the SUV was turning over. I saw moving sky with all the bright stars. My first thought was: "God, save my baby!" My Isuzu ended up on its right side. Two small boxes with baby food fell from the back seat onto Jessef's head. I took my seatbelt off and helped crying Jessef free from his car seat. Some good Samaritans, who had to hit their brakes while my SUV was crossing from one highway lane to another, helped me to get out of the vehicle. Baby Jessef and I were absolutely unharmed. The front and two side windows were not broken. The air bag did not pop-up. We didn't have one bruise.

Someone brought me a blanket. Someone offered for me to sit in their car while we waiting on the police. Some people were picking up my canned goods that had spilled all over the highway.

You know Russian propaganda says that Americans are uncaring, cold-hearted, selfish people. I keep finding every year of my life here that that it is not true. The funny thing was that I did not know that my car would be towed. I was so naïve, thinking that all these people who had helped me out would roll the SUV over and I would continue on my journey!

Keith did not realize that I was missing. He thought that I might have gotten a flat tire so he slowed down. He was driving all the way to Arkansas waiting for me to catch up. No bad thoughts crossed his mind. We did not have cell phones. Our wireless contract was up in October and we had not renewed it.

Jessef and I, on the other hand, were spending the night on a floor at the sheriff's police department in Greenville, TX. In the early morning I called Keith's parents. I knew that he would finally call them. Then a gentleman came up to me at the sheriff's department and introduced himself. He was Joe Knight. He offered me three choices: I could go to rest at a women's shelter, to his house or to a hotel. I chose the hotel. I wanted privacy, a shower and some sleep. It was easier to childproof one small hotel room than the whole Knight house. Mr. Knight took us to a hotel. Then he checked me in, paid for it and drove to Wal-Mart to get some diapers and toothpaste for me. He left me with a prayer. My knight in shining armor was a constable and a part-time pastor at a church which name I do not remember. How can you forget such generous, caring, extraordinary people like that? How did I deserve to attract them in my life?

Jessef and I had our first roll-over accident. After Keith found out my hotel number from his parents he drove back to Texas. When he stopped to call me for better directions a police car stopped and the officer came up to Keith: "Are you the husband who got separated from his wife last night?" Keith and I were reunited. We drove to a towing place to unload our SUV. Keith could not believe how totaled it looked with a big hole on the side of a back door. I rolled over some sharp sign sticking in the ditch between highways. It was a miraculous car crash. Not one other vehicle or people were involved. No one was harmed. We were not harmed, but touched by God's grace again.

CHAPTER 12
HOW TO GET ALONG WITH IN-LAWS AND YOUR INNER SELF.

Five years ago I was taking seriously how my pictures were taken. If I had closed eyes on pictures, I would tear them up. In 2003, I was tearing only pictures where I looked way too fat.

One day my Mom was reminding me about her former friend Tanya. This woman won a greencard and came to the USA. My Mom told me about her concerns: "Tanya practiced magic in Tashkent like you did; she had our pictures and might be doing something with them." This time I did not agree with my Mom. I laughed at her and answered in my email: "Dear Mama! Tanya struggled her first time in America to get by, to learn English, to buy her first used car, to get a job. Do you think she brought over here our pictures as extra luggage, to carry them from one rental place to another? Mom, Americans are not as superstitious as Russians and Uzbeks! In America you have to work very hard, you have no time for stupid stuff. I, personally, do not."

Before our fifth year anniversary, I bought Keith pants in WAL MART with a tag – "made in Uzbekistan". Can you believe it?

It took me 5 years to cook perfect Uzbek pilaf here in the USA! I buy "French cut" carrots, which exactly how Uzbeks cut them for their pilafs. I also buy parboiled long grain rice. Parboiled is the best health wise if to believe South Beach Diet. When I want to make Holiday Style Uzbek pilaf, I put in a pilaf garbanzo beans and yellow raisins, but I cook them with the meat, onions, carrots and caraway seeds together.

Finally, after 5 years of trial and error, I got a decent job. How? I went to Orthodox Church in Fayetteville and met Sherry there. Sherry was speaking almost perfect Russian and married to a Russian man. She told me about her job, and I applied there, too.

I had to get my police record check, go through training to learn how to do paperwork, CPR and CPI (how to restrain a violent child).

My degree in education was useful! I am a TSS (therapeutic staff support). I work individually with special needs children in a school setting or home/community. I observe and correct client's behavior when needed, transfer him/her organizational skills, teach manners. For example, when a client forgets to thank peers or teachers for favors, I remind them. I remind them to say "please", "sorry", etc. I prompt the client to stop making noise and to follow directions. I praise a child if he deserves it. I reinforce positive behaviors. This way the Special Ed teacher can concentrate on teaching and not on behavior problems. TSS work with autistic children, with oppositional defiant disorder, learning disabilities, and attention deficit disorder. As a TSS, I had to spend time with clients in a home and community settings. At home, I would teach them how to cook and bake, and how to play certain table games to fulfill goals in client's treatment plan like "self-esteem builder" and "following directions". IT is a very rewarding job, because kids do change, become more mature, more polite, when individual work is being done on daily basis.

I also became a part time mystery shopper, here in Pennsylvania. I get assignments by email, go to a certain store and check them out. I am making an inspection on their cleanliness, service, uniform, friendliness. I act like a regular customer, use store's bathroom, to check it out, too. Then I come home, I use internet to fill out my report online. I need a scanner to scan my receipts to get reimbursement. It is a great job if you like to spy, to observe, to pay attention. Keith supported all of my job decisions.

I am not embarrassed to tell people about my occupation, for the first time in 5 years of living in the US. However, this chapter is not about my new job, but about schools.

I admire the American elementary school. I worked in the Chambersburg and Mercersburg elementary schools. Oh, my God! Every classroom has a clock! Every classroom has a phone so the principal does not have to walk around the school to notify teachers about important phone calls or meetings! Every classroom has a big American flag. I'll bet teachers did not have to buy those with their own money! Playgrounds have swings, slides, monkey bars and benches! Students can borrow the school's balls and jump ropes to have fun outside! This country is rich and spends a lot of money on school supplies!

I like the system of supervised recess. Teachers guard their students of elementary schools quietly in the school halls to the cafeteria, playground, and another classroom. There is no knocking each other down, running and kicking walls here.

I like that American students are separated by age. There are no first graders running with high school students in the same school building like it is in Russia, Uzbekistan and other former Soviet Union republics. When I was a student or a teacher in Tashkent, I hated recess. Every 45 minutes the school bell would ring. Students of all ages would try to find their classroom, taking a bathroom break in 5 minutes.

I was attending school in the 80's. I had to wear a uniform. I had to wear either a blue or brown dress with a black apron. My Mom bought me dresses and sewed my aprons.

GYM class was 3 times a week, 45 minutes long. We had to go to a locker room, change our clothes and attend the class. One of the girls had to stay in this changing room because it did not have locks. If left unattended, someone could steal your lunch money, for example.

I saw one health room at Mercersburg elementary school. I talked to the nurse and got some answers to my questions. I was impressed to find out that parents donate shoes and winter jackets to the school so that needy students can use them! I saw with my own eyes how one girl walked into the health room and asked for sneakers. She forgot hers at home! Nobody in Russia would even think to borrow sneakers from the school.

What a country!

I hated to be sweaty after gym class and had no possibility of taking a shower. We had only 5 minutes to put our uniform on and find the next classroom.

There are no yellow busses for students in Uzbekistan or Russia. Children live close enough to walk to the school or take a public bus.

We never had a subject named "science". We had separate lessons like zoology, botany, biology, chemistry, astronomy, and physics. We even had a lesson called "military preparation" in the 8th grade. We learned about poison gases, atomic reaction, and all kinds of bombs. I remember learning how to put together and take apart an automatic gun called Kalashnikov. We had to go to a school yard and throw fake grenades as far as we could.

All boys, my peers, had to learn carpenter skills. All girls were taught how to sew and make salads. Zoology teachers never cut up frogs or rats for the study and the student's amusement. I remember studying very carefully about insects and animals. We had no VCR's to watch in the whole school because the government could not afford it. All we had were schoolbooks. I was amused that American students and teachers do not know the difference between bees and wasps. School playgrounds and cafeterias were visited by yellow jackets, the most aggressive types of wasps, pretty often. To me it was weird that students and teachers were calling them "bees". Zoology in Russia and Uzbekistan covers such differences.

I was impressed by the American music class! Children do not have to write songs by hand. They have access to books of songs right in the classroom! What a country!

Art classrooms I found stunning in the USA. Schools have such a great supply of glue, crayons, scissors, construction and crepe paper for kids! Russians and Uzbeks, Ukrainians and Georgians have to bring all of that stuff with them to school! Russian students do not work with glitter, aluminum foil, or chalk in their Art lessons. I never saw glitter in my life before I came to the USA.

American elementary schools have scheduled lunch and outside recess time. Student in Uzbekistan and Russia have one big recess for 15 minutes. This is the time for everybody in the whole school building to take a bathroom break, eat at the cafeteria, and run home to get forgotten homework.

American students are "blessed" with playground equipment like swings, slides, benches, monkey bars and basketball courts. Schools offer them jump ropes and balls to play outside! Classrooms have games so that students can enjoy their free time during harsh weather! My goodness, how can some American children hate school?

American students can enjoy a variety of foods in their cafeteria. Russian students cannot get bananas, slices of oranges, puddings, burgers, pizzas, or

PBJ sandwiches in their school cafeterias! They have never heard about vanilla or strawberry milk! They have tea, regular milk or compote for lunch! There are no hot turkey sandwiches and no gravies for mashed potatoes in Russia or Uzbekistan.

I remember having mashed potatoes and cutlets, barley or garbanzo bean soups or porridges, pastas or rice for school lunches. I did not even know what pizza was! I went to school in 80's!

When I had to use the school bathroom, I took paper with me because nobody put it there for people's use. Trust me—things have not changed much since that time.

American teachers and the staff I have observed are very respectful of student's feelings. They do not call their students names and do not put them in the corner. If an American teacher is wrong he will apologize to the student.

I want to share one story. I was 14. It was a physics lesson. My peers were making noise. The teacher thought it was me and ordered me to stand in the corner for the rest of the lesson. I obeyed. My classmates were afraid to be bullied and did not speak up. Someone told the teacher later what really happened. The teacher took me to his lab and apologized in private. He embarrassed me in front of 25 students and apologized just to me. So this apology did not mean anything.

I remember my math teacher in 6th grade was calling us "rams, real stupid rams".

(In Russian language people say "ram" and "chicken" when they mean "brainless".)

I like that American students get a lot of respect and care from teachers and staff. I doubt the level of education, but supplies and materials in the USA schools are outstanding! I am happy to know that my son will attend an American school one day.

Speaking of my son, Jessef, it is a challenge to raise any child. However, it is more challenging to raise a bilingual child.

Keith speaks English to Jessef most of the time. I speak English to him a lot also. This is my problem. I like English. It has a lot of shorter words than the Russian language does. I catch myself speaking to Jessef the easiest way – in English.

The other day I was writing a plan for a chapter for my book in Russian. All of the sudden I realized that I was writing in English. I do the same thing when I make my shopping list. Keith does not need to see it because he does not usually shop.

I am Russian so why am I making my shopping list in English? When I speak to my Russian friends in the USA, I catch myself using English words, also. I cannot say that I am losing my Russian language. However, I realize that I substitute it with English a lot. I am very concerned that my son will not know Russian.

Both of his grandmothers have their concerns also. His American grandmother was concerned that Jessef would not know English because she heard me speaking to him a lot in Russian.

His Russian grandmother was concerned that her American grandson would not know English because she heard me speaking to him in Russian on a videocassette. However, if I spoke to him in English on the video, I would be criticized in Tashkent that I am not teaching my son my native language and that my relatives do not understand what I am saying to him. I feel that the grandmothers' concerns are silly. If a child is being raised in a family where one parent speaks to him in one language, the child will learn it. If a child watches American cartoons, sees his American relatives, goes to child care, how in the world would he not know English? I know Russian-speaking families in the USA who do not teach their children English because they do not speak it at home. However, the children pick up the language anyway from cartoons, other children and child care. If I speak too much Russian to my son, why is his vocabulary content only 10% Russian? I am lacking consistency. I should speak to Jessef only in Russian. Maybe I should stop mixing Russian sentences with English.

Everybody knows that children learn animal noises very early. It was an issue for me because Russian and American animal noises are different. Russian frogs say: "kva-kva", a horse says: "igo-go", a rooster says: "kukareku", a pig says: "hru-hru-hru", a duck says: "kryak-kryak", a birdie says: "pee-pee". At first I was going to teach Jessef the Russian way. Soon I realized that, since he is communicating to English-speaking people the most, he needs to know the American way of animal noises. I said to myself: "Well, at least Russian and American cows, dogs and cats speak the same language."

Most Russian children have no room of their own. When I was born, my parents lived with my grandmother in a one-bedroom apartment. My grandmother slept in the bedroom and my parents slept on the sofa in living room. I had my crib. I slept in that crib for six years until my parents bought an apartment. Russians are amazed that Americans let their children sleep in different rooms from infancy. For me it was very inconvenient that Keith cleared up his office in our Texas townhouse to make it Jessef's bedroom. I remember nights when I would jump from my bed when I heard him crying and run down the hall to his room to nurse. Then I would put him down and he would scream. He hated to be alone…to be jailed in the crib! He would wake up every time I put him down! I could not handle that because I was not getting enough sleep. Jessef ended up in our bed.

When we moved to a new place, after living with Mom and Dad, Jessef decided to be independent. He realized that he loves his room and sleeping bag on the floor. He quit demanding milk bottles two or three times at night. He was 22 months old then so he outgrew his need of security in sleeping with us and eating at night. My family was unhappy to read my letters when I was writing to them about the American custom of letting babies "cry it out". We tried this method with Jess twice but it was horrible for all of us and did not work. Russians believe that it is a luxury to have a separate room for a toddler. I had a hard time overcoming this belief. Keith was insistent on Jessef being out of our bedroom. I believed that it was most important to have a master bedroom and office than a master bedroom and a toddler's room. Keith combined the master bedroom with the office. Jessef grew independent. Everybody is happy.

I think that the hardest thing in raising a Russian-American child is the fact that it is not easy to establish interacting for a child with his Russian relatives overseas. We as immigrants move to the USA for a better life. Most of us do not plan on suppressing our Russian roots. We are proud to be Russians in America and create a better future for our children.

It was November, 2003, when we moved to Pennsylvania with my in-laws.

We lived with Mom and Dad five months until could get back on our feet. I believe they saved us from bankruptcy. They did not charge us anything for staying in their house.

We had some money saved. Keith had not gotten any unemployment checks since January. We were only getting small checks from the furniture consignment store and our renters. We weren't making money on renting our house. We had to come up with more than 500 dollars every month to pay for the mortgage, pool loan, pool maintenance, sewer and alarm. Thank God the insurance company paid off our car loan and sent the remaining balance to us. We could buy a small used car and paid cash for it.

My car crash helped us financially because we did not have to pay the high monthly payments on the Isuzu anymore or the expensive insurance. Owning credit cards saved us from bankruptcy also. Our moving to Pennsylvania, gas, food, Christmas presents, and books for Keith to study for his MCSD were all charges on our credit cards for months. We figured that if Keith did not get a decent job we would lose the house in Arizona anyway. So we would go through bankruptcy and would not have to pay our credit cards either. On the other hand, if we did get jobs we would start paying our debts down anyway.

We were going into more debt while looking for jobs, but still paying house bills and minimum credit card payments. It was a horrible thought for us that we might lose our house and good credit history.

Family-wise, living with my in-laws was good for me. I learned how to make meat loaf, spinach and mango salad, Hershey Bar cookies, strawberry shortcake, and sour kraut and pork. I was raised, hearing Russian proverb that "A road to men's heart lays through his stomach". If you care about your relationship, you should know how to cook your spouses' favorite meals if you are the one who is in charge of kitchen. Of course, if we want pizza or sushi, we will be heading out to eat.

I had no idea that I could cook rice in a microwave and make my baked potatoes in it.

I did not know how to make sure that vegetables and salads stay longer and fresher in a fridge. I learned those tricks from Jo Ann. It was important to me to learn from mom-in-law certain recipes Keith was used to, so he does not miss her cooking and his childhood too much. I tried my best to adapt to Keith's taste, learned new recipes. He tried to adapt to eat Russian, Uzbek and Ukrainian meals.

I feel that I was almost jumping over my head to keep in-laws house clean, especially the kitchen. It was impossible with the baby around. I did not want to upset Mom. However, after five months living with her, I became a better homemaker than I had ever been before. Before I could go to sleep and leave dirty dishes on the kitchen counter. (Keith had a rule that the sink should not be filled with dirty dishes, but clean and dry at all times if not in use.) At my in-law's house I had to adjust to their rules: no dishes should sit on the kitchen counter but in the sink. Anyway, now at our new rental townhouse I never leave dishes sit overnight, neither on the counter nor in the sink.

Mom would forget that I am from another culture sometimes. It was good for her to get to know me better. She learned that I like to drink my coffee with sweetened condensed milk sometimes. I grew up having sweetened condensed milk on bread or pancakes. I never saw maple or any other pancake syrup in my life before I moved to the USA. I made buckwheat porridge for breakfast several times. It was common breakfast for me as a child. I taught Jessef to eat it. Keith likes it sometimes with an egg on a side. I even could sneak hamburger meat in it, since my son refused to eat animal proteins. I offered to Dad to try my porridge once. He did not want to taste any of that. I could not understand how he eats cereal almost every morning.

It was hard on Mom to deal with a young independent Russian woman who likes to do things her way. I would start making dinner without talking to Mom first. Sometimes I would use foods which Mom had bought, planning to make something herself. I felt that she should be happy that I was taking over the kitchen.

Most families in Russia and Uzbekistan live together and share kitchen duties. Stay-at- home grandmothers usually cook and baby- sit their grandchildren, while their children and children's spouses work. I took for granted Mom's hospitality too often. I did not realize it most of the time. I was sure that a retired, sick woman would appreciate the fact that I was protecting her from getting tired from working in the kitchen. Well, I did not protect her feelings from being hurt by me by ignoring her desire to plan her meals, to work on her kitchen, etc.

How to get along with in-laws? Remember, they love their child, whom you married, and they wish that child all happiness in the world. Listen to what they have to say, and do not talk back too much. Keith did a great job interacting with his Russian mom-in-law. When he had something against her, he would never tell it to her face; he would speak to me first. I helped him to understand why did she said what she said, and why did she do what she did. Remember Russian saying: DO NOT SPIT IN A WELL, YOU MIGHT DRINK FROM IT.

While we were living with Richard and Jo Ann Leslie, I read several books, to see, who wrote what on the same subject.

Lynn Visson in her book WEDDED STRANGERS goes back to the early 1920s, and searches for different stories throughout 20th century on the subject of intercultural marriages. This book answers questions, how it was before, and after perestroika, cultural differences, and problems couples faced. The author collected stories from interviewed Russian-American couples. I did not like some statements in this books like "All Russians love vodka, all Russians are always late, all Russians eat bread with their food." However, it was very interesting book.

Irina McClellan in OF LOVE AND RUSSIA writes about her marriage in the early 1970s and the eleven-year separation from her spouse. This book is about the Soviet Union autocratic regime, hard times obtaining visas and reuniting with her American spouse. The book is out of print.

Frank Coleman, Rodger Weston, and Billy write about their personal experiences with Russian and Ukrainian women, here in the US and in Russia. Their books are specifically for men seeking Russian brides and traveling to Russia.

Frank Coleman in TO RUSSIA FOR LOVE advises American bachelors to meet as many Russian women as they can. He provides internet sites with addresses of single Russian women. Coleman tells American men how to court a Russian woman, including which gifts to buy.

Rodger Weston's story is on CD. LOVE LETTERS FROM RUSSIA lets readers read many letters written by Russian women corresponding to him. This book is full of pictures and maps. This is also a sad story of a man, who married an immature girl, and how the marriage was struggling.

Billy Conn in HOW TO HAPPILY SURVIVE MARRIAGE TO a RUSSIAN WOMAN takes American men systematically through important phases of courtship with a Russian woman. He gives good advices on how to write letters, which websites to look up, how to get married overseas, and how to succeed in this kind of marriage.

Zita Dabars with Lilia Vokhmina wrote THE RUSSIAN WAY as a manual for travelers and educators. This gives an insider look into how Russians feel about all aspects of life from family to entertainment. This is a good book for people who are interested in learning some Russian phrases, which are woven into every chapter. THE RUSSIAN WAY also provides a historical background, prices in restaurants and hotels, and the current ecology situation.

I was working on my book since 1998. When I read the books I described above, I was searching for my competitors.

HOW TO SURVIVE IN INTERNATIONAL MARRIAGE: This is the first book written by Russian wife in the 21st century about her personal experiences in America, and the influence of Americans on her. Coleman, Rodgers, Conn wrote what they think about Russian women. The Leslie discusses what a Russian woman thinks about American men, society, and culture. Leslie takes readers through stepping stones of her life in America, from non-professional baby-sitter and food service jobs, to a professional one in behavioral health as a TSS (Therapeutic Staff Support). Adjustment and courage are two qualities you need to make it in a multicultural relationship.

This is the first book written by a Russian wife from Uzbekistan, a Muslim Republic, who describes Uzbekistan and creates rules for a happy international marriage.

When Keith got a job and we could finally move out from Mom and Dad's, we all were very happy. While living with them I learned to appreciate my own space. I am almost in love with my cute two-bedroom townhouse. I never enjoyed living in an apartment so much. Remember, in five years we had lived in Georgia, Arizona and Texas. I was taking for granted having my own address before! Now I am enjoying the space that I have. My Carrollton townhouse in Texas was crowded with coffee tables, end tables and heavy furniture. Now I do not spend so much time polishing furniture. I do not yell at Jess: "Stop banging on the wood!" I do not have to kiss so many boo-boos like he used to get from our furniture corners before. I am free! Oh, God, in Arizona I was very proud of my possessions. Bad times helped me to realize that my life is easier without them.

At first we had no furniture in the living room and only our in-law's card table in the dining area. Soon Pastor Bob Cook and his wife Shirley brought us their old sofa and matching chair. Also, we got from them an old oak dining table and three chairs. Later, we borrowed from them a cot for Jessef to sleep on. Prior to this, our son was sleeping in his own room on the sleeping bags on the floor for months.

Now I do not feel like I did before: "that is too cheap" or "this is too old". I feel like I outgrew my old self. I am fine with what I have. I have our office in the master bedroom. We have no bed frame, but a king size orthopedic mattress which is tall and comfortable.

I use carton shelves from Wall Mart in my closet to store my socks, underwear, and shoes. I want to possess things which are practical and easy to move since I have no feeling of stability and home in my life. Two or three years ago I could not stand the thought of getting rid of my furniture and my plants. We had to pay a lot of money for a three-bedroom place. Now I am saving on rent because I do not need a lot of square feet!

For my thirtieth birthday, Keith's parents presented me with a nice red purse. They put a coin in it, as American superstition calls. It surprised me; because Russians do the same thing then they give wallets and purses as gifts! Wow, culture crossing took place!

Two years ago I paid a professional to edit my book. My literary agent did not find me a publisher in two years. So I wrote more chapters and asked Shirley Cook to edit them for me. She agreed! How did I deserve to meet her in my life?

I am thankful to God for the entire pruning we had. I am glad to live in Pennsylvania, because Keith, Jessef and I can see his parents often and our other relatives. There is nothing like a family. I am thankful to God for the hardships. Not too many people can say that they have lived in four states in five years. Not too many people can admit that miracles have happened to them.

Especially I am thankful to God for bringing me into the church family. I believe that the United Methodist Church has made a tremendous impact on my life. Aldersgate Church in Carrollton did.

Three years ago, I did not see myself doing a stand up comedy routine or singing in Russian during a Saturday church dinner. I did not see myself playing bells for the church bell choir. I did not see myself writing a check with a church's name on it. I did not expect anybody from a church to deliver food boxes to my home or record Russian songs on a CD off the Internet just for me! I feel that the church helped me to open up to Americans, for my husband's family and for myself. I believe that I am a better person now that I came to the USA.

I remember that I used to look down on people a lot before, expecting too much from them. I cared about impressing my Russian family and friends with my possessions. I cannot believe I used to be so superstitious! It was a baggage, I am telling you! Now I am free from that heavy baggage I brought with me from Uzbekistan. America made me better. American people did. Thanks to the church, thanks to everybody whom I met, thanks to God. I feel that I am different, but I did not lose my inner self. It is because my spouse's support of my hobbies, interests, choice of friends and jobs. I was supporting his choice of jobs (that is why we moved so much), friends and hobbies.

I married a mature man, who helped me mature, so we both can take care of our family and be happy. It is important to both partners to be dedicated to adapt, to adjust, to listen, to learn, to transform in international marriage. People do change. If you are not ready for a change, you are not ready for international marriage. People can grow mature, learn from their mistakes. Keith and I found that love, patience and dedication to stay married will help people to survive in multicultural marriage.

About the Author

Oksana Kornienko Leslie is a Russian from Uzbekistan, married to an American for six years. Oksana possesses a Master's degree in Secondary Education and Russian Language.

Printed in Great Britain
by Amazon.co.uk, Ltd.,
Marston Gate.